ANNALS OF PORNOGRAPHIE: HOW PORN BECAME 'BAD'

Revised & Updated Edition

BRIAN M. WATSON

for a.g., s.m. & j.s., for the years in time
and for z.b. & k.b., for the time in years
love always,

b

CONTENTS

1

Introduction

Omnium rerum principia parva sunt.
(The beginnings of all things are small.)
Cicero, *De Finibus Bonorum et Malorum*, V. 21.

*Truth! stark naked truth, is the word, and I will not so much as
take the pains to bestow the strip of a gauze-wrapper on it.*
John Cleland, *Fanny Hill*

begin, v1 /bɪˈgɪn/
Of common West Germanic or ? Germanic formation:
Old English bi-, be-ginnan is identical with Old Saxon
and Old High German bi-ginnan. . . . The latter (Old
High German and Middle High German) had the senses
'to cut open, open up, begin, undertake'; hence it is
inferred that the root sense of *ginnan was 'to open,
open up,' [and] Old English gínan 'to gape, yawn,' from
a stem *gi-, appearing also in Old Church Slavonic zij-
ati, Latin hiāre 'to gape, open'[1]

ONE REASON I begin, well, with 'begin,' is to draw attention to words. The entries in an etymology dictionary look much like the description above for the
word 'begin'—they typically list the earlier formats of the

word, such as biginnan or begouth, and their meanings (to 'undertake' or to 'open up'), and how those meanings changed and developed into the word we use today. These entries can be incredibly detailed and expansive—the entire entry for 'begin' is nearly 500 words long—far longer than this paragraph. However, even the most detailed etymology does not tell the full story of a word's origin, purpose, or intention. For example, here is the entry for pornography:

> **Pornography, Brit. /pɔːˈnɒgrəfi/, U.S. /pɔrˈnɑgrəfi/**
> Hellenistic Greek πορνογράφος (adjective) that writes about prostitutes (ancient Greek πορνο- (see porno-comb. form) + -γράφος -graph comb. form) + -y suffix (compare -graphy comb. form), perhaps after French pornographie treatise on prostitution (1800), obscene painting (1842), description of obscene matters, obscene publication (1907 or earlier)[2]

Do you see the difference? This entry, in its entirety, is not even 50 words. The usually-verbose Oxford English Dictionary simply says that it is a Greek word literally meaning 'writers about prostitutes.' It doesn't tell you that this word is only found once in Ancient Greek, where Athenaeus comments on an artist that painted portraits of courtesans. Then the word fell out of use for *1500 years* until it was used in 1842 to describe a proposal on how to regulate prostitutes and then the erotic wall murals depicting prostitutes uncovered at Pompeii.[3] What happened? Why was a word resurrected after so long? Why was it needed? Why weren't the murals at Pompeii just called the Pompeii Murals, or referred to as the Erotic Art in Pompeii and Herculaneum like Wikipedia does today?

Consider another comparison: On January 20th, 1674, John Wilmot, the 2nd Earl of Rochester, delivered a poem he had promised to King Charles II. In a rather unfortunate moment for the history of poetry, Rochester accidently delivered into the hands of the king *The Island of Britain*, also known as *A Satyre on Charles II*. Upon discovering his mistake (and hearing that the king wanted his head), he was forced to flee the court for his safety. By February, however, the king seemed to forgive him, granting him the title 'Ranger of Woodstock Park' and allowing him to return to court.[4]

Two centuries later, in October of 1869, Daniel Gabriel Rossetti published *Jenny*, in his *Exhumation Proofs*, a poem that had originally been buried with his wife in 1862. This poem also met with considerable controversy, but Rossetti was not as easily forgiven. Even years after the fact, he was accused by Robert Buchanan, a Scottish dramatist, of being "fleshy all over, from the roots of his hair to the tips of his toes...snake-like in [his] eternal wriggling, lipping, munching, slavering and biting," and responsible for a host of offences, including "decency outraged, history falsified, purity sacrificed, art prostituted, language perverted, religion outraged," among others.[5]

When the texts of the two poems are compared, however, it is Rochester's poem that seems to outrage decency and religion, falsify history, prostitute art, and so on. The poem begins in earnest with "In th' isle of Britain, long since famous grown / For breeding the best cunts in Christendom, //[lives] the easiest King and best-bred man alive," and goes on to describe both the Kings whoring and 'tarse' (penis) in obscene detail, complaining that Charles is "starving his people, hazarding his crown. //...for he loves fucking much."

The language of Rossetti's poem, by contrast, hardly perverts language—it begins with "Lazy laughing languid Jenny, / Fond of a kiss and fond of a guinea, / Whose head upon my knee to-night / Rests for a while," which hardly seems obscene.[7] The most 'suggestive' the poem gets is to speak of Jenny's "dainties through the dirt" and the only 'action' seen in it is "one kiss."[8]

What changed in the two intervening centuries? Why did Rossetti's poem, so tame in comparison to Rochester's, inspire such a diatribe? Why do our modern eyes immediately peg Rochester as the 'libertine poet' or 'a profane wit,' as a 2004 book and movie did?[9] This book is an attempt to answer these questions, an attempt to trace a history through the 'underside' of Western culture, its art, literature, philosophy, sexology, psychology and its changing laws. It is an attempt to explain the modern view—to explain exactly why, where, and how porn became 'bad.' The other reason I began this chapter with the word 'begin' is found in its older meanings of 'to gape' or 'to open up'—sometimes history needs to be cut open, revealed, and stripped. Sometimes the past is not as clear as battle dates or body counts. Sometimes it is hidden in the shadows, buried beneath tons of rock and ash, or taking place behind a bedroom door.

Because, like it, love it, use it, or hate it, modern society has a tortured relationship with pornography. This relationship manifests in a number of ways, like 2013's anti-pornography rules in the United Kingdom, which aimed to cut off both children and adults from internet pornography by default, the 2015 ruling that adult eBooks could only be sold after ten pm in Germany, or the raft of anti-pornography "Public Health Crisis" bills passed in 17 US states.[10]

Books condemning the corrupting effects of pornography appear with regularity, with such titles as; *Pornland: How Porn Has Hijacked Our Sexuality, Getting Off: Pornography and the End of Masculinity,* or *Wired for Intimacy: How Pornography Hijacks the Male Brain*, which claims that "our culture has become pornified." Online communities like Reddit's NoFap have over a quarter-million 'Fapstronauts' who seek to "abstain from pornography and masturbation. . . as a test of self-control" or to 'quit' pornography all together if "excessive masturbation or pornography has become a problem" in their lives.[11]

The fapstronauts encourage and compete with each other by daily updating the community on their abstinence from PMO (Porn, Masturbation, Orgasm). Websites like yourbrainonporn.com claim that "Evolution has not prepared your brain for today's Internet porn," and that it causes PED, porn-induced erectile dysfunction.

On the other side of the debate, doctors such as David Ley have published books such as *The Myth of Sex Addiction* attacking the science and the pseudoscience offered up by these sources and arguing that: sex addiction is a "a shell game, a game that is using smoke and mirrors to hide moral judgments and to deny personal responsibility."[12] At the same time, pornography companies are increasingly profitable— one example of this is the $14.5 million purchase of the old San Francisco Armory by Kink.com, a company specializing in BDSM pornography, or the wild proliferation of 'tube' sites like YouPorn or RedTube that are increasingly getting into the porn business themselves.[13] Pornography use and acceptance is also increasingly widespread; a 2013 *Gallup* poll found that nearly half of Americans 18–34 years old found porn morally acceptable, compared to 19% among those 55 and older.[14]

Additionally, pornography is becoming increasingly legitimized—2014 saw the first publication of the journal *Porn Studies,* which ran articles from a diverse array of fields. Whether the opinion is that "increasing accessibility provided by various media technologies. . .[has made] pornographies of all kinds accessible to a wider range of audiences," or that "evolution has not prepared your brain," pornography's detractors and supporters both claim that modern pornography marks a radical break from the past—this is not your daddy's *Playboy*.

But as the history of the word reveals, 'pornography' *does* have a history, albeit a relatively short and modern one of about a century and a half (1850 onwards). But this does not mean that obscene works never existed or were not understood as obscene—such a claim would be wrong, as the history of human perversity is as long as the history of the species. Instead, these earlier works were different. One example is the anti-Catholic caricatures of Louis Cranach in support of Martin Luther, which often depicted—graphically—the Pope as the 'Great Whore,' or the Whore of Babylon. Or even Luther's scatological jokes about the Pope.

These pre-pornography works are just as capable of being as graphic, shocking, or titillating as modern-day PornHub videos, but they often integrated social, religious, or political critiques between sex scenes, or used erotic dialogue as a means of critiquing society at large. The earliest surviving forms of what might be considered pornography, by our modern eyes, circulated in private among elite, upper-class readers in manuscript format. In this format, for this audience, it was used to critique political figures, such as the King, or to cast suspicion on whether nuns and monks were really chaste, or to criticize the Catholic Church for its involvement in politics. It was only the advent of Gutenberg's printing press in 1436 that, as in so many other fields, changed everything.

The short answer to the question of 'why porn became bad' is that the printing press made the reproduction of 'immoral' texts and images remarkably cheap and easy. When this was joined with increasing middle- and lower-class literacy, and book markets such as Holywell Street in London or the Grands-Boulevards area of Paris, it created a type of work that supposedly had an 'undesirable' effect upon the general population. Various European churches and states attempted to control this effect through moral reform and legal regulation. The short answer, however, does not capture the entire story. That is the purpose of this history.

The long answer touches on a variety of colorful characters who do not get their historical due: from the already-mentioned 'profane wit,' Rochester; to the Renaissance 'porn star' and 'Scourge of Princes,' Pietro Aretino; to the "Divine" Marquis de Sade; to the 'unspeakable' and flamboyant Edmund Curll (the first Hugh Hefner); and to tax-dodging street pornographers and radicals in the streets of London, Paris, Rome and Amsterdam. Featuring in this history too are the organizations that fought against their type: The Society for the Reformation of Manners, the Proclamation Society, the French, and English governments and their Kings and most famously, the Society for the Suppression of Vice. The long answer takes us to locations as far-flung as the hallowed halls of the Council of Trent where popes and cardinals fought over the future of the church, to a narrow alley in London filled with hack writers, aspiring poets, cheap bookstores, dirty drunks and aggressive prostitutes, lovingly and disgustingly referred to as Grub Street. It touches on the underside of Western culture, the history of sexuality, the creation of privacy (and public life), and the 'invention of manners.' It brings together, in one place, the history of Western culture's tortured and blissful relationship with erotic representation.

Over the past three decades, several historians have engaged with erotica/pornography as a field: in manuscript form (Ian Fredrick Moulton, *Before Pornography*; Lynn Hunt, *The Invention of Pornography*), in the seventeenth and eighteenth-century developments (the works of Julie Peakman, Sarah Toulalan and James Turner), in the events of the nineteenth-century that created obscene libel (Karen Harvey, *Reading Sex*; Bradford Mudge, *The Whore's Story*), or by focusing on the events after the creation of the Obscene Publications Act of 1857 (Lisa Z. Sigel, *Governing Pleasures*, and too many others to name), or simply focusing on the history of visual pornography in Hollywood and elsewhere. But except for a few attempts in the 1960s (such as the Hyde and Ernst summary) there has been no attempt to aggregate these disparate perspectives into one text that that would serve as an introductory work and a textbook—until now.

This work originally began life as a Master's Thesis in History and Culture at Drew University under Jonathan Rose, founder of The Society for the History of Authorship, Reading and Publishing. After it received the David Kohn award, I decided to expand it into a larger survey, and I began a six-month archive tour through England, France, Italy and the United States to track down primary sources, verify hunches and suspicions and to get a sense for the breadth and development of pornography as a genre. The original intention was to publish the book as a popular history through a trade press but, due to squeamishness over the subject matter as well as an academic focus and a refusal to sensationalize the material I decided to self-publish the text in March of 2016, and it managed to have popular success, including a number of interviews, lectures, and an appearance on the Conan O'Brien show. The text you are currently reading is an extensive academic re-write of the original text, along with the usual apparatus of footnotes and citations.

This study attempts to place and center erotic writing and pornography as a mode of discourse and a genre with a history, as too often 'pornography' gets treated as if it sprung fully-formed from the head of Zeus. I do this by breaking up the history into four separate parts, which roughly correspond with the type of story I am trying to tell here, which is an ideological move from the upper to the lower and then to the middle classes, as so far as it is possible to talk about classes and pornography. Geographically, the (hi)story begins in Florence with Boccaccio before traveling to Rome and Venice with Aretino and then over the Alps into Germany through Trent with Martin Luther and the counter-reformation and into France via Avignon with Pallavicino. We tarry there for a while to explore the foundational texts that were then carried over the English Channel to London by libertine figures such as Rochester and where pornography as such reached its most recognizably modern form.

The following chapters are divided into four separate sections, in a sort of hat tip to the progress of the erotic enumerated by Aretino and others. Part one, Foreplay, examines (from 1338 to 1644) the 'prehistory' of pornography in Renaissance erotic discourse as used by Boccaccio, Chaucer and others, until it was brought into its most realized form in the sixteenth century under Pietro Aretino, the 'father' of literary pornography. This carries us then into the radicalization of the form in the radical years following the Protestant Reformation and then the Catholic Counter-Reformation, where a sort of mildly erotic social, religious and political discourse/satire becomes religiously radicalized, dangerous, and subversive, literally to the point of Luther and his critics hurling shit at each other.

Part two, Rising Action(s), examines (at a slower pace) the period of time between 1647 and 1740, which gave us the classics of literary pornography, if any works could be said to be pornographic classics. The School of Girls (*L'escolle des filles*), Chorier's *Aloysiæ Sigeæ Toletanæ satyra sotadica* (Luisa Sigea Toledana's Sotadic satire, on the secrets of love and sex), and Rochester's *St. James Park* and other poems. Though these works were still intended for mostly upper class readers, literacy and literature were becoming far more widespread, and the danger of the lower classes and (gasp) women and children reading them became abruptly recognized with the tidal wave of obscenity that Edmund Curll's activities represented —resulting in the category of obscene libel.

Part three, Climax, delves into the so-called Golden Age of erotic/obscene libel from 1741 to 1857, which marks the creation of pornography as a regulatory category (the Obscene Publications Act) and the increasing widespread usage of the word itself. The Golden Age, so far as there was one, resulted in the works of the two greatest erotic writers, John Cleland and the Marquis de Sade and the resulting works of *Fanny Hill* and *Justine/Juliette*. These two of course stand out for the usual reasons of their insane popularity, but they also mark a key division in our story here, a key turning point or a before-and-after. Before Cleland and de Sade (and others of their time), erotic discourse or obscene libel is notable

Brian M. Watson

for its combination of social, religious or political critique/
satire with erotic language or situations. Cleland's *Fanny Hill*
strips (pun possibly intended) all sort of even slightly dangerous criticism away from unadulterated eroticism, resulting
in the most recognizably modern form of pornography. De
Sade, however goes the other route and layers and heaps and
nearly drowns his sexy material in critique of the church, the
state, philosophy, love, culture—you name it. The two men's
different fates signal to their contemporaries and descend-
ants what is possible and what is not—there are attempts to
prosecute Cleland but he escapes unscathed, whereas de Sade
would spend nearly the entirety of his life in prison either for
libertine actions or libertine writings. The rest of this section
details the explosion in erotic, porn-for-porn's sake works
that sprung up following Cleland, the types of works we normally think of when we think of Victorian and early literary
pornography (though, in fact, it is late literary pornography in
this timeline). Finally, Part Four, La Petite Mort/Futuumeshi,
closes us out by bringing us, in a roughshod way, away from
the out rightly erotic texts to the other works of literature
that were threatened and damaged by a too-robust Obscene
Publications Act, which included Havelock Ellis, James Joyce,
E.M. Forester, Radclyffe Hall, and of course, D.H. Lawrence,
which could be said to be the inheritors of the Sadean type or
erotic critique or discourse. The closing section will examine
the birth' of Hollywood-style pornography through filmog-
raphy and photography and how the current permissive conditions developed.

Throughout each of these sections, the development and
back-and-forth of Western European (specifically British, but
also French) histories of sexuality, marriage, the family, and
privacy are explored in tandem as to fully contextualize the
meaning of erotic works, obscene libel, and then pornography.
From this I draw three primary conclusions: i) pornography is
a creation of class conflict as much as anything can be, that

10

is, it was something that the middle and working classes were prosecuted for, not the upper—it was perfectly acceptable for the 'right' audience to have access to this material; ii) erotic writing (and then obscene libel and pornography) function(s/ed) as a way to critique societal, political and religious figures, traditions and morality; and iii) the pendulum-swing between sexual restrictiveness and permissiveness, the action of libertine writers and the reaction of authorities or reformation societies is one of the most important macro-trends in history—there is no pornography without obscenity, no obscenity without erotica. Obscene books, plays, poetry, art, and engravings were the ones that created and shaped our modern ideas about the pornographic—the arrival of photography and film didn't change anything. Indeed, photos and videos would follow the same path that books and poetry had decades and centuries earlier—only faster.

As suggested by the very definition of the word—"the explicit description or exhibition of sexual subjects or activity in literature, painting, films, etc., in a manner intended to stimulate erotic rather than aesthetic feelings"—an aesthetic judgment is inseparable from the thing itself. As such, I am aware that my individual judgment of what is 'extreme and obscene' may be different from another's—this definitional issue is prevalent throughout the field—but I have attempted to compensate for my judgment by focusing on works that aroused public controversy and criticism. This is not only because those works that created a particular splash or resulted in legal proceedings created more records and therefore more sources and material to work from, but also because they demonstrate the material that contemporaries found the most disturbing and therefore the most deserving of note or censorship.

In a recent work, Ian Moulton has strongly argued that to slap together the usual list of erotic libertine works (including many of the erotic works touched on in this research) into a canon of pornography creates a "compelling but in some ways dubious teleology:"

> a movement towards modernity, the market, and the public sphere. They also arguably demonstrate an increasing focus on sexual activity as an end in itself, at times creating what Stephen Marcus has memorably called a 'pornotopia' in which sex has no relation to procreation, family, society, or politics, but exists only as a utopian source of physical delight: a fantasy world primarily structured to stimulate the masturbatory fantasies of heterosexual male readers. . . But libertine narrative constitutes only a part of early modern erotic writing as a whole. Not only were erotic texts written in a wide range of genres – verse satire, lyric poetry, epigrams, and drama, as well as dialogues and novels – their content went well beyond the limits of libertinism, if by libertinism we mean the celebration of rebellious elite masculine sexuality. [15]

And I agree thoroughly, and have sought to reach into other fields and types of works that would not necessarily fall into the usual (hi)story of pornography—such as the works of Boccaccio, Martin Luther, Radclyffe Hall, and others. For me, pornography—beginning with Pietro Aretino—is made up of two competing trends or styles running alongside of and wrapped up inside of each other that eventually diverge. One is the motive of social, religious, and political critique that I have identified as being a distinguishing feature of early erotic discourse, obscenity, and reaches perhaps its highest form in the scathing and blistering works of the Marquis de Sade (and of course, survived in other formats beyond him). The other is the purely sexual, commercial, reader-arousal motive that perhaps reaches its finest form in the work of John Cleland, various Victorian scribblers, and the backalley photographic and Hollywood visual distributors. The cases and examples picked here are indeed small or singular examples, especially in light of the tidal wave of erotic material produced from the middle of the nineteenth century onwards, but these examples are selected because the impact that they had.

I have attempted throughout this text to use three different words for the material covered —erotica, obscenity, and pornography—to refer to three distinct phases in the development of pornography. Generally speaking, I use the word *erotica* or *erotic literature* to refer to material from the fifteenth and sixteenth centuries, publications that combined the erotic with social, religious and political criticism. *Obscene literature* and its formulations refers, generally, to the period of time between the British publisher Edmund Curll (who I identify as a key figure in this history) to the passing of the British Obscene Publications Act in 1857. I have tried to use the word *pornography* where I am injecting modern judgment or in describing post-Act works. However, there are several places where the word overlaps for stylistic or readability purposes. In addition, this story is as much a (his)story as it is a history—just as most of our surviving sources from the past are written by men, for men, and with a male audience in mind, pornography and obscenity is more aggressively so. While some historians have pointed out that we can't rule out female readership (especially in the late 1700's and beyond—with one exception in the 1600s, where a group of maids in the French royal court were discovered with a bad book) it is much harder to document and trace than male involvement, consumption and production of pornography and obscene works. But I have tried to do my best to address both contemporary and modern ideas in the pages that follow. Any mistakes are my own.

PART I: FOREPLAY
(1338-1644)

2

1338 – 1556: Arentine and Tridentine

Perverted Humanists

W E BEGIN our history where the modern world is so often said to have been "born"—the Italian Renaissance, the great rebirth and flourishing of European humanism after the (not so) dark centuries of the Dark Ages. That is a tautology as much as it is inaccurate, and has been remarkably disrupted by recent scholarship and scholars of the Middle Ages that have shown just how vibrant, colorful and alive the era was, and how much this vibrancy helped contribute to the Italianate outpouring that would later be called the Renaissance. There were of course many erotic works that circulated among small groups and communities during the Middle Ages, but the main reason we are beginning with the Renaissance is because it is necessary to talk about the cultural and philosophical reasons, as well as the technological ones, that helped to contribute to 'pornography' as a genre.[16]

Italy at the time of the Renaissance was not the country of Italy that we know today—after the collapse of the Roman

Empire and the prolonged breakup of the post-classical era, the peninsula had settled into several powerful city-states, from the Duchy of Milan and Republic of Venice in the north to the Church-ruled 'theocracy' of the Papal States in the peninsular heart, to the Kingdom of Naples (and Sicily) in the south. The various powers were locked in a perpetual state of rivalry, backstabbing and shifting alliances that caused political headaches but spurred economic and cultural competition. By far the most significant in the cultural realm (for our discussion here) was the Kingdom of Florence under the Medici banking family. Over the course of decades, the Medicis almost single-handedly ignited the Renaissance, giving birth and sponsorship to many of the giants of Western culture— Leonardo da Vinci, Donatello, Fra Angelico, Michelangelo, and Galileo. But before all of them, came Giovanni Boccaccio— the man that laid the fields that would bear such fruit, one of would be pornography in its earliest forms.

More specifically, came *The Decameron*. *The Decameron* has a long history of catching unprepared readers and underprepared undergraduates who are shocked (shocked, I say!) to discover such an early and respectable author dealing with such 'taboo' subjects. Although Boccaccio's book is not usually labeled as 'pornography,' it remains important as a starting point for us, both for how it would go on to influence Pietro Aretino, and as an example of a pre-Aretine humanist work that utilized erotic discourse without any significant blowback.

Put simply, Renaissance humanism was the belief that the present world of living people deserved as much attention as the future world of lost or saved souls.[17] Although this idea doesn't seem terribly radical today, at the time it was a revolutionary idea in a culture that was very much focused on the afterlife. The fact that this idea doesn't seem all that insane is a testament to how successful humanism was as a philosophy. In actual practice, humanism was a study of the legacy of Roman and Greek antiquity that concerned itself with the rediscovery, restoration, retranslation and reinterpretation of them. As scholars have pointed out, it ranged from archeological digs to uncover of dusty scrolls in monasteries and attics, but it comes to pervade "almost all areas of post-medieval culture, including theology, philosophy, political thought, jurisprudence, medicine, mathematics and the creative arts... And in this way it was to become the embodiment of, and vehicle for, that very classical tradition that is the most fundamental aspect of the continuity of European cultural and intellectual history." [18]

Humanists (lead by the Florentine poet Petrarch) opposed a school of thought known as scholasticism, which had dominated Christian and European thinking throughout the Middle Ages.[19] They argued that it created scholars secluded in their libraries, quibbling over abstract theology like how many angels could fit on a pinhead, or if God could create a boulder he could not lift. Instead, the humanists argued, education should create a citizen (that is, upper-class white male citizens) trained in the skills that would enable them to lead others in pursuit of public and moral good. They rejected theology and educational hierarchy and exegesis, instead advocating for people to look at 'the text itself,' and to use vernacular (common) languages over Latin or Greek. Humanism was primarily tied to northern Italianate (especially Florentine) and urban elites, where the need for well-educated secular civil servants and bureaucrats was the strongest.

In this, they were inspired by the Greek idea that the human should be the center and measure of all things, like in Leonardo da Vinci's famous *Vitruvian Man* diagram. In the eyes of humanists, Mr. Vitruvian should, from a young age, study ancient Greek and Roman texts on rhetoric, philosophy, history, grammar and poetry, which would teach him *humanitatis*, or the humanities. The result would be a citizen imbued with the Roman virtue of dedication to the common good of society—which humanists believed was consistent with the Gospel and was the hallmark of the devout Christian. In theory at least, the Humanist ideal was directed not so much at clerics and the upper classes, but to laymen (and everymen like Mr. Vitruvian) who spent their lives 'in the world.' Boccaccio was a perfect example of this: after convincing his father to let him study Church law at what would become the University of Naples, he would also spend much of his free time studying literature and then go on to writing poetry, which he considered his true vocation.

As a result, education in the humanist style became a powerful instrument for the reform of the church and of society. And humanists justifiably felt that a reform of the church and society was desperately needed. Under popes such as Alexander VI and Julius II, the papacy and the church had become corrupt; used as a means for personal and family profit over the Christian ideals of charity and poverty. Pope Alexander VI, for example, ignored the rule of clerical celibacy, both keeping mistresses in the Vatican and legitimizing the children he had by them. His successor, Julius II, also fathered illegitimate children and became known as the 'Warrior Pope' for leading armies across Italy —in contempt of such commandments as 'thou shalt not kill.' The abuses of the church extended far beyond Rome and the Curia: in fact, the ecclesiastical system was abused from the top down: "The most obvious was the absence of Bishops from their dioceses. . . . The same holds true for pastors of parishes. . .superstition and ignorance of the basic tenets of Christianity were. . .rampant."[20]

In answer, reformers and satirists launched regular attacks on the church the gluttonous monk, lecherous friar, and gullible priest became commonplace stereotypes in literature of the time. The reason I emphasize this is because these sorts of satires are the first seeds of modern pornography. As I noted in the introduction, the earliest forms of pornography were a 'type' of work used for religious, social, and political critique.

In fact, to critique the church of the time was to indulge in all three forms of criticism—the pope, after all, was both a religious and a political figure who engaged in incredible social scandals.

One of the first and finest examples of this sort erotic satirical critique is found in Boccaccio's 1353 *Decameron*. *The Decameron* is a collection of 100 short stories supposedly told over the course of ten days by seven young women and three young men who are taking shelter from the Black Death in the countryside outside of Florence, Italy. Each day, one of the ten is elected as King or Queen of the party, and chooses a storytelling topic such as 'misadventures that end happily' or 'things lost and regained' or 'tricks wives play on husbands.' Based on a topic, each King or Queen is charged with telling a story. The stories run the gamut from tragedy to humor to the erotic, and many of them are recognizable as satires of a particular group or idea, such as the ideal of fidelity. While there are a number of original stories, most of the *Decameron* was not Boccaccio's original work, they were stories that were already known or circulating around medieval Europe. With that said, the church and its officers—nuns, priests and abbots —are by far the most satirized and mocked.

For example, the first story of the compendium tells the story of 'Saint' Ciapelletto, who is actually a notoriously wicked man who takes "great delight in giving false testimony... particular pleasure in stirring up enmity, discord, and bad blood between friends, relatives and anybody else. . .he often found himself cheerfully assaulting or killing people with his own hands. . . He never went to church . . . He was perhaps the worst man ever born."[21] However, when he visits Burgundy, he falls deathly ill and a friar from a nearby convent comes to give him his last rites. Ciapelletto proceeds to tell the friar about his life in a way that makes him seem innocent and saintly while actually mocking the dimwitted friar. Upon Ciapelleto's death the friar preaches a sermon and the townspeople come to revere him as a saint. Thus Boccaccio starts off strong by having the first story be a deliberate ridicule of the practice of saintly canonization by the Catholic Church.

Boccaccio does not back off from his satire, as the second story of the same night is about the conversion of a Jew, who concludes after a visit to Rome that the papacy was so corrupt, the church had to be of divine inspiration. The members of the church, "from highest to lowest were flagrantly given to the sin of lust not only of the natural variety but of the sodomitic [homosexual], without the slightest display of shame or remorse." They were all "gluttons, winebibbers and drunkards without exception."[22] Returning home to his friend, who had tried to convert him, the Jew concludes that since the church still existed, even though the papacy and the Curia were working so hard to tear it down, it was proof that the church must be of divine origin, and he converts. In both of these stories Boccaccio is very careful not to say that the church as a whole is not divinely inspired, or that God is not real, but that the mortal caretakers of Christianity are failing to live up to their roles—first by ridiculing the people at the bottom, who are superstitious and ignorant of the basic tenets of Christianity and then by ridiculing the top, who should know better and be better.

In the fourth story of the first day and the first story of the third day, he turns to monastics, who were frequent targets of satirist and accused of scandal. The first one, 'A Monk and His Abbot,' is about a monk who sees a young woman and is "fiercely assailed by carnal desire," seduces her, and brings her back to his cell. While indulging in sin he is "carried away by the vigor of his passion," and loudly throws "all caution to the winds."[23] His abbot, walking down the hall, hears the couple, and spies on them through the peephole. Instead of confronting them immediately, he decides to wait until they are finished. The monk however, seemingly recovered from his passion, realizes he has been caught when he hears the abbot outside the door. Grasping for an escape, he tells the abbot he must go outside to bring in the firewood. Laughing at how doomed the monk is, the Abbot enters the room and finds the terrified and ashamed young lady. However, the abbot also succumbs to his desires, with the justification of, "Why not enjoy myself a little when I have the opportunity?...This is a fine-looking wench and not a living soul knows she's here...No one will ever find out and a sin that's hidden is half-forgiven."[24] The story goes on, narrating that, "he settled down beneath her instead of laying on top, and in this way he sported with her at a considerable length."[25] Meanwhile, the monk, who had only pretended to leave, snuck up and watched them through a chink in the wall. When the abbot finished, he found the monk in his office, saying, "I had failed until just now to [realize] that monks have women to support...but now you have shown me...and I shall always follow your good example."[26] The abbot, knowing he had been outwitted, swore the monk to secrecy and Boccaccio concludes that, "we can only assume that they afterward brought her back at regular intervals."[27] There is of course a good deal of humor in these episodes, as well as a bit of the carnivalesque tradition of the lessers getting the better of their betters, but there is also the very real suspicion about the authenticity of the chastity of monks and nuns.

Another story, 'Masetto of Lamporeccio,' is similar in the sense that it involves the sexual adventures of supposedly chaste monastics. The main character, Masetto, fakes being a deaf-mute and begins work as a gardener for a convent. A bold nun, realizing that he is unable to talk, begins talking about exploiting him for her own pleasure. Horribly offended, another nun cries out, "Don't you realize that we have promised God to preserve our virginity?" "Pah!" said the bold one "We are constantly making Him promises that we never keep! What does it matter if we fail to keep this one?"[28] Masetto, who has heard all of this, goes along with their plan until eventually, nun by nun, the entire convent is sleeping with him. Eventually, even the head of the convent, the abbess, attacks him in his sleep. For Masetto, this is the final straw, and he decides that if he "continu[es] to be dumb any longer he might do himself some serious injury,"[29] and confesses to the abbess. The abbess realizes that all of the nuns have outsmarted her and she reaches an arrangement where they tell the town that their praying managed to cure Masetto of being a deaf-mute and then hire him as their permanent 'caretaker.' Masetto lives happily ever after, "father[ing] quite a number of nunlets and monklets."[30]

By far the most obscene of the text is that of Alibech and Rustico, the tenth of the third day. Until quite recently, many translators refused to translate it because it involved forthright sexuality as well as the sexual awakening and desire of a girl. The story concerns a "graceful and young"[31] 14-year-old girl named Alibech. As it turns out, she is not Christian, but takes a liking to the Christians in her town and asks one of them to tell her the best way to serve God. They tell her that "the ones who served God best were those who put the greatest distance between themselves and earthly goods, as happened in the case of people who had gone to live in the remoter parts" of the desert. The very next morning, Alibech decides that she should set out into the desert to learn about herself and to learn how to serve God.

After a few days of wandering in the desert, she is dehydrated and delirious, but manages to stumble into the hut of a recluse monk. "On observing how young and exceedingly pretty she was, the good man was afraid to take her under his wing lest the devil should catch him unawares,"[32] so he sends her deeper into the desert, to a monk even more ascetic and holy than he. This second monk comes to the same conclusion as the first, and sends her onward, to the most holy and pious monk he knows, Rustico. Rustico, determined to prove that "he possessed a will of iron," decides not to turn her away. Unfortunately, a few days later he falls into temptation, and eventually surrenders to it. Discovering that she is completely innocent on the subject of sex, he tells her that God most loves putting the 'Devil back in hell.' When she asks what he means, he has her undress with him to demonstrate. When she asks what is 'sticking out' from him, he tells her that it is the Devil, and continues with, "But you have something instead, that I haven't . . . You have Hell. [And] if you are prepared to take sufficient pity upon me to let me put him back into hell, you will be giving me marvelous relief, as well as rendering incalculable service and pleasure to God."[33]

As you are no doubt guessing, the girl agrees to help Rustico 'put the devil back into hell,' and although it is painful at first, over the next few days, every time the devil rages hard, Alibech was more than willing to help Rustico put him under control, and soon develops a 'taste' for it. A very powerful and overwhelming taste. In fact, she develops such a love of serving God that, "the girl took so much stuffing out of him that he eventually began to turn cold. . . . Rustico, who was living on a diet of herb roots and water, was quite incapable of supplying her requirements."[34] This story plays on the contemporary stereotype that women were the much more interested and aggressive sexual partners, and that Rustico was dwindling because he was using his limited supply of sperm without resting. But luckily for Rustico, a group of the Alibech's countrymen come to his aid by tracking her out into the desert and then returning her home to be married.[35]

Many translators refused to translate this scene. For example, in Payne's 1931 translation, a comment reads that: "The translators regret that the disuse into which magic has fallen, makes it impossible to render the technicalities of that mysterious art into tolerable English; they have therefore found it necessary to insert several passages in the original Italian."[36] This should be evidence enough to indicate that *The Decameron* was considered, even the twentieth century scandalous and disturbing enough to be obscene or pornographic; unfit to be rendered into English. But Boccaccio never faced trouble or prosecution from the church or the government of Florence, where he lived. Indeed, why would a translator in 1931 be too afraid to translate this story, whereas Boccaccio, living in a far more 'oppressive' time, where the church had far more power, could write these stories and achieve great fame? To answer that, we need to zoom out a bit larger and look at the technological and epidemiological status of Europe.

While we have had our nose stuck in the tales and adventures of *The Decameron*, it probably became easier to ignore the framing story of death and destruction. Indeed, many of the readers that turned to Boccaccio's stories may have been doing it to escape the disease raging around them. The Black Death (1346-53) was a monumental event in European history, and one of the greatest pandemics in history. As Philip Ziegler recounts in his book on the subject, the plague caused the deaths of one to two thirds of the European population, anywhere from 75-200 million people, and it took a century and a half for the population to recover to pre-plague levels.[37]

The symptoms and causes must have been utterly bewildering to a culture that did not have an understanding of germ theory or infectious diseases—the plague was blamed on everything from the alignment of the planets, to earthquakes that released bad air (*mal-aria*), to an incredibly angry God. No doubt some of the critiques of the church originated from that last line of thinking. A quote from our Boccaccio serves to illustrate some of the impacts, "They sickened by the thousands daily, and died unattended and without help. Many died in the open street, others dying in their houses. . . . Consecrated churchyards did not suffice for the burial of the vast multitude of bodies, which were heaped by the hundreds in vast trenches. . ."[38] But in some roundabout ways, the plague had 'positive' effects. For example, demands for labor

Brian M. Watson

and luxury goods increased the wages of both rural and urban workers, and this contributed to the decline and collapse of the institutions of serfdom and feudalism—or the societal systems most resembling feudalism—in many countries. It also had a major impact by decimating the numbers of a particular small group of urban workers; scribes.

One question that is commonly asked by students is "why did it take Europeans so long to develop the printing press?" After all, wooden block printing was developed and used in China and Japan by the year 200CE, over a millennia before Gutenberg's little machine. Even granting that technology takes a long time to spread, the idea of wooden block printing and movable type were known to Europeans before Gutenberg—in fact, some enterprising individuals used wooden block printing to create playing cards in the 1200s and 1300s. So why didn't one of them make the logical leap to printing books? After all, there was a large market for books: like today, students attending university would have to get copies of the books assigned by the professor. Like today, these books would be absurdly expensive and burdensome. Like today, there was also a market for graduating seniors to sell their secondhand books to incoming freshmen. However, *unlike* today, the books were not printed with highly efficient printing presses and at huge profit margins. Instead, the books were so expensive because each copy was produced by a scribe who would write and illustrate the books by hand. As a result, in cities such as London, Paris, Venice, Florence and Rome, there were a great number of competing scribes, which had the effect of keeping the prices (relatively) reasonable. Along came a little rat called the Black Death—which hit the urban areas occupied by scribes the hardest—and prices shot up. To make things worse for the destitute students, literacy was becoming increasingly common as every wealthy lady or man clamored for their own copies of religious and romantic texts written in the vernacular (the common tongue, such as

26

English, French, or German), thus straining the scribal output to the breaking point. Furthermore, by 1400 books had begun to move from ecclesiastical and religious contexts such as churches and monasteries to homes, town halls, and into the personal libraries of wealthy lay people.[39]

By 1300, for the first time, "everyone knew someone who could read and there were books in every church and every village."[40] The scribes, decimated and dwindling after the plague, could simply not keep up. Suddenly, there was space for an entrepreneur, someone who could take techniques learned as a blacksmith and goldsmith to make something new, someone who was in incredible debt and needed to pull off something really profitable—someone, in fact, just like Johannes Gutenberg. The combination of old technologies, such as movable type (used to quickly copy any text), and old skills (the abilities of a blacksmith or a goldsmith to create letter molds and fonts), with new technologies (Gutenberg's invention of a new ink that lasted longer), in the perfect storm of cultural and economic conditions, made the Gutenberg printing press a revolutionary breakthrough. The printing press was embraced with great fervor by everyone in Europe—Protestants, Catholics, Humanists, Scholastics—everyone. Less than 25 years later, there were nearly 200 printing presses across Europe; London, Paris, Venice, Florence, Rome, all the places where scribes had once ruled supreme.

As already noted, works in the popular tongues became increasingly in demand, so printers began churning out works in French, Italian, English and German. Though it predates the print revolution, one popular French text, *The Song of Roland*, commented on this trend of popular language, saying, "No one now says anything much about the Greeks and Romans—there is no more word of them; their glowing embers are extinguished."[41] Although Greek and Latin would hobble on for a few more centuries in classrooms and the Vatican, the poet of *Roland* was correct; Greek and Latin were declining and the common tongues were on the rise. When William Caxton, the first printer in London, was opening his print house, the first work he chose to publish was not an esoteric or astute Latin text, instead, it was Chaucer's *Canterbury Tales*, which has its own bawdy language and jokes, much in the vein of Boccaccio. It is undoubtedly obvious how scandalous Chaucer's *Tales* would have been to some of his contemporaries. So why *The Canterbury Tales* not considered obscene? Where were the popes, kings and assassins that would move against later works and authors? The answer is, basically, too little, too soon. Although, yes, *The Canterbury Tales* does fuse the erotic satire of Boccaccio with the availability and accessibility of a printing press, Chaucer did not write for the larger audience the printing press enabled. In fact, he was writing for a small audience of upper-class individuals who would have recognized the characters as based on notable figures. Secondly, Caxton published the work in 1475, nearly 75 years after the death of Chaucer—the work was no less scandalous, but it had been addressed and written for a different time and different people. Finally, only a third of the copies appear to have been published in the cheaper paper format intended for a general audience. The other 60% were published on much more expensive parchment which probably exceeded the purchasing power of a middle or lower class individual, even if that individual could read.

The power and potential of the printing press had yet to be realized. It would take a more scandalous and pioneering individual to harness the power of print—an individual that could force kings and princes to cower and beg, one that was courted and flattered by the most powerful figures of his time. The Scourge of Princes, the divine and obscene Pietro Aretino.

The Scourge of Princes

THE REASON we didn't begin our story with Pietro Aretino, the 'father' of pornography, is because he is as much a person as he is a moment. All of the things we have discussed up to this point—Europe after the Black Death, humanism, the printing press, the corrupted church and the rise of the common vernacular—came to a head in the mind of Aretino. Simultaneously genius and madman, Aretino was a man without rival in the history of Western Europe. He was the first one to hit on the idea of combining titillating erotic dialog in the vernacular, high-brow cultural and religious critique, and the proto-capitalistic potential of the printing press. Even though he was a force of nature in his own time, he is almost totally forgotten today—largely because of the scandal around his 'invention' of pornography.

Aretino was a 16th century Italian author, playwright, poet, satirist, and socio-cultural critic. He is perhaps the best-kept secret of the Renaissance, and perhaps the best-kept secret in all of literature. Among other things, he has been credited with the first public relations campaign, the first gossip rag, the first overt literary extortion attempt, and being the first *vox populi*. He was lauded as the "Divine Aretino" in the same breath that he was cursed as the 'Scourge of Princes.'

More than any other person of this star-studded era, Aretino represented a man of the times, a consummate self-fashioner, and a demonstration of what the printing press was capable of in the right hands. Although he was born out of wedlock in an obscure backwater, and banished from his hometown as a teenager, he managed to survive with wits, intellect, and a heavy dose of good luck. By the time he died, he had survived assassination attempts by the Church, been honored by popes he had mocked, manipulated the kings of France, Spain and the Holy Roman Empire into competing for his praise, and been knighted as a Knight of Rhodes and a Knight of St. Peter. His works inspired Shakespeare, Ben Johnson, John Donne, Rabelais, Machiavelli, Michelangelo, Titian and others.

To begin, well, at the beginning, Pietro Aretino was born in the little cathedral city of Arezzo (Aretino meaning 'from Arezzo'), on the night of April 19th-20th, 1492. It was the same year that Christopher Columbus 'discovered' the New World. A few days prior to his birth, Lorenzo de Medici, called the Magnificent, had died. Lorenzo was, more or less, the ruler of the Florentine Republic, and one of the great sponsors of humanism and the Italian Renaissance. Though Lorenzo's death marked the beginning of the decline of the Florentine Renaissance, his life had managed to create an atmosphere that was perfect for the nourishing and flowering of someone like Pietro.

PETRVS ARRETINVS ACERRIMVS VIRTVTVM AC VITIORVM DEMOSTRATOR

Figure 1: Pietro Aretino, drawn by Marcantonio Raimondi.

He was the son a lower-middle-class cobbler named Luca del Tura and Margherita Bonci, a woman of supposedly great beauty and minor fame—she was used as the model for Saint Mary in a fresco at a local church. Despite modeling Mother Mary, she may not have been a model for all the virtues; her husband discovered she was carrying on an affair with a local nobleman and left in a huff, joining a group of mercenaries, and was never heard from again. This nobleman, Luigi Bacci, raised Aretino more or less as his own, having him educated in the humanist style that was common in Italy at the time. Pietro would later assert in his very self-serving way that "I was born in a charity ward, but with the soul of a king."[42]

Two things in his childhood seem to have had major impact on him. The first were the burlesque scribblings of a local poet and barber named Burchiello, "whose Muse was a hobo Venus of crossroads bred among taverns and the low haunts of vulgar company" (e.g. the town whore).[43] It seems that he memorized Burchiello's vulgar Italian poetry and then began to imitate and outdo him, something that would provide the key for his success later in life. The second event was a riot in the town that started when a Florentine tax collector showed up to collect taxes. The people of Arezzo had been harboring resentment at the high taxes and low rewards that the Florentine Republic had been subjecting them to. The visit of the tax collector triggered the gathering of a large crowd in the town square, which turned into a large mob, and, in the words of biographer James Cleugh, the "houses of the rich, mainly supporters of Florentine policy were plundered, some were burnt to the ground. A priest. . .was dragged from his hiding spot and butchered in the streets. . . . Other pro-Florentines were hanged from balconies or tortured as 'sodomites' by having a lighted torch thrust between their naked buttocks. . .finally, the castle, the symbol of Florentine rule, was destroyed."[44]

Brian M. Watson

The next day, the Florentine army burst into the town, sacked it, and carried off 30 of the top citizens as hostages. To the young Pietro, "these turbulent scenes of merciless carnage, destruction and plunder, the gossip of treachery and deceit on all sides," seemed to inspire in him a lifelong aversion to violence and hatred.[45] Even when chased down by the assassins of the church, he would never harbor much hatred towards the people sent to kill him.

One way or another, he left home in 1505 or 1506, at the age of 14, for the nearby city of Perugia and became a bookbinder's assistant. This experience no doubt gave him a great appreciation for how the printing press worked and the intricacies of the trade; information that would aid him greatly in the future. He may or may not have observed the dalliances or heard gossip about the monks and nuns at a nearby monastery, something that would go on to feature strongly in his writing, but the truth is difficult to ascertain, as Aretino was a promiscuous liar his entire life. While in Perugia, it seems that he roomed with one Agnolo Firenzuola—who would later become a famous abbot. During his early days however, Firenzuola engaged in debauchery and drunken antics with Aretino, once even appearing buck naked in their apartment window in order to scandalize the elderly women of the town. It seems Pietro was forced to flee the city after he vandalized a statue of Saint Mary Magdalene by painting a lute in her hands and makeup on her face, which would have marked her as a prostitute. The prank, unsurprisingly, did not appeal to the clergy, the town, or the ruling Baglioni family. It was discreetly explained to him that if he did not make himself scarce, he would face investigation by the Inquisition, an idea that did not seem to appeal to him at all, so he took off for Rome.

Arriving in Rome at the age of 24, penniless and homeless, things looked bleak for the boy from Arezzo. However, his ten years of wandering seem to have made him a great authority in the gutter jargon and low-class style of Italy's underside.

Surprisingly (or perhaps not, when we consider Boccaccio's descriptions!), 16th century Rome ended up being the perfect home for him. He began to be known for his wit and his ability to party; he ended up in the services of Agostino Chigi, a self-made millionaire, and made himself popular at Chigi's lavish dinner parties. These dinners were famous throughout Italy, and were frequented by both Roman nobility and major figures in the church. The drunken carousing of these parties became legend. For example, at one these dinners, an intoxicated Chigi told Pope Leo X that he was so rich that he had no idea how much money actually owned, and to prove his point, he took plates and bowls made of solid gold and threw them out the window, into the Tiber River. Unknown to Leo and the others, Chigi had secretly installed a net below the window to catch the crockery.[46]

Aretino had found the perfect audience for his obscene and witty poems, and became Chigi's unofficial jester for the next couple of years. However, this was not enough for Pietro Aretino—according to Cleugh, he was determined to be the "one to give rather than receive orders, he intended to have all of Rome at his feet. . . . He knew he could only do it in one way. Most people, he could see, succeeded by force or fraud."[47] Aretino however, recognized a third avenue; by combining his pen and satirical eye with the untapped power of the printing press, he realized he could become a sort of Boccaccio on steroids (for what it's worth, he was a huge fan of Boccaccio, and his favorite story was the Masetto one). He only needed a topic that would entertain all of Rome. Finally, in 1516, an opportunity fell into his lap; the death of the pope's elephant.

The pope's elephant? Indeed, Pope Leo X had been given a pet elephant by King Manuel I of Portugal as a gift in 1514. A letter between two German diplomats describe what happened two years later:

> You have no doubt heard that the pope has a great
> animal, called Elephant [Hanno], and that he holds

it in great honor and loves it much. Now you must know that this animal is dead. When it was taken sick the Pope was in great distress, and summoned several physicians and said to them: "If it is possible, cure Elephant for me." Then they did their best; made a careful diagnosis and administered a purge that cost five hundred golden florins, but it was in vain, for the animal died. The pope grieved much for Elephant. They say he gave a thousand ducats for Elephant; for it was a wonderful animal, and had a long snout of prodigious size.[48]

Leo was heartbroken. He commissioned Raphael to paint a life-sized portrait of the elephant, and he wrote a pompous Latin epigraph for it himself. All of Rome was still gossiping and snickering behind Leo's back when suddenly, hundreds of copies of a pamphlet titled *The Last Will and Testament of the Elephant Hanno* appeared on the streets of Rome. *The Last Will and Testament* was a resounding satire, mocking nearly every single cardinal and authority figure in Rome:

Item to my heir, the workshop of St Peter, I give the golden covering which I wear on festal occasions, on condition that they do not put the alms of the said workshop to unholy uses. . . . Item to my heir, the Cardinal Santa Croce, I give my knees, so that he can imitate my genuflections [cocksucking], but only on the condition that he tells no more lies in Council. . . . Item to my heir, Cardinal Danti Quattro, I give my jaws so that he can devour the revenues of Christ more readily. . . . Item to my heir, Cardinal Grassi, I give my [generative organs] as he is the most incorrigible fornicator. . . .[49]

If another pope had been in power, Aretino would have faced

immediate arrest, torture and imprisonment. However, Leo X was, like Pietro, a Florentine that enjoyed seeing the Roman cardinals around him mocked. The boy from Arezzo found himself in a private audience with the pope, who hired Aretino a sort of personal court jester, stealing him away from Chigi. In just a few years, Aretino had gone from penniless to fawned-over by the pope—and now he could really begin to shine.

The Positions and 'The Reasonings'

WITH GREAT ACKNOWLEDGEMENT and reward came, unfortunately, great suspicion and inspection. Aretino had not won many friends with his caricature of the cardinals and their sins, and in 1521, when Pope Leo X died from a bout of pneumonia after a very un-Papal hunting trip, Aretino lost his protector. As the common saying went, Leo had "taken office like a fox, and ruled like a lion [and he] died like a dog."[50] As usual, the cardinals met at the Vatican and began their arguments over who would be the next pope. Also as usual, kings, queens, dukes and lords competed with each other to get their candidate elected pope. As with any major event in early modern Europe, pamphleteers, propagandists and satirists took to the streets of Rome and did quick business, supporting or decrying particular candidates to anyone who would listen (or pay). Aretino, of course, was unable to resist such an explosive scene, and as he was the greatest writer of jargon and gutter Italian, he entered the fray with his own pamphlets:

> If Filisco's pope he'll go for a whole year without a lawsuit...[if] Mantua's pope he'll try to avoid [touching] small boys...Ponzetta will spend all the money in lavish parties...and Grassi will have to desert his [illicit] wife, poor dear.... And though his poor heart bleeds, Valle'll have to give up his brats, Cesarini his whores, and Trani [will give up] his poor ma, who

Brian M. Watson

loves him so.[51]

Unlike some of the other writers, Aretino had an eye on increasing his own reputation and notoriety, not that of others, so he would openly sign his ribald songs with lines such as: "It's really surprising that the Cardinal's College / Can find no way of stopping Aretino's Verbiage."[52] Aretino's strategy was to get a friend or family member of Leo X elected and guarantee himself many more years of financial support and renown. However, the strategy failed. Unable to compromise on a candidate, the Cardinal's College elected Adrian of Utrecht as Pope Adrian VI, a cardinal who had not even bothered to attend the voting session. Adrian was reputed to "scorn the vanities of this world, including everything Pietro so hugely enjoyed—witty literature, grand painting, gorgeous young women, brilliant banquets and dazzling garments." According to biographer Thomas Caldecot Chubb realizing his bind, and thinking over the verses he had written, Aretino decided to flee Rome and spend some time in the countryside with a friend, rather than risk, that "forgiveness might not be on the long list of Adrian's Christian virtues." [53]

Luckily for Aretino, Adrian VI's papacy lasted barely a year before his unfortunate death and his successor was Clement VIII, another Medici. Unluckily for Aretino, when he tried to take the same strategy of mocking the power-hungry individuals around the new pope, he managed to directly upset a man known as Giovanmatteo Giberti, who held an important role in Clement's Datary (a papal office). Giberti was infuriated, saying "Let that lewd speaker [speak] as he will. But since he has dared to snarl at me, I shall find a way to cut his tongue from his loud mouth." In a very roundabout way, Giberti would find a justification within the year.

That summer, an artist named Giulio Romano was working on painting saints in the Vatican. In the spirit of bored workers and doodling schoolchildren everywhere, he decided to dash off 16 sketches of obscene character to amuse his friends. In the words of one contemporary, these sketches "dealt with the various attitudes and postures in which lewd men have intercourse with lewd women." Had this been a century beforehand, a good number of rich and powerful nobles would have had a laugh at the sketches, passed them around to their friends, and then they would have disappeared forever. However, along with the printing press, another German technology with great and terrible potential had filtered down into Italy—engraving.

Inspired by the printing press, artists looking for mass reproduction had turned to carving a block of wood, filling the gaps with ink, and then pressing them on paper, resulting in what was called a 'woodblock print.' These woodblocks were capable of several thousand impressions, and were often colored in with watercolors or by hand. In fact, woodblocks were most often used to create playing cards. The downside to using wood was that the images would begin to fade and wear down after a few thousand impressions. Additionally, like with the printing press, demand very quickly outstripped supply, and an alternative method was needed. This alternative was found in copper, first by goldsmiths (who had a right to metal engraving under feudal law), and then by painters, the most famous and influential of which was Albrecht Dürer. Dürer, much like Aretino, realized that the developing middle class could not yet afford to own beautiful paintings or decorations, but they could afford copper engravings, which could be sold by the hundreds of thousands.

Although Dürer was the first to realize the potential profits and fame, he was not the only one. One Marcantonio Raimondi (who drew our picture of Aretino above), from Bologna, stole Dürer's engraving technique and used it to print a few hundred copies of Romano's dirty pictures, arguing in a letter to his friend that "they will circulate, and [you and I] will at the same time become both rich and famous." And they did. However, Raimondi perhaps sold the engravings far too eagerly and recklessly, to every possible customer, which, even in Rome, led to his arrest and imprisonment by Clement VI. In a lucky break, his friend Pietro Aretino managed to secure his release. The thankful Raimondi showed Aretino the engravings that he had been imprisoned for, and Aretino declared that he was inspired by them, and wrote 16 sonnets to go along with them, dedicating them in a letter to "all hypocrites [such as Giberti], for I am all out of patience with their scurvy strictures and their villainous judgment and that dirty custom that forbids the eyes to see what most delights them. What harm is there to see a man possess a woman? Are the beasts freer than we?" The pairing of the engravings with Aretino's dirty poems created something really unique—perhaps the first *Playboy Magazine* in all of history.

Figure 2: from a 1602 edition of Aretino's poetry.

Each poem is imagined as a sort of dialog between a courtesan and a client, who mutually urge each other, in the crudest possible terms and details, to make the most of their intercourse. In several cases, the courtesans or the male lovers were given the names of actual political figures and notable women, continuing Aretino's trend of satirizing religious, social, and political figures. As mentioned before, this trend is probably the key to the difference between early obscenity and modern pornography. Here is a polite and proper translation of one of the *I Modi* poems by Samuel Putnam in 1923, who went to great lengths to avoid offending propriety:

> At sylvan tourneys let us joust, dear one,
>> As Adam did, and Eve, in Eden's shade;
>> And if I break a lance, don't be afraid:
>> That is the sequel to our rustic fun.
>> Speaking of Adam, it is sad that he has run
>> His last brave course and no more bends a blade;
>> Sad, too, that in that dull and heavenly glade
>> One cannot do as one on earth has done!
>> I know, they blame the apple: that's not true;
>> Look at the birds and beasts, and you will see
>> That we on earth do merely what we must.
>> But this is not a time for jest; do you
>> Not feel the wave that's swelling up in me?
>> Then, come! Take arms! against a sea of -- Lust!
> [54]

Here is a much more literal 1989 translation by Lynne Lawner:

> **He:** Lets' fottere [fuck], my love, let's fottere,
>> Since all of us were born only to fottere.

You adore the cazzo[cock] and I the potta [pussy].
The world would be nothing without this act.
If it were proper to fottere after death,
I'd say let's fottere ourselves to death,
Then we could fottere Adam and Eve,
Who died such a dishonourable death.
She: Truly, if those truants hadn't eaten
that treacherous apple in the garden,
Lovers would long ago have quenched their lust.
But let's stop chatting. Stick your cazzo in
So that it reaches my heart, and crush the soul
That lives or dies issuing from the cazzo.
He: Don't leave out my balls [don't stop my orgasm] -
Take [it] inside the potta,
those witnesses of every extreme pleasure[55]

It is perhaps a testament to Aretino's style that these poems continued to shock and disturb moralists for centuries. You can almost hear the pain one 20th century historian was in as he wrote that, "these sonnets have no literary touches, unlike the author's later pornography. The wit is coarse and blunt, meant to shock like a blow to the face."[56] And shock it did, like a blow to the face of Giovanmatteo Giberti, Aretino's sworn enemy. Through some malicious hand, the 16 poems, one of which parodied Giberti, found their way to his desk, and he ordered Aretino's imprisonment. When the guards arrived to arrest the poet, however, they found his rooms empty. Aretino, with his amazing self-preservation instincts, realized he had overstepped and fled Rome. Writing from Mantua, Aretino continued to assail Giberti and the pope poetically, writing mockery after parody after satire, and distributing them to the masses. Giberti found himself the butt of jokes across Italy.

Deciding that normal, legal retaliation was out of his grasp, Giberti elected to retaliate with a knockout blow. Around two in the morning of July of 1525, Pietro was attacked while riding home after a night of drunken carousing and partying with his friends. A masked man on foot, carrying an 18-inch dagger, seized the horse's reins and stabbed him twice in the chest. He was picked up by the city guard shortly thereafter, and brought to the city's *medicus* (doctor). Although the physician treated him as well as he could (the medical profession was just in its infancy in the 1500s), Aretino lingered on the threshold of death for weeks. By some miracle, he managed to recover. While he was on the mend he was visited by a young man called Achille della Volta. Della Volta asked Aretino accusingly if he had written a love sonnet to a maid named Lucrezia. In his way the Aretino replied that *of course* he had written the poem, it was an amazing bit of work. Della Volta was violently upset and asked Aretino how he was supposed to ignore a poem written to a woman that he loved, and admitted that he had been responsible for stabbing Aretino a few weeks prior, and that his confessor had set him to apologize for the stabbing.

Who was his confessor? Well, it was the maligned Giovanmatteo Giberti. However, Aretino also knew that Giberti would not have acted without permission from the Pope. This meant that his sonnets were having the desired effect, and his power had grown enough that the pope and the Datary recognized him as a threat. If the attempt on his life hadn't come so close to ending it, Aretino probably would have considered it a sort of backhanded compliment. In the following weeks he managed to crawl out of bed and relearn how to write with his left hand, his right hand having been so mangled in the assassination attempt that it took him years to recover the use of it. The first thing he did was to fire off letters demanding that his assailants be arrested. Nothing happened. The second thing he did was to threaten to publish Giberti and Della Volta's names. Still nothing. Then he published them, but due Giberti's political position, these demands were ignored too.

Deciding that Rome, and even Mantua, were too dangerous

for him while Clement VI and Giberti remained in power, Aretino relocated in March of 1527 to Venice, the city which he would call his home until his death. Although Venice is part of the country of Italy today, that was not the case in the 16th century; it was its own country, The Republic of Venice, and it was one of the most powerful of the era. The Republic and the city of Venice had become generally regarded among Italian intellectuals as a refuge for individuals chased from their native states for political, social, or religious reasons. The city was ruled by a powerful oligarchy called the Council of Ten, who more or less allowed freedom of speech as long as it did not threaten their profits.

Setting up a small house on one of Venice's canals, Aretino quickly discovered that he could be more daring in his satire and broadcast his voice far wider than it had ever been before. By using the printing press, his sharp tongue, and his eye for satire, he could use his pen to get nearly anything he wanted. Over the course of the next few years, protected by the generally permissive culture of Venice, he reached the height of his power. One of his tricks was to write to a powerful nobleman (most of who came to know him by his nickname; the Scourge of Princes,), and threaten them with publication of various true or false gossip he had heard, unless they compensated him. In this manner he managed to provide himself with patronage from nearly all of the Italian princes, King Francis I of France (who sent him an elaborate gold chain as a bribe), and even Charles V of Spain and the Holy Roman Empire. In writing a biography of Aretino, one historian noted that "since the collapse of the civilization of Ancient Rome, no private individual had exercised so considerable an influence on politics and social behavior both by his written works and the force of his personality. Nor did any of his contemporaries achieve equal effects in either field, though many tried to do so."

One of the first works he published in Venice, was his *Ragionamenti,* which translates as *Dialogues* or literally, *The*

Reasonings. The Dialogues, credited as the first realized work of 'literary pornography,' is Aretino's most famous and influential work. It was published in two parts—*Capricciosi raigonamenti* (Capricious Discussions, 1536), and *Piacevoli raigonamenti* (Pleasing Discussions), published in 1556, the year of his death. Although both are available in modern translations, the first one is perhaps the best known, and was published in three parts by Hesperus Press; *The Secret Life of Nuns, The Secret Life of Wives,* and *The School of Whoredom.* This is the work more or less established what erotic and obscene writing would look like for the next two centuries, and indeed, still influences pornography today.

The 1536 *Capricciosi raigonamenti* begins with this introduction: "This begins the first day of conversation in which Nanna, beneath a fig tree in Rome, tells Antonia the life of the nuns, composed by the Divine Aretino for his amusement and to set forth correctly the three conditions of women." The titles of the Hesperus editions, and the introduction, suggest both the structure and the purpose of the *Dialogues*— women in the 15th and 16th centuries only had three acceptable choices open to them, as the men in power did not allow any more. They could become a holy nun, a wife, or a whore, and that was it. Additionally, the tripartite structure of the *Dialogue* allowed Aretino to criticize the church, society, and politics in turn for maximum effect.

Aretino, of course, was building off of earlier models of cultural critique. For example, the stories take place beneath a fig tree in a grape arbor, and over the course of three days involves one woman (Nanna) telling dozens of stories to Antonia, a fellow whore. *The Dialogues* is a much more stripped-down version of Boccaccio's *Decameron,* but Aretino was deliberately setting himself up as the descendant of both Boccaccio and Chaucer. The work opens in the grape arbor, when Antonia sees the worried and visibly upset Nanna in the arbor and comments:

Antonia: "What's troubling you, Nanna? Do you think that woe besmeared face befits a woman who rules the world?"

Nanna: "The world you say? [My] dear Antonia, there are troubles for everyone, and so many of them, just where you'd imagine there would be joys, that you'd be astonished. Take my word for it, this world is a filthy place.

Antonia: "You are right! The world is filthy, but for me, not for you. Why, you can afford the most fantastic delicacies, and everywhere, in all the piazzas and taverns, one heard nothing but "Nanna this" and "Nanna that." Your house is always packed like an egg, and all Rome danced around you.

Nanna: "And so it is, yet, I am not happy. . ."[57]

The reason for Nanna's unhappiness, we soon discover, is that her daughter Pippa has turned 16, and Nanna must decide her future. Unlike a son, whom she could send off to school or the military, or to anything he desired with her riches, her daughter can only become a nun, a wife, or a whore, so she is stuck in a conundrum. "But," Antonia asks, "Weren't you a nun, a wife, and a courtesan?" "Yes," Nanna replies, but "nowadays nuns, wives, and whores live different lives from what they used to." "Hah!" exclaims Antonia "Life has always been lived in the same way: people have always eaten, have always drunk, have always slept. . .and women have always pissed through the crack. Now, I would dearly love for you, Nanna, to tell me about the lives of the nuns, wives, and whores of your day, and I will tell you what you should do with your darling Pippa."[58]

Nanna agrees to this, saying that "today I shall tell you the life of the nuns, tomorrow the life of the wives, and the day after the life of the whores," and immediately begins her story. When she was a child, her father decided to make her into a nun, even against her mother's wishes—largely because then he would not have to pay for her dowry. She describes how she was dragged into the convent by her father, as every member of her family, and the boy she was in love with, mourned. As she entered the convent "the door slammed behind me and I heard a loud 'alas!'. . .that door shut so suddenly I didn't even have time to say goodbye to my family, I was sure I was stepping alive and half-breathing into the grave, and imagined I would see women half-dead from austerity and fasting." But when she enters the refectory (dining room) of the nunnery, she finds, to her great confusion, that "fresh, gleaming rosy" nuns and "handsome, well-groomed and gay young" monks and friars welcomed her eagerly by kissing her, "even vying with each other to see who could give the most honeyed ones [tongue kisses]." [59]

Still innocent and pure, and unaware of what was going on, Nanna sits down to eat with the nuns and monks, when suddenly, a man appears with a gift for the diners which are the cause of much laughter and appreciation. Nanna relates that, "They were glass fruits made in Murano near Venice to look like a prick. (But I was too innocent to realize that at the time)." This is perhaps one of the first references to dildos in (post-Roman) Western literature, though they were not called dildos as of yet—that word entered the English language later, in about 1590 and is likely from the Italian *deletto*, meaning delight—perhaps originating from the works of Aretino. Bewildered, Nanna leaves the refectory and walks down the hallway to her cloister.[60]

Along the way she spots a painting of "all the various modes and avenues by which [one] can fuck and be fucked," a not-quite-so-subtle reference to Aretino's *I Modi* and also to Boccaccio:

On the second wall is the story of the muse Masetto

> de Lampolecchi, and I swear to you upon my soul the two nuns looked positively alive as they lead him to the hut. . . On the third wall, is my memory serves, were portrayed all the nuns who had ever belonged to the order, with their lovers beside them and their children too. . . The last picture depicted all the various modes and avenues by which one can fuck and be fuck. In fact, before beginning their jousts with their partners the nuns must try to assume the same positions in life as the nuns painted in that picture.[61]

When she enters her room, she sits and weeps quietly, thinking she will have to become chaste and starve herself when all of a sudden she hears laughter and, "since the sound kept growing louder and louder," she put her eye to a crack in the wall (there are a lot of cracks in walls and people peeking through doorknobs in early pornography), and is astonished to see:

> [F]our sisters, the General, and three milky-white and ruby-red young friars who were taking off the reverend father and putting him in a velvet coat [like a prince]. . .meanwhile the sisters removed their habits and the friars took off their tunics. The latter put on the sisters robes, and the sisters put on the friars, except one, who put on the reverend father's cassock, seated herself pontifically, and began to imitate a superior laying down the law for the convent.[62]

Part of the reason this scene is so shocking—aside from the fact that monks and nuns are having sex in the other room—is that in Renaissance and earlier times, it was illegal on punishment of death for a woman to wear the clothes of a man.

Indeed, it is hard to emphasize just how concerned officials in early modern Europe were about clothing and rank. Although alien to a modern culture of consumption and consumerism, there were incredibly detailed 'sumptuary' laws from the Middle-Ages onward. According to Maria Muzzarelli these laws "regulated the consumption of goods, consisting in the analysis, quantification, or prohibition of various demonstrations of opulence displayed during banquets, feats, funerals, or in one's attire."[63] The effect and purpose of these laws "allowed residents of a city and even foreigners to distinguish at first sight knights, lawyers or doctors...sumptuary legislation thus functioned as an instrument to maintain and reinforce social barriers."[64] For example in Spain, sumptuary laws were incredibly specific: one thirteenth-century law detailed the amount of outfits knights could own in a year (four), the materials that could be on saddles (no silk, no plush), the colors that 'infidels' could wear (white, black or brown) and the types of beards Jews or Moors could have (only long).[65] When Shakespeare wrote in *Hamlet* "costly thy habit as thy purse can buy, / But not express'd in fancy; rich, not gaudy; / For the apparel oft proclaims the man" (*Hamlet*, lines 556-58) he was offering very real and contemporary advice. For officials and moralists, even the "idea of female cross-dressing and the mobility it allowed becomes an anxious refrain in moralistic and anti-theatrical tracts of the time."[66] Katy Emck notes that

> for moralists [and authority figures, I might add] female cross-dressing becomes a potent symbol of social and moral disorder frequently associated with a public theater which, in   England and Spain, cut across class boundaries and allowed its audience to imagine themselves in different roles and stations in life and, in theory at least, to actually try them out.[67]

So the cross-dressing, along with the nudity and mocking of

religion, were all combined by Aretino to create a powerful and hilariously satirical image for his readers.

If this was not shocking enough to the "sweet and innocent" Nanna, the reverend father ordered the friars to strip him, and "grabbing ahold of the youngest, prettiest nun, threw her tunic over her head. . .then, deliberately prying open the leaves of her asshole missal, contemplated her crotch. [Then] he placed his paintbrush, which he first moistened with spit, in her tiny color cup, and he made her twist, as women do in the birth throes or the mother's maladyi." At the same time, Nanna watched as another friar took the reverend father in the behind, and the other two priests "pound the sauce in the mortar" of the other two sisters. Being so 'innocent,' Nanna of course "began rubbing my dear little monkey with my hand like cats in January rub their backsides on a roof."[68]

The rest of the so-called *The Secret Life of Nuns* continues along in this manner, satirizing nuns and abbots, sisters, priests, monks and friars, accusing them all of breaking their vows and being hypocritical in their pursuit of fleshly pleasures. Nanna eventually has sex with the bishop of the convent a few times before he catches her *in flagrante delicto* with one of his students, another monk. She describes how he dragged her through the nunnery and then whipped her within an inch of her life. She escapes from the nunnery and heads back home to her mother. Thus ends the first day of Nana's dialogue, and she instructs Antonia to come the next day at the same time so the tales can continue.

Returning to their spot under the fig tree in the vineyard, Antonia declares that she cannot believe, "those crazy mothers and foolish fathers who believe that their daughters who become nuns do not have teeth to bite with, like the girls who get married. . .they ought to know that these girls are also made of flesh and bone and that nothing whets desire so much as forbidding it."[69] Although Aretino has been very obviously critiquing the church throughout the first dialogue, this is where he comes out clearest in his motivation. Antonia's statement is a very clear-cut denunciation of the Catholic Church's position on clerical celibacy—a policy that came out of the First and Second Lateran Councils (1123 and 1139). Aretino and his characters are pointing to the fact that many priests, bishops, and monastics continued to engage in illicit and secret marriages three centuries later, much to the detriment of the church, which is something the Protestant Reformation and the Catholic Counter-Reformation would address, and which we will turn to in the next chapter. Having finished satirizing religion and religious figures, Aretino (and Nanna) move on to social and political criticism in the second day of the dialogues.

After having been beaten out of the nunnery by a jealous and hypocritical bishop, Nanna's mother decides that it is best to marry her off to a rich old man, in order to secure her daughter's future. Her mother, of course "knew that my virginity had gone straight to the dogs, and so she filled an eggshell with chicken blood [and placed it in Nanna's vagina], instructing me on how to appear chaste."[70] When her new husband went to bed, Nanna pretends to cry out in fear, and her mother rushes in and holds and coaxes her daughter "to accept the staff of the good shepherd who was laboring mighty to open [Nanna's] thighs."[71] Although it seems insane to modern eyes that a mother would rush into a bedroom while her daughter and her new husband were consummating their marriage, weddings and sex in the 16th century were much more public events than they are today. Wedding guests would often stay in the bedroom to sing, watch, offer ribald jokes and helpful tips to the new couple—whose privacy was usually only the bed draperies, if any at all.[72]

The ruse works perfectly, and Nanna's new husband is wholly convinced of her virginity. The along with being a series of ribald tales, the satirical focus of the *Secret Life of Wives* is the male social and political obsession with purity and virginity. Specifically in sixteenth century Italy, many women during the Renaissance were married at an young age (around 14) to ensure their purity, and many of the Italian kingdoms decreed that virginity was an absolute necessity in a bride and that adultery by a woman was punishable by death. Nanna goes on to discuss how she became friends with a number of wives that told her about their affairs. The first story she tells is about the wife of a "big merchant, young, good-looking witty,"[73] exactly the sort of man who would be ruined by adultery.

However, he fails miserably at pleasing his wife in bed and, when he is out of town, she sneaks lovers in through a back entry. Mid-coitus, she declares to the watching Nanna that she'd much rather that, "people know me as a horny woman who is content than a good woman who is desperate!"[74] Another story tells of Nanna's near-rape as she slept in the bed of a married friend. As she lay asleep, the drunken husband of her friend returns home, and seeing his chance, attempts to take Nanna by surprise. Her friend was not in the room with her because she was too busy having sex with the tutor she had convinced her husband to hire. When Nanna screams, the friend and the tutor run into the room naked and the husband sees them. Far from ending in disaster, the wife uses her rich family connections and economic power to force her financially poor husband into cuckolded obedience.

Two stories tell of women who outsmarted their husbands and seduced religious figures (showing both the sexual corruption of the church and the stupidity of the husbands). The first tells of a wife who saw the, er, 'attributes' of well-endowed priest when he was urinating in the street and then, falling into a faint, pretended to be on her deathbed until her husband called for the same priest to give her last rites. Finally getting him alone, she "sank her claws into his robe and pulled him on top of her."[75] When the wife begins to seem much better, her pious husband comes in and declares it a miracle, saying "there is no better physician than the God Almighty!"[76] The second story tells of the wife of a powerful doctor and how she wormed her way into a monk's cell and begins to take advantage of him. Unfortunately, she is too loud in her hosannas, and the entire monastery and town comes to her rescue, thinking she was being murdered. The townspeople kick in the door and find the pair in the midst of a very sweaty and terrible 'exorcism,' or at least that's what the pair convince the townspeople of! And so on. Sometimes these stories have obvious morals—for example, a story about an younger wife who takes her elderly husband's ten valets as lovers ends with the pointed comment that, "she was absolutely right, and so much the worse for the old idiot. He should have taken a wife of his own age, not a girl who could have been his daughter a hundred times over."[77] But other times, the stories are just meant to mock the social and political policies that force women into unhappy marriages:

> **Nanna:** Feminine chastity is like a glass decanter which, no matter how carefully you handle it, finally slips out of your fingers when you least expect it and it shattered completely. If you don't keep it locked up in a chest it is impossible to keep it whole; and the woman who does can be considered a miracle, like the glass that falls and doesn't break. [78]

"Blessed are the women who can fulfill their desires,"[79] Antonia declares in the midst of the stories, and Nanna agrees: "once I had seen and understood the lives of the wives, in order to keep my end up, I began to satisfy all my whims and desires, doing it with all sorts, from porters to great lords, with especial favor extended to the religious orders. . .and not only did my husband know about it, but he saw it too. Yet I heard people all around me whispering: 'That woman is giving him just what he deserves'" for marrying a young girl he could not please. And, "after a thousand cuckoldries [that I forced] him to swallow down as someone mentions a burning mouthful, one day he found a beggar mounted on me."[80] Her husband lunges at her with his fists in order to break her face, but she pulls his dagger out and stabs him in the heart with it. Aretino's sexual suggestions here are intentional—the wife not only makes him swallow 'burning mouthfuls,' but also penetrates him with his own knife, the ultimate cuckoldry. Having satirized men economically, religiously and socially, Aretino even has Nanna mock them legally as she escapes punishment from murder by becoming a courtesan in Rome.

Thus begins the third dialogue, *The School of Whoredom.* It tells the tale of Nanna's life in Rome, from poverty to the height of her power as a courtesan. Arriving in Rome with very little money, Nanna and her mother rent an apartment on the ground floor of a house, and Nanna, with the guidance of her mother, plays the 'pure innocent virgin' card again. Her mother, "who taught me all I have done, all I am doing, and all I shall ever do in the future," dresses her up and tells her to stand by a window that faces the street and pretend to let men 'catch' her in compromising positions:

> **Nanna:** Have you ever seen a sparrow perching at a window of a granary? He pecks up ten grains of wheat and flits off; then, after staying away for a while. . .he comes back to the booty with two more sparrows, flies off again, and returns with four, then ten, then thirty, and finally a huge flock. That's just how my panting suitors swarmed around my house, trying to poke their beaks into my granary.[81]

She describes "affecting the modesty of a nun, staring straight at them with the self-confidence of a wife, and all the while making the gestures of a whore," until men were lining up and pounding at her door desperately.[82] Then, with the aid of her mother and her landlady, they spread the word that she was an 'innocent virgin' that had fallen on hard times. The men, of course, fail to see through the trap and the triumvirate manages to sell her 'virginity' again and again at absurdly high prices. Unfortunately for these desperate (and desperately mocked) men, on the night when they show up to 'have her,' Nanna plays the virgin role even harder. She pretends to be horrified and afraid and only lets her customers get a little bit further each night (kissing, the glimpse of a thigh or a bosom), and forcing more payments and gifts from them until finally 'giving in.'

The rest of the third dialogue continues in much the same way, telling how Nanna manipulated everyone from princes to merchants, even overcoming the men who thought to outsmart her. In all of these escapades, Nana declares that "I never behaved like [a dumb whore]. A whore without brains is the first to suffer from it. You've got to know how to handle yourself in the world, and not try to set yourself higher than a queen."[83] In one episode, she amuses herself by hiding three rivals to her love in various closets in her house until they all discover each other and fight, in another, she convinces a rich merchant to use all his money buying jewels to please her (jewels that she already owned) and bankrupts him. Finally, she concludes by noting, "I can't give you a detailed account of all the swindles with which I stripped my lovers bare," and asking Antonia which role (nun, wife or whore) she should pick for her darling daughter Pippa.[84] Antonia considers it for a moment and then says that making her a whore is the best option, since: "The nun betrays her sacred vows and the married woman murders the holy bond of matrimony, but the whore violates neither her monastery nor her husband." She concludes by comparing the work of a whore to that of a soldier, and adds, "from what I have understood of your talk, a whore's vices are really virtues."[85] Nanna agrees, and they (literally) ride off into the sunset.

The Ragionamenti were published while Pietro Aretino was

at the height of his power. He created and sustained a reading populace in Italy that made him feared and nearly invulnerable. A contemporary describes what it was like when a new Aretine text was published:

> Even at the opening of the papal law courts, I never saw such a press of litigants striving to be the first to enter as there were men striving to purchase [Aretino's book.] Suddenly, there was a great crowd of people, followed by as much noise and jostling as there is. . . when they give alms to the poor. . . Had I not taken care to be among the first, and consequently I would not have been one of these if it had not been for a certain courtier [who set a copy of the book down for a moment]. No sooner did he do this than I snatched it up and withdrew. . . He cried and begged and screamed, but I made off with the book and have read it ten times over.[86]

The fact that Aretino's contemporaries were stampeding booksellers and fighting like teenagers over the release of the newest *Harry Potter* book should signal just how early on book commodification and obsessive cults of authorial celebrity had begun to develop, something that is usually attributed to later centuries. It is not really clear how much of this is singular to Aretino himself and how much of it was just an augury of things to come but it is a remarkable piece of evidence at how widespread the culture of reading and the ability for a large group of people to read, and it should have been a signal of just how much power the printing press and the reading masses would come to have.

The boy born in a charity ward on a cold April night had reached a position of power and fame that far outstripped nearly everyone else around him. In the final decades of his life he would correspond with popes, Francis I of France, and Charles V of Spain and the Holy Roman Empire; playing them off of each other and profiting handsomely in the process. His correspondence heavily influenced Titian, Michelangelo and other Renaissance painters and thinkers. Even today you can visit one of the most famous artworks in the world, the Sistine Chapel in Vatican City, and see Pietro Aretino painted as St. Bartholomew holding the flayed skin of Michelangelo —a reference to the fact that Aretino wrote a bad review of the painter. Finally, in many ways, Pietro Aretino's use of the printing press to create his own audience was a major inspiration and influence on Martin Luther, the German priest who would shake Western civilization to its foundations, and whose story we will turn to in the next chapter.

Aretino lived until 1556, dying at the ripe old age of 64, and having seen the passing of some of the most significant figures in European history: Martin Luther in 1546, Francis I of France and Henry VIII of England passed in the year 1547, and although Charles V had not yet departed the mortal plane, 1556 was the year he abdicated his throne, split his empire in half and withdrew to a monastery for the rest of his days. The boy from Arezzo however, lived his final years as joyously as his life—indeed, his death came about when, laughing loudly, he tipped his chair too far back and fell, cracking his head on the stone floor. Words carved into the Church of San Luca in Arrezzo near Aretino's grave read:

> Although base-born, Pietro Aretino rose to
> towering height
> by blaming the foul vices of the world
> therefore those to whom the world pays ransom
> paid ransom to him
> lest he should tell the truth about them.[87]

In many ways, Aretino was to become a symbol of what it was like and how to become a self-made man through the printing press. For decades afterwards his name was used both as a compliment to public intellectuals, and hurled as an insult to suggest moral corruption, depravity, lasciviousness, and other faults. Although Aretino's stock has somewhat fallen throughout time, he remains perhaps one of the most modern of the early moderns. His legacy, however, was in how he used the press in such a self-enabling way and the legacy of his work leads to him being credited as the inventor of "literate pornography," as Wikipedia does today. Nearly all of the figures that we shall touch on following used, referenced, and enjoyed Aretino, and if literary pornography is nothing else, it is perhaps a collection of authors that have read Aretino.

3

1556 – 1644: To Reform and Counter-Reform

To Reform: Sex, Scat, and Sin

A BOUT A YEAR AFTER Pietro Aretino published *The Last Will and Testament of the Elephant Hanno* (1516), a very serious middle-aged priest and professor of theology was wrestling with an idea. If Aretino's satirical pamphlet had any influence on him, it is not recorded, but there is no doubt the he knew of some of Aretino's works. Like Aretino, this priest had grown up on the works of the humanist Renaissance, and (like Aretino) he was inspired by authors such as Boccaccio and his *Decameron*. One of his favorite stories was the tale of the Jew who travels to Rome and finds the papacy and the Roman Curia so corrupt that the church must be of divine origin. Indeed, when this priest visited Rome in 1511 he found that Boccaccio's story was not an exaggeration. He later wrote about the corruption, lies, and generally sinful behavior of Rome. Among other things, he declared that, "the true Antichrist is sitting in the temple of God and is reigning in Rome—that empurpled Babylon—and that the Roman Curia is the Synagogue of Satan."[88]

Although he and Aretino had the same target—Rome—it is easy to see the vast difference between Aretino's mocking tone and sharp wit, and the righteous and burning fury of the middle-aged priest. The author of this invective was Martin Luther, a name that would soon come to shake the very foundations of the Church and trigger decades of conflict across the continent. In 1517, however, he was a little-known professor of theology at Wittenberg University in the Holy Roman Empire. The Holy Roman Empire is a topic for a different book (or hundreds of them), but for our purposes here it is important to understand that it—generally speaking—occupied the area that modern-day Germany does. However, like Italy of the time, it was fragmented into thousands of subkingdoms, duchies, free cities and bishoprics. What this means, is that when the Reformation got underway, and certain kingdoms converted but other ones did not, it allowed Luther and his supporters to flee a relatively short distance to a friendlier territories. It would also have truly disastrous effects when the wars of religion broke out, but more on that later.

Aretino's ripping satires were the first time in the history of the church that a mass-produced (and massively-accessible) work had attacked the cardinals and gotten away with it. Martin Luther's *Ninety-Five Theses* was the second, and was far more disrupting. In the *Ninety-Five Theses*, Luther attacks abuses of the pope and cardinals on all fronts, but especially on the topics of nepotism (giving positions to relatives), simony (selling church positions or lands), usury (lending money with high interest), pluralism (holding multiple church offices at once), and the sale of indulgences. Inspired either by Aretino or his own genius, Luther realized that the printing press allowed him to broadcast his pamphlets and arguments far and wide across Europe. With a strategy remarkably similar to Aretino's, the works that Luther and his supporters mass-produced tied together visuals and text in order to reach the largest possible audience. If Pietro Aretino is the best-kept secret of the Renaissance, then Martin Luther is perhaps the best-known but least-understood secret. Luther, and the Reformation that he ignited would have a dramatic influence on history. But how does a German monk play into our little story of pornography and obscenity?

I turn to Luther in this chapter to both address the role that sexuality played sixteenth century status quo and to observe how obscenity was used in parallel and post-Aretine traditions. In other words, the Aretine erotic discourse/satire was radicalized to the extreme in the Reformation and Counter-Reformation. Before we turn to the how and why of Luther's *Theses*, and his use of an obscene/erotic style, we need to sketch the details of what European sexuality was like, because, as one historian put it, "sex was central to the Reformation's reshaping of the world."[89] Between the death of Jesus and the 1500s, church leaders had developed a curious array of sexual regulations; more or less a blend between the Greco-Roman and Judeo-Christian ideas. One historian, James Brundage, described European sexual morality as "a complex assemblage of pagan and Jewish purity regulations, linked with primitive beliefs about the relationship between sex and the holy, joined to Stoic teachings about sexual ethics and bound together by a patchwork of [new] doctrinal theories."[90]

Both Stoic and Hebrew thinkers, in general, distrusted sex and saw it as a corrupting and defiling pleasure. Stoics (or rather, the Stoics seen as influential by Christian thinkers) saw it as disturbing to an ideally calm and 'stoic' mind, and the early Jews had dozens of purity laws and taboos around sex. When these combined, they could be quite formidable—Saint Paul, for example, argued "I would that all men [and women] were [chaste like] myself it is good for them if they abide even as I. But if they cannot contain [lustfulness], let them marry: for it is better to marry than to burn." (I Corinthians 7.1-40). Saint Augustine also saw lust as evil: "it intrudes where it is not needed and tempts the hearts of faithful and holy people with its untimely and wicked desire. Even if we do not give in to these restless impulses. . . [we would] want them not to exist in us at all, if that were possible."[91] As Kyle Harper puts it, the "legacy of Christianity lies in the dissolution of an ancient system where status and social reproduction scripted the terms of sexual morality," which is to say Christians were both *shamed* by their society for improper behavior as well as seeing this improper behavior as a cosmological *sin*.[92]

As a result, marriage and the rules and regulations surrounding marriage became one of the church's primary concerns. Between 1100 and 1300, the church tried to discourage concubinage (multiple sexual partners) and loose moral standards among both the upper and lower classes, with greater or lesser success. Surviving records of English Church courts indicate that sexual and marital cases made up 60-90% of all litigation—the same holds true in France and elsewhere.[93] Although this control was somewhat successful, one of the places it was completely unsuccessful was in Rome, the capital of the church and the center of the Christian world. This is something that was frequently satirized and mocked by humanist reformers such as Boccaccio and, of course, Aretino.

The topic of sex was a key issue in the Reformation, and how it changed the face of European life. The Catholic Church's permissive attitude to sexual morality and prostitution was of major concern to Protestants. As Dabhoiwala notes: "Its priests were lecherous parasites: the ideal of clerical celibacy was no more than a joke. [Church] courts were not nearly fierce enough in pursing sexual offender and punishing their moral sins. . ."[94] More than anyone else, Boccaccio and Aretino were responsible for the stereotype of priests as 'lecherous parasites' and for pointing out that the ideal of clerical celibacy was a joke. Luther harnessed these pre-existing stereotypes of corrupt priests and a corrupt Rome in order to leverage his moral position. Dabhoiwala continues: "[Luther and other] Protestants advanced a purer, more rigorous morality. The Catholic aspiration to celibacy was jettisoned as unrealistic and counter-productive. . . . On the other hands, God's many pronouncements against whoredom were to be taken even more seriously: all sex outside marriage should be severely punished."[95] When the legal codes were revised in the newly-reformed countries, the laws against adultery and prostitution became increasingly harsh.

Although this is not the place to trace the intricacies of the Reformation, Luther's primary dispute with the church in Rome was the selling of 'indulgences.' Indulgences were a way for sinners to pay their way out of sins or Limbo. Originally, the profits were used by the church to raise money for charity or good works, but it was eventually corrupted into a profit-making enterprise by professional 'pardoners.' One pardoner in specific, Johann Tetzel, aggressively marketed indulgences in the German region as a way for any Christian to achieve salvation. Furious at some of his claims, Luther wrote up *The Ninety-Five Theses on the Power and Efficacy of Indulgences*, and so started the Protestant Reformation.

Initially, he just began by nailing his protestations to the door of the All Saints' Church in Wittenberg, which acted a bit like a bulletin board for local priests and clergy—the theses were written in Latin and in an academic style. Once they were translated into the German vernacular however, they quickly exploded. Luther wrote to a publisher that his "purpose was not to publish them. Thus I [decided to] either destroy them if condemned or edit them with the approbation of others. But now that they are printed and circulated far beyond my expectation, I feel anxious about what they may bring forth," and later said that "should have spoken far differently and more distinctly had I known what was going to happen."[96]

As the Reformation got underway, the Lutherans used the printing press and the newly developed copper-engraving method to pursue multiple avenues of visual anti-Catholic propaganda. Three (of many) examples of these are *The Donkey Pope, The Pope as The Whore of Babylon,* and *The Papal Devil.* The first represents the pope as a monstrous beast with the head of a donkey and the genitals of a woman, a mocking caricature to the perversity and bestiality of the church. The second graphically represents the pope as the biblical Whore of Babylon, riding a seven headed dragon and selling indulgences. The third represents the pope as the devil or the Antichrist, who has the breasts of a woman. The common theme uniting these —and indeed, much of Lutheran propaganda,—was an effort to paint the church as feminine, weak, and especially, to tie it to a sensual and sexual component, making the argument that the church was sensuous and corrupt.

Another propaganda effort was to print sheets of song lyrics to distribute in the streets. An example is *"Nun treiben wir den Babst hinaus,"* a translation of which (by John Hartmann) reads:

> Now we drive out the pope
>> from Christ's church and God's house.
>> Therein he has reigned in a deadly fashion
>> and has seduced uncountably many souls.
>> Now move along, you damned son,
>> you Whore of Babylon.
>> You are the abomination and the Antichrist,
>> full of lies, death and cunning.
>> Your indulgence, bull and decree,
>> now they receive their seal in the toilet.
>> Thereby you stole the good from the world,
>> and defiled Christ's blood as well.[97]

The goal of these propaganda efforts was to paint Luther as the "German Hercules" and inspire German nationalism against the soft and sensuous Italians. In contrast to the weak, languid, corrupted and effeminate Church, Luther was depicted as strong, virile, and active, crushing the enemies of the

Reformation and the German people, driving them before him and hearing the lamentations of their effeminate priests. Specifically, German propagandists would use scatological (shit or piss-related) humor, which was the most popular sort of humor in Germany, the people's humor, in order to make a point about the distant and upper-class pope. One example shows German Landsknecht mercenaries "adoring the Pope as an earthly God," that is, by defecating all over papal symbols. Another image shows "the birth and origins of the Pope," where he is literally shat out and nursed by a she-devil.[98]

Figure 3: The Birth and Origins of the Pope

Figure 4: Luther as German Hercules, destroying his enemies.

By using the language and the humor of the common people, as Aretino did with his back-street and vulgar Italian, Luther was able to both catch their attention and keep it. Furthermore, it allowed him to demean the pope and the church directly:

Gently, dear Pauli, dear donkey, don't dance around!

> Oh, dearest little ass-pope, don't dance around--
> dearest, dearest little donkey, don't do it. For the ice
> is very solidly frozen this year because there was no
> wind--you might fall and break a leg. If a fart should
> escape you while you were falling, the whole world
> would laugh at you and say, "Ugh, the devil! How the
> ass-pope has befouled himself!"[99]

Luther's language was likely seen as so childish and immature by the well-educated humanist church authorities that in many cases they were unable to muster a response to him and could not understand how he managed to rally followers across Germany.

In 1521, the Catholic Church assembled a formal meeting called the Diet of Worms to try and resolve Luther's concerns and to bring him back into the fold. In Protestant depictions of this scene, Luther appears as a reserved and conservative figure, tonsured in the style of a monk and wrapped in a simple black robe held together with a tattered leather belt. His eyes and his hand are extended to heaven, and a holy light glows forth from him. In contrast, Charles V and the Church officials are wrapped in crimson robes earthly luxury and splendor, loaded down with heavy golden ornamentation but shrouded in darkness and off to the side of the paintings. Things had gone too far. Luther declared "here I stand, I can do no other, God help me. Amen." He would not recant or repent his heresies.

After the failed reconciliation attempt, it did not take long for things to start happening very fast. First, several German territories began converting to Lutheranism. Next, other branches of the Reformation 'broke out' in Switzerland with the Calvinists and the Anabaptists. Then, then it snowballed to the point where Henry VIII of England (who had ironically just been named defender of the Catholic Faith) broke with the Catholic Church between 1532 and 1534 and initiated the English Reformation For various reasons, the Pope and the Church were incredibly slow to react to the threat of the Reformation. In fact, looking back on it now, many people see the nearly half-century delay between the start of the Reformation and the start of the Counter-Reformation as foolish and irresponsible on the part of the Church. This would be an unfair characterization, though; over the centuries, the Church had seen many heresies, such as the Lollards and the Hussites, come and go. Also, the pope had good reason not to call a Council. The previous council, Fifth Lateran, had pushed controls on his power, and a new Council carried the threat of further limits on papal power, especially considering how 'corrupt' the Curia was.

Unfortunately, there was a new player in town—the printing press—and the Church did not realize how much of a threat it represented to their previously monopolistic methods of control until it was too late. Just like the fall of the Soviet Union is partially attributable to the photocopy machine's ability to mass reproduce pamphlets, and part of the modern Arab Spring is attributable to internet technologies, the printing press marked a new development in communication. And in a strange way, its power was recognized by both the most libertine and the most religious forces of Europe at that time. This is a trend that will repeat throughout our story; the pendulum swings from toleration to increased religious enthusiasm, until excesses in either generate their own opposites.

The strategies followed by Martin Luther and Pietro Aretino throughout their lives were remarkably similar. In fact, as the two men worked mostly within the same time frame, their strategies throughout their lives almost seemed to develop in tandem. Both used the power of the printing press in a new and unique way to broadcast their ideas and personalities to the greatest possible audiences, both were pursued by authorities who sought to kill them, both moved to places or areas where they could not be reached, and both lived their lives out more or less in peace, publishing until the end. Truly, Aretino and Luther were the first to utilize a printing press for their own powerful intentions and were probably the last who were able to use an unrestricted printing press. The reason I put it like that—unrestricted printing press— is because the Reformation touched off by Luther absolutely shook the Catholic world, and eventually, a response was needed. In 1545, Pope Paul III called the Council of Trent to- gether to organize both defense and offense against the Refor- mation. This council, more than anything else, would have a major impact on the people and countries of Europe, and is a major landmark in the history of sexuality and pornography. The Council of Trent was not only the first major attempt to suppress or ban literature, it was also the Council that helped create marriage and privacy as we know it today.

To Counter-Reform

THE COUNCIL OF TRENT took place in two main stages. The first lasted from 1545-1547 and broke up due to political concerns and fears of plague in the city of Trent. Not much was accomplished during the first part except considerations on how the council should be run, where people should sit, and reaffirmations of Catholic beliefs against Lutheran ones. When the first meeting broke up, they had only made eight decisions (called sessions) out of an eventual total of twenty- five. For various political reasons, the council did not meet again until nearly twenty years later, from 1562-1563. As the Rev. John W. O'Malley, a professor of theology at Georgetown, says in Trent: What Happened at the Council, "Luther set the agenda for the Council. His challenge to the church was two- fold. Its origin, as well as its center was an idea, an idea about how we are saved, namely 'by faith alone' and not by 'works,' not by our own striving. . . [Second was] a cry for reform of various ecclesiastical offices and religious practices."[100] Our interests lie with the second part of Trent and this second issue, the reform of religious practices, so we will focus on that. O'Malley points out the differences between the "faith and morals" which the Councils focused on, and how they are more accurately seen as "doctrine and public behavior."[101] The Church Councils, "as legislative and judicial bodies dealt not with "faith" as an inner sentiment of the believer but with dogma or teaching publicly professed by the church." Likewise, morals as approached by the Councils are not "ethical theories or principals but [with] observable public behavior."[102]

In this way, the Catholic Church and the Counter-Reformation were not as concerned with interior beliefs and internal faith as Luther and the Reformation were—they were concerned with outward behavior and outward action. At its core, the disagreement between the church and the Reformers was a disagreement over what was more important; public or private life. As I noted earlier, sex and marriage were essential to the Reformation's worldview. So they also became essential to the Counter-Reformation. Envoys at the Council of Trent pointed out that some of Luther's critiques were correct: "Citing information garnered from an extensive visitation of Bavaria in 1558, [an envoy] painted a dark picture. The vast majority of the parish clergy was ignorant and infected with heresy. Out of a hundred, only three or four were not secretly married or keeping concubines, to the great scandal of the faithful."[103]

Furthermore, it was common for upper-class men to clandestinely marry, or promise marriage to, women of lower station to 'get into their pants,' and then, if she got pregnant, to deny ever having been married.

The result was the *Tamesti*, which stated that, "whereas clandestine marriages had previously [been] declared valid, though blameworthy, all would be deemed invalid unless celebrated before a priest and at least two witnesses."[104] In O'Malley's view, "No single provision of the entire council affected the Catholic laity more directly than *Tamesti*. . . [It] meant that in the future the church recognized no marriages between Catholics as valid unless it had been witnessed by a priest."[105] Non-Catholic countries, such as England, were slower to reform, but their eventual marriage reforms (Such as Lord Hardwicke's 1753 act) followed a similar process as the *Tamesti*. The intention and effects of *Tamesti* (and indeed, other marriage legislation) were, in a way, feminist, in the sense that they sought to protect women from being taken advantage of and abandoned through clandestine marriages. This is pretty remarkable to modern people, who normally assume that the Church was responsible solely for oppressing and controlling female sexuality, not for trying to protect them.

The debate over privacy and marriage, probably more than anything else, has had a profound impact and influence on our lives today. For example, in modern times we often consider anything that has to do with sex or sexuality as 'private' and something that should occur 'behind closed doors.' In the 16th, 17th, and even the early 18th centuries, this was not necessarily the case (though it became increasingly so as time progressed). In fact, it was not abnormal for a wedding party to carry them to the bedroom on their first night, nor was it uncommon for sexual acts to take place in a bar, in a dark alleyway in London or Paris, and witnesses would think very little of it.[106] Again, this was a period where entire families would share the same bed and children were likely to know just how their parents made new siblings. Indeed, family life of the medieval era to the 16th century is nearly unrecognizable to modern eyes. Lawrence Stone states perhaps the most extreme reading of this and describes the early 16th century home as one with no real boundaries to the outside world or privacy: "it was open to support, advice, investigation and interference from outside, from neighbors and from kin."[107]

The splitting of the private and public world that happened as a result of the Reformation and Counter-Reformation had an impact on both the architecture of the home and the attitudes around sex. This occurred first among the upper classes, who were likely already accustomed to formalized and public marriages. These changes then began to be adopted by middle and lower classes, slowly at first and then with increasing speed, as shown by the architecture of homes, in which to the trend moved from one-room 'cruck' houses where bedrooms were "common living areas (in lower-class homes) or sites for social gatherings (in upper-class ones) to being what they are today—private spaces for the single person or couple who sleep in them." [108]

Of course, this is not to say that no one before this had attempted to hide intercourse or tried to achieve privacy —in fact, much of the erotic work we've discussed so far was so disturbing to authorities because it involved a narrator spying on, or seeing, sex that broke societal boundaries (nuns and monks, upper and lower classes, and so on). The Council, therefore, had to deal with the two types of works represented by Pietro Aretino and Martin Luther—religious critique (Luther) and sexual critique of religion, society and politics (Aretino). When I mentioned that Luther and Aretino were the last to use the power of the printing press without restrictions, it was because the Council of Trent initiated the very first *Index Librorum Prohibitorum*, or Index of Prohibited Books, in response to the effects of Aretino and Luther on the people.

Index Librorum Prohibitorum

THE DECREE OF THE Council consisted of ten 'rules' that were to be followed in prohibiting books. The first few rules prohibited the books of heretics such as Luther, Zwingli, Calvin, and others, and it also prohibited translations of the Old Testament from falling into the hands of the common people—only "learned and pious men" should be allowed access to these texts. The reason for this was that it was now "clear from experience" that allowing vernacular (common-tongue) translations would lead to mischief (such as Luther). Additionally, the Council prohibited all books and writings on divinations, magic, or the mixing of poisons, and finally, "books which professedly deal with, narrate, or teach things lascivious or obscene are absolutely prohibited," claiming that they were the source of corruption. The possession of such books was ordered "to be severely punished by the bishops."[109]

This would clearly target obscene and pornographic writing. However, the rule did not end there, but went on to dictate that, "Ancient books written by heathens may by reason of their elegance and quality of style be permitted, but may by no means be read to children."[110] The exception for ancient Greek and Roman texts that are 'elegant' and have 'quality of style' gives us the evidence that the church was not necessarily targeting or offended by sex in books—they were targeting the contemporary use of the erotic to criticize religion, society, and politics by individuals such as Aretino. The ancient Roman poet Catullus, of the eloquent lines "I will sodomize you and face-fuck you," was still allowed—in Latin, of course, as were Virgil and other poets that would be later considered questionable or obscene, and not acceptable to translate in later centuries.

The other interesting aspect to this exception is the commandment that these types of books should never be read to children. This is one of the first "think of the children" arguments against dirty or erotic writing—humanist Catholic thinkers were thoroughly convinced of the need to raise children in the right manner, to the point where the first *Index* banned works that suggested alternative methods of children's education—texts such as *The education of children and also, and rightly, their formation studies, & behavior, & c.* were utterly banned. The Reformation made this protectionist conviction even stronger—both the laity and the children needed to be protected from the obscene, dirty Romans. So why did Trent allow 'ancient books written by heathens may by reason of their elegance and quality of style' to continue? Well, for one, they were written in Latin, and Latin provided a barrier both between the upper and lower classes and between men and women, as only Catholics educated in Latin (mostly upper-class men) could read them.

Puberty being what it is, and teenage boys being who they are, many found ways around this prohibition—the eighteenth-century Italian playboy Casanova, for one, wrote about the pleasures of discovering dirty Latin literature as a boy. The fact that texts survive from this era means that many people found their way around Tridentine regulations. Unscrupulous authors used the 'elegant writing' loophole for their own texts, claiming that they were simply translations of Latin works, the originals of which had been (conveniently) lost. Publishers would also pay cash-strapped students to translate the dirty bits of Latin texts. They would then run off a few hundred copies with a false publication date and location, and then sell them under the counter to their more discriminating customers.

The results of *Tamesti* and the *Index Librorum Prohibitorum* on the development of erotica and sexuality was mixed. While the *Index* prohibited hundreds of authors and works and even targeted certain publishers for prosecution, it was only retroactive and after-the-fact, since it was impossible to keep the *Index* current when the book market began to take off and hundreds of new books were published a year. What's more is that the *Index* gave no particular guidance on how to deal with a newly publicized work. The real censorship and control came from The Holy Office of the Universal Inquisition (where the French, Spanish, and Roman Inquisitions got their names). It fell on the office of the Inquisition to actively prohibit and censor the works of new authors, along with their usual crackdowns on infidels and heretics. Though the Inquisition today is commonly thought of as the butt of a joke (nobody expects the Spanish Inquisition!), it was anything but funny during the times it was active. Persons that had been denounced as heretical could face the loss of their property and lives, not to mention hours of torture.

One author that discovered this for himself was Ferrante Pallavicino, the best satirist and writer of his day. He was born in 1615 to the old, wealthy, and powerful Pallavicino family —whose names still grace several palaces in Vienna, Genoa, Rome and Bologna. He received the best possible humanist education of the time (including Latin and Greek), and joined the Augustinian holy order. Highly intelligent, well-read, and a prodigious writer, he seemed to be destined to be a powerful figure in the Catholic Church, as many of his ancestors had been. Destined, that is, until he accompanied a friend on some of the expeditions of the Thirty Years' War, an experience that changed him for the rest of his (rather short) life.

The Thirty Years' War started in 1618, a few years after Pallavicino's birth, and continued until 1648, four years after his death. He lived his entire life in the shadow of the war between Protestants and Catholics. Originally, it had started as a series of border conflicts between the Protestant and Catholic provinces in the Holy Roman Empire, but eventually it managed to involve (and eventually bankrupt) just about all of the major European powers, including France, Sweden, Denmark, Spain, Norway, and Poland, among others. It was one of the most brutal and devastating wars in European history, resulting in over eight million deaths, a body count that was unheard of and wouldn't be exceeded until World War I.[111] Pallavicino and many of his contemporaries were horrified. Pallavicino was also outraged at the current pope, Urban VIII, who had taken advantage of the Thirty Years War to launch his own private war for control of the Duchy of Castro in Italy. Edward Muir comments that "this grubby little war [was] scandalous for the opportunism of the Barberini [the pope's family], even by the scandalous standards of the seventeenth century."[112]

Returning home from Germany, Pallavicino settled in Venice and published *Il Corriero svaligiato* ("The Post-boy Robbed of his Bag"), which pretended to be a series of letters that had been robbed from a mailman. This frame story allowed the author to adopt numerous viewpoints, and insult, critique and mock a wide variety of individuals, including the pope, the Curia, the Inquisition, various Italian cities, and leaders involved in the Thirty Year's War. Particularly, Pallavicino loathed and attacked the Jesuits, who were a highly-regarded but highly-controversial Catholic religious order, known for being the enforcers of the Counter-Reformation.

This was not the only book that offended the Church. In fact, nearly all of his works were placed on later editions of the *Index*, including *The Whore Church Mocked*, the *Heavenly Divorce caused by the sluttiness of the Roman Bride* and *The Whore's Rhetorick*. It is these last two books we will touch on briefly. Although it is nowhere as 'pornographic' as Aretino, *The Whore's Rhetorick* is an example of pornography writing after Aretino and after Trent, and shows how much the political situation had shifted. *The Rhetorick* is largely an anti-Jesuit work, in the sense that Pallavicino took Jesuit ideas and turned them on their head by having prostitutes and whores speak them. If that is not enough it is also organized deliberately like a Jesuit text, specifically Suarez's textbook for future Jesuits.[113] In a pattern we've seen with *Raigonamenti* and will see again, the work is a dialogue between two women, an older one and a younger one. The younger girl, Dorothea, is an innocent virgin and the daughter of a man who "had much more nobility in his Vein then Money in his Purse."[114] There is not enough money to support his family, and they suffer from lack of sleep and food. One day, she sits by the window, wailing about her fate and her poverty in terms that would cause eyebrow raises from a member of the Inquisition: "[I would] fly in the face of heaven. I would boldly approach the Almighty's Throne to know what one action of [my] life has merited this rigid penance, this complication of misery and pain."[115] Luckily for her, an old woman appears, although she is given the most unfortunate description: "so loaded with years as to be scarce able to support the burden. . . her breasts appeared like a pair of bladders. . . her Chin was acute and bending upwards, it was graced with a dozen hairs placed much after the same order as they are in an old pussy only they were not so pungent. . .[she] rather resembled dogshit."[116] This lovely presence is Madame Cresswell, who has come to help Dorothea.

Admiring Dorothea's beauty and charm, Cresswell says that she formerly happened to be "a lady of pleasure" who had reached the height of the trade in her days. Unfortunately, she had become corrupted by reading too many Jesuit texts and had fallen into poverty after spending all of her money on their books—an interesting reversal of the later religious argument that dirty books would destroy one's health, or the modern one that porn 'rewires' our brain. After a long speech, she convinces Dorothea to be her student, and she will teach the younger girl everything she needs to know in order to be a "first-rate whore," as long as Dorothea will agree to support the older matron with her profits. The two women strike a deal, and on the following day, Cresswell begins her education.

There is not much to be drawn from Cresswell's speeches for our purposes here—she is not as aggressively erotic or obscene in the way that Nana or other characters were. But, at this early stage, it was not the supposed sexiness of the works that was disturbing to authorities, it was the erotic combined with social, religious, and political critique. And in that sense,

The Whore's Rhetoric has all three. For example, Madame Cresswell uses the same language as a Jesuit or humanist teacher in
saying that "I have promised you a Rhetorick, and therefore to
make good on my word. . .the four parts are Oration, Elocu-
tion, and the Doctrine of the Tropes and Figures. . . I will only
omit the barbarous and insignificant names" of the Greeks and
the Romans. Cresswell mocks the entire system of humanist
teaching in a few lines, and applies the rhetoric that that the
fathers of the church would find disturbing. But Pallavicino
does not stop there:

> The Regular Priests of the Romish Church do seem-
> ingly take their Vows of Chasity, Poverty and Obedi-
> ence, but instead of these they wisely devote them-
> selves to Luxury, Avarice and Dissimulation; in
> like matter you must put on a seeming modesty
> even when you exercise the most essential parts
> of your Profession. . .you must pretend a contempt
> of money. . .a counterfeit humility. . .while in the
> meantime your main and sole aim must be to im-
> pose on all men.[117]

Cresswell advises that Dorothea cultivate "an inevitable
decree to satisfy the most lascivious appetite provided he
comes with Gold in his purse." She also suggests that she ignore any social or class distinctions, basing her business solely
on money: "money removes all stench, from the meanest action by virtue of its purging quality," and encourages women
of England to "cuckold their Husbands all their lives."[118]

Not only does *The Whores Rhetorick* criticize and satirize
the Jesuits, the church, and the Catholic hierarchy, Pallavicino
also manages to invert the entire system of Catholic belief
by having a prostitute say that money washes away all sins
—not the church, or Jesus. As Muir explains: "By systemat-
ically pursuing the parallels between rhetorical persuasion
and erotic seduction, Pallavicino demonstrates how the high

art of rhetoric has the same instrumental character as the lowly deceptions of the prostitute."[119] Furthermore, the *Rhetorick* argues that all sexual desire is completely natural and good, something very much at odds with post-Tridentine Church thinking. It is quite easy to see why the pope, and various other authority figures, wanted his head. Almost immediately after publication, the papal ambassador in Venice stormed into the city hall and demanded Pallavicino's arrest, and the city obliged—for a short time anyhow: Pallavicino was eventually freed because he had avoided criticizing Venice itself in his works.

Indeed, he had done a great deal of brown-nosing in favor of Venice, such as his first book *Il Sole ne' pianeti, cioè le grandezze della Serenissima Republica di Venetia* (The Sun in the planets, that is, the greatness of the Most Serene Republic of Venice). As Muir notes, "as long as authors did not attack the government of Venice itself, they could publish almost anything...and they did...and Pallavicino's work was a panegyric that brought him the protection of the Venetian Senate."[120] The Republic of Venice, as it turns out, was remarkably liberal for its time, and so long as you didn't critique the oligarchy running the city, they did not care—this is one of the reasons Aretino had settled there nearly a century beforehand. The imprisonment and then later release inspired a hugely productive period for him, and his biting erotic satire was enough to make him a popular author as well as an intellectual hero—Muir observes that his "books were so popular that booksellers and printers bought them from him at a premium."[121]

After being freed from jail in Venice, he went on to publish several more satires and mockeries of the church in general, and the hated Pope Urban VIII in particular. Urban, however, was not one to take such critique laying down, and unlike the popes of Aretino's time, he recognized the danger of allowing such satire to circulate. Through an intermediary, the Church approached a 'friend' of Pallavicino, bought him out, and gave him a forged letter that said the King of France wanted to award him some money. Traveling under the assumed name of Raimondi (a hat tip to the Raimondi that drew the *I Modi*), Pallavicino followed his 'friend' into an ambush in the city of Avignon, a French city under Papal control.

Immediately jailed, Pallavicino used his alias and insisted that he was not responsible for the insulting works. He might have gotten away from prison if it was not for the fact that another one of his books hit the book market and caused so much rage that he was discovered. *The Celestial Divorce caused by the sluttiness of the Roman Bride* was another obviously controversial work for the church—it depicts Jesus Christ asking God for a divorce from the Catholic Church because of its vice and sin. God, utterly flabbergasted and confused, sends Saint Paul back down to earth to investigate the Catholic Church, and the story concludes with Paul being so scandalized that he urges God to grant Christ's divorce. On March 5, 1644, the twenty-eight-year-old Pallavicino was decapitated in Avignon for the crime of *lèse majesté*. In many ways this execution marked the end of the Renaissance in Italy, at least the end of unfettered and uncensored satire and critique of the church and state. It definitely marked the end of erotic book innovation in Italy—future writers and publishers would come from north of the Alps.

PART II: RISING ACTION(S) (1647-1740)

4

1647 – 1690: The Girls, The Earl, and The Reforms

L'escolle des filles

A S THE CATHOLIC Counter-Reformation carried on and the 17th century spun itself out, Italy ceased to be the center of pornographic and obscene literature in Europe. Instead, the trade moved north and west, entering a second phase, part of the so-called 'Northern' Renaissance. In this sense, the erotic works of Aretino and Pallavicino were some of the final products of the 'Italian' Renaissance before its 'decline and fall,' and led poets such as Thomas Nashe in England, or Jean de La Fontaine in France to model themselves after Pietro Aretino as an example of a man of letters and a political independent. Critics, however, demonized them for being dissolute and perverted (like those damn Italians), cautioning parents against allowing their sons to pursue music, dancing, and 'modern poetry' with warnings such as: "If you would have your sonne soft, womannish, uncleane, smooth mouthed, affected to bawdry, scurrility, filthy rimes, and unseemly wickednes of talking" then let them read this Italian trash.[122] The Italian trash proved incredibly influential, but it also took on some uniquely French and English characteristics. James Grantham Turner argues that the last flourishes of the Italian Renaissance were pornographic works that "provided transmission of key ideas to France and England," among which included "the replacement of the trickster-whore by the domestic-affective mistress. . . the cultivation of extreme sexuality as *summum bonum* and sublime aesthetic masterpiece. . .the rhetorical construction of desire. . . the lascivious genius of the writer [and the] the naturalness of unnatural perversions."[123]

Although there are earlier examples of erotic works none of them really matched up to Pietro Aretino's lascivious genius; his *Ragionamenti* (1536) was translated and seen in London by 1658 and earlier in Paris, though even earlier editions likely existed in Italian (and circulated among the upper classes). As a final flourish of the Italian Renaissance, Aretino's book inaugurated obscene French and English Renaissances, where writers were inspired to produce their own versions, such as *The Crafty Whore* (1658), a free rendering of the third dialogue of *Raigonamenti*, which deals with the life of whores. According to historian Ian Fredrick Moulton, *The Crafty Whore* "is much more bland than the *Ragionamenti*—there is no explicit description of sexual acts, for example. It is also strongly moralistic; some passages warn of the dangers of venereal disease, and the dialogue ends with both whores renouncing their past sins and resolving to retire to a "remote Cell or Hermitage."[124] Other Italian translations included *La Puttana Errante*, which was written in 1550 by a student of Aretino named Nicolo Franco and translated into English as *Accomplished Whore* (1660). And of course there was Pallavicino's *La Retorica Delle Puttane* (1642) was translated as *The Whore's Rhetorick* in 1683, which we have discussed in the previous section. But none of these works were even remotely original or lived up to the obscenity or eroticism of Aretino, and indeed some of them were entirely religious and non-erotic, losing any elements of cultural critique and becoming just moralistic tales. The next work or some originality to make a major splash was *L'escolle des filles* (*The School of Girls*) in 1655.

On January 13th of 1668, Samuel Pepys, who was an English Member of Parliament and a naval administrator, but is now famous for the detailed diary he kept when he was young, decided to visit a bookstore and buy a novel in French for his wife, who was just learning French. Unfortunately for his wife, he was not successful. He wrote:

> I saw the French book which I did think to have had for my wife to translate, called L'escolle des Filles, but when I came to look into it, it is the most bawdy, lewd book that ever I saw, rather worse than Puttana Errante - so that I was ashamed of reading in it. [125]

So ashamed, in fact, that he left the bookseller's immediately and did not manage to purchase anything for his wife. What he had read of this notorious text, however, seemed to stick in the back of his mind and stay with him. Eventually, a few weeks later, on February eighth, he writes that:

> Thence away to the Strand to my bookseller's, and there stayed an hour and bought that idle, roguish book, L'escolle des Filles. . . . I resolve, as soon as I have read it, to burn it, that it may not stand in the list of my books, nor among them, to disgrace them if it should be found.[126]

The next day he writes, becoming perhaps the first recorded person in history to read a dirty novel 'for research purposes only:'

> [I've been] at my chamber all the morning and in the office, doing business and also reading a little of L'escolle des Filles, which is a mighty lewd book, but yet not amiss for a sober man once to read over to

inform himself in the villainy of the world. . . . [after a night of drinking with his friends] I to my chamber, where I did read through [that] lewd book, but what doth me no wrong to read for information sake but [he writes in code here but it's easy to figure out] it did hazer my prick para stand all the while, and una vez to decharger; and after I had [finished], I burned it, that it might not be among my books to my shame; and so at night to supper and then to bed. [127]

What was this book that could inspire such shame in Samuel Pepys, a man who records his causal sexual assaults against his servant's wife and who brought his telescope to church to examine women in the audience up close? What could shock the man who frankly discusses hooking up with his friends' wives in public places and carriages? Where does it stand in our history of obscenity? This book, *L'escolle des Filles* [The School of Girls] and its sequel *La Philosophie Des Dames* [The Philosophy of Women] became both incredibly popular and incredibly censored. It was quickly translated into Italian, Dutch, and English, and spread like wildfire across Europe. The text is also known by its English name, *The School of Venus: Or, the Ladies Delight Reduced into Rules of Practice*. It was put together by two men, Michel Millot and Jean L'Ange, likely in the winter of 1664-65. The writing of the text is sometimes attributed to Millot, due to an unauthorized Dutch edition which credited it to him. This is unlikely, to say in the least, as *L'escolle des Filles* was printed secretly and with false names in order to cover the identities of Millot and L'Ange. As far as historians can piece together, the real 'author' of the text was a 'print collective,' which included Millot and L'Ange along with a financier, publisher and author.[128]

In fact, the only reason we know the two names we do is because one member of this collective, the publisher Louis

Piot, ratted them out in order to secure his own safety. In 1655, Piot agreed to publish 300 copies of *L'escolle Des Filles*, of which 50 were on high quality paper—the fact that over 80% of the books were made in the cheaper and lower quality format shows that authors were beginning to understand that there was a wider market middle-class audience. After taking payment from Millot and printing off the books under a fake name and location (a strategy publishers used to escape prosecution), Piot either had second thoughts or decided he could profit, and reached out to the Parisian printer's guild for protection. It seems like the guild reported the two men to a public prosecutor, who ordered their arrest. On June 12th L'Ange was captured and his copies of the books were destroyed. It seems that Millot was also captured, but he managed to make a daring escape from police custody and over the border into Belgium.

The resulting court testimony gives us all the information about the two men we have: Jean L'Ange was born in 1610 in Paris, and was an *écuyer*, which translates literally as an 'esquire,' or horseman, but what his role was is unclear. Millot appears to have been a tax auditor of some sort, and would later become a mercenary after fleeing France. As Millot had financed most of the cost of publishing the books, the court decided that he was liable, and ordered his execution and seizure of his property. Unfortunately for the court, he has escaped into Belgium, but he was burnt in effigy on August 9th, 1655 along with all of the remaining copies of the books. L'Ange was imprisoned until October, banished from Paris for three years, and fined 200 livres (roughly $45,000 today). As Joan DeJean notes, in many ways, this was a precursor to the modern obscenity trial, and was amazingly underwhelming and unsatisfactory for the French government—"they could not have been convinced that the trial had put an end to the matter not that they had found their man in Millot, because fifteen years after the book police were still torturing suspects, hoping at long last to learn the true story."[129]

Although all of the copies in Paris were destroyed when the authorities ransacked Millot and L'Ange's homes and burnt them with Millot's effigy, it is obvious that some of the copies must have survived and made it into other countries, as there was a Dutch translation the following year, and is was translated to English in 1680. As Bradford Mudge noted in his recent anthology of erotic works, the "translation changes the names of the original protagonists--Susanne, Fanchon, and Robinet--to Katy, Frances, and Roger but otherwise remains faithful to the original. Like the French, it appears in two dialogues. Unlike the French, it contains twelve engravings, or 'cutts.'"[130] The only other difference in the English edition was that the first and second dialogues were split into two separate books, even though they had been originally written as one. The motive of the publisher was capitalistic profit— the same intention that Hollywood movie studios have when they split the last movie of a trilogy into two separate parts). In this way, *The School of Venus* is a good example of how the book market was developing extremely capitalistic characteristics; books were one of the first goods to become commodities. Another sign of this is that *The School of Venus* was the first obscene book to be advertised in a newspaper. It would take another century or so before the full potential of this format was realized. Either way, in the introduction to the English edition, the translator claims to be publishing the book with purely "charitable" intentions:

> [T]hough our English Ladies are the most accomplished in the world, not only for their Angelical and Beautiful faces, but also for the exact composure, of their Shape and Body; yet being bred up in a cold Northern Flegmatick Country, and kept under the severe, though insignificant Government, of an Hypocritical Mother or Governess, when they once come to be enjoyed, their Embraces are so cold, and

> they such ignorants to the misteries of swiving [sex],
> as it quite dulls their lovers Appetites, and often
> makes them run after other women, which though
> less Beautiful, yet having the advantages of knowing
> more, and better management of their Arses, give
> more content and pleasure to their Gallants. . .so
> have I finished this [book] to the ignorant Maid. I am
> sure this must be a welcome book.[131]

These sorts of somewhat amusing, tongue-in-cheek introductions where the author or the publisher swears that he is just publishing erotic text for information's sake, for the good of the general public, or at the behest of a rich noble person, were extremely common. In some cases it was used as a sort of legal defense if they were arrested. This was one of the defenses that the infamous publisher Edmund Curll would use in the 18th century. Of course, the author and the reader knew that this introduction was tongue-in-cheek, but it allows for the figment of plausible deniability, like a handy fig leaf.

The story follows nearly the same model as Aretino and Pallavicino by having a much older and more experienced woman teach the younger and more innocent one how to have sex and manage her affairs. The one major difference however, as alluded to above, is that the trickster-whore (such as Nanna or Cresswell) is replaced by a more domestic mistress, a woman who clearly belongs to middle-class society. In a way, this reduces female power because they cease to deceive and exploit men, but on the other hand, it is a more 'realistic' character, one who is truly part of society. Critics such as the Society for the Reformation of Manners or the Society for the Suppression of Vice went on to argue that this was much more dangerous because it blurred the lines between reality and fantasy, like a modern video game—or modern pornography! — supposedly does.

The dialog begins when Frances, the wiser and more experienced cousin, comes to visit her younger and innocent-to-a-fault younger cousin, Katy. Frances asks her what she is up to, and Katy says that she is at 'work,' meaning the domestic work of cooking or cleaning, etc. Frances comments almost snidely:

> **Frances:** I think you do nothing else, you live here confined to your Chamber, as if it were a Nunnery; you never stir abroad, and seldom a man comes at thee.

> **Katy**: You say very true Cousin, what should I trouble my self with men; I believe none of them ever think of me, and my Mother tells me, I am not yet old enough to Marry.

> **Frances**: Not old enough to be Married, and a young plump Wench of Sixteen; thou art finely fitted indeed with a Mother, who ought now to take care to please thee. . .art thou such a Fool to believe you can't enjoy a mans company without being Married?[132]

Katy, in her 'sweet and innocent' way, says that *of course* she enjoys the company of men; her uncles and male cousins come to visit her. "Pish," Frances cries "they are your kindred! I mean others." Katy says that there is a certain 'Mr. Roger' that comes to visit her, but he only pretends to love her, speaks of things that she doesn't understand, or compliments her beauty. She says, "Indeed they do little else but commend my beauty, kissing me and feeling my Breasts, telling me a Hundred things, which they say are very pleasing to them, but for my part, they add nothing to my content."[133]

With this comment, Frances sees that Katy is hopelessly innocent, calls her an ignorant fool, and demands to instruct her in the ways of love. Katy demurs, arguing "What can an innocent Girl learn from men, whom the world account so debauched?"[134] This line provides Frances with a way to begin her educating dialogue, but it is also interesting because it reveals the shifting attitudes towards male and female sexuality. In earlier works, like Aretino's, or the poems of Thomas Nashe women were stereotyped as being more sexually voracious and aggressive. It seems that by the mid-to-late seventeenth-century that society began to represent men as the sexual aggressors. European culture had not, at this point, reached the highs (or lows) of male libertinism, but it was beginning to incline that way. A rather hilarious bit involving Mr. Roger and Katy follows this when Frances tells her there is a great pleasure in men's company that she has not yet tasted, and asks her how Mr. Roger behaves while he is alone with her. A puzzled Katy, oblivious to the facts, recounts Mr. Roger trying to hide an erection in her company, saying that, "he sighs and bemoans himself in my presence, I (far from being the cause thereof) pity him, ask him what [ails him], and should be glad with all my heart if I could give him any ease." To which Frances responds, "Yes, yes, you have touched his cloaths, but you should have handled something else."[135]

Frances, being such an obliging, kind soul, describes exactly what Katy should have been holding in blunt details, which she says is necessary: "Pish, you are [too innocent], if you are minded to hear such Discourse, you must not be so Scrupulous. . .I must use the very words without Mincing: Cunt, Arse, Prick, Bollocks, &c." Aside from being a clear communication of Frances ideas and language, this is also an amusing hat-tip to Pietro Aretino's *Dialogues* where Antonia tells Nanna to

> Speak plainly and say "fuck," "prick," "cunt," and "ass" if you want anyone except the scholars at the University of Rome to understand you. You with your "rope in the ring," your "obelisk in the Coliseum," your "leek in the garden," your "key in the lock,"

your "bolt in the door,". . . your "leaves of the missal," "arrow," "carrot," "root," and all the shit there is--why don't you say it straight out and stop going about on tiptoes?[136]

Aretino's Nanna argues that, "Don't you know that respectability looks all the more beautiful in a whorehouse?"[137] With the shift in character from public whores to private, domestic women, the roles are reversed, and the listener, Katy, blushes at the Frances' use of the word 'prick' and cries: "Oh Lord Coz, you Swear?"[138]

Figure 5: Frances educating Katy in female anatomy.

It is obvious how the text is supposed to be amusing for the reader—even today, Katy's description of a penis as a "white hogs pudding" is hilarious, but also educational—Frances doesn't mince words in her description of a penis, and she also gives her younger cousin (and the readers) several different names for it. Nor does she mince words in describing how the sexual act takes place either, though the way she describes it is rather energetic:

Frances: He usually takes courage, throws her backwards, flings up her Coats and Smock, lets fall his Breeches, opens her Legs, and thrusts his Tarse into her Cunt (which is the place through which she Pisseth) lustily therein, Rubbing it, which is the greatest pleasure imaginable.

Katy: Lord Cousin, what strange things do you tell me, but how the Duce doth he get in that thing which seems to be so limber and soft? Sure he must needs cram it in with his Fingers?

Frances: Oh, thou are an ignorant Girl indeed, when a man hath a Fucking Job to do, his Prick is not then limber, but appears quite another thing, it is half as big and as long again as it was before, it is also as stiff as a stake, and when it's standing so stiff, the skin on the Head comes back, and it appears just like a very large Heart Cherry.[139]

Frances then goes on to describe the female aspects of genitalia, noting that "in plain English it is called a Cunt, though they out of an affected modesty mince the word, call it a Twot [twat], and Twenty such kind of Names." And, of course, when the twot meets the tarse, "it is called Fucking!" But, she cautions, "don't talk of such kind of thing before Company, for they will call you an immodest bawdy Wench, and chide you for it." Frances quickly moves into her educational lecture on basic male anatomy, including other names used: "Thing with which a Man Pisseth, is sometimes call'd a Prick, sometimes a Tarse, sometimes a Mans Yard. . . . Besides they have Two little Balls made up in a Skin something like a Purse, these we call Bollocks, they are not much unlike our Spanish Olives." [140]

This particular section demonstrates how much sexual education went into early modern erotica and obscenity.

Many of the works that we will be discussing from this point forward do not necessarily assume sexual knowledge on the part of an elite reader as Aretino's dialogues did. Instead they point to one of the motivators for both the author and the reader or purchaser: to catalogue (on the part of the author) and to learn (on the part of the reader) about different aspects of human sexuality, anatomy and physiology. Another important work, *Aristotle's Masterpiece* also occupied this liminal space—with far less focus on sex—and will be discussed in the next section. To us, it might be surprising to see this sort of heavily-detailed sex-ed, but these sorts of educational lectures become incredibly common in erotic literature in the 17th and 18th centuries. Part of the reason was that, well, they *were* sex-ed. As Frances points out, it was not polite or common to talk "before Company," so the need for sexual education from other sources became increasingly common, just as modern pornography is becoming a means of sexual education for the generations raised on the Internet. This was definitely the intention of L'Ange and Millot, whose title (*The School of Girls*) and introduction encouraged people to give these books away for educational purposes.

It seems that at least one young man took this advice, as historian Sarah Toulalan documents: "Louis XIV clearly thought that *L'escolle des filles* was utterly unsuitable reading for young women, as not only was the particular maid of honor who was discovered to have the book expelled from her position, but also all the others [who came in contact with it] (although the book was apparently given to her by a man rather than acquired by her own choosing)."[141] It is not clear what specifically would have been offensive to King Louis XIV, but there are a number of possibilities. First is the possibility that the combination of eroticism with cultural critique was seen as dangerous. This is especially true when Frances argues that "all People of all ranks and degrees participate [in adultery], even from the King to the Cobler, from the Queen to the Scullion Wench, in short one half of the World Fucks the other."[142] As Mudge notes in his edition, this would have been seen as rather dangerous and incendiary because sex was frequently used in erotic texts as "the great leveler, that which —regardless of class differences—makes us all the same. In keeping with its connections to satire, this material targets hypocrisy and pretense as it establishes sexuality as a natural, materialistic "real" against which we are to measure social and cultural restriction."[143]

Secondly, the *School of Venus* is rather insulting in its attitude towards religion, especially when Katy seems to have a case of moral horror for going against the church's instruction to be chaste and pure. Ever-clever Frances manages to reassure her by saying, "God who sees and knows all things will say nothing, besides, I cannot think leachery a sin." She continues with the idea that if women were in charge, rather than men, "you would soon find they would account fucking so lawful, as it should not be accounted a Misdemeanor...and were it not for fear of great Bellys, it were possible swiving [sex] would be much more used then now it is."[144] This is further compounded when Frances describes in great detail (keeping with the sex-ed) primitive birth-control methods, which will be discussed in a moment.

The 'subversiveness' of the text is not the only thing of interest from *The School of Venus*—in fact, it also provides a look at the 'one-sex' model of humanity, when Frances notes:

> Listen then. A Prick hath a fine soft loose skin, which though the Wench take it in her Hand, when it is loose and lank, will soon grow stiff and be filled: 'Tis full of Nerves and Gristles. . .over this Head is a Cap of Skin which slips backwards when the Prick stands, underneath there is a pipe which swells like a great vain and comes to the Head of the Prick, where is a small slit or orifice; as for the Womans Cunt, I know not what it is within, but I am told

[that the vagina] is nothing but a Prick turned inwards.[145]

Before modern anatomy and understanding of sexual differences, the one-sex model of human biology was based on similarity rather than differences, and was popular in European medical theory from ancient Greek times until the 18th or 19th centuries. As Mudge puts it, "Anatomists, physicians, and philosophers from Aristotle and Galen to Leonardo da Vinci believed in a "homology," a visual and structural likeness, between male and female reproductive organs."[146] Of course, there has been a great deal of recent discussion and questioning around the idea in recent years, especially by recent historians of the body. The argument for the societal transition from a premodern one-sex worldview to a two sex binary originates, in its strongest and most influential form, from Thomas Laqueur's 1990 *Making Sex: Body and Gender from the Greeks to Freud*, which Lauren Kassel calls "a sort of creation myth for binary ideas about sex difference."[147] Michael Solberg, in a recent essay has most forcefully rejected Lacquers thesis and argued that "the major anatomists and the overwhelming majority of late medieval and early modern physicians clearly did not advocate a one-sex model. On the contrary, they stressed anatomical difference and its fatal effects on female health."[148] While this may be true of anatomists and physicians specifically, it is apparent from the erotic texts of Millot and L'Ange, as well as Chorier in the next section, that these ideas were not reflected across society. These works, in fact, lend support to Laura Gowing's argument that "that one-sex and two-sex models co-existed with ideas about sexual difference that were embodied from head to toe and determined by the balance of humours in the body."[149]

After some discussion on sexual education, Frances and Katy turn to Frances' personal experience with her husband, where she describes the various sexual positions, none of which were 'church-approved:'

> You may see there are more ways then one to put a Prick into a Cunt, sometimes my Husband gets upon me, sometimes I get upon him, sometimes we do it sideways, sometimes kneeling, sometimes cross-ways, sometimes backwards, as if I were to take a Glister,11 sometimes Wheelbarrow, with one leg upon his shoulders, sometimes we do it on our feet, sometimes upon a stool, and when he is in Hast he throws me upon a Form, Chair or Floor, and fucks me lustily, so these ways afford several and variety of pleasures. . . [150]

She continues in detail. After this, the first dialogue abruptly ends when Frances hears Mr. Roger on the stairs, and she and Katy agree that Katy will pursue an affair with him. Frances quickly leaves her cousin behind, saying that she will call on her again soon. And she does return shortly afterwards, for a second dialogue that delves even deeper into morality and philosophy.

The second dialogue begins with Frances acting like an ex-cited schoolgirl, asking Katy to tell her all the hot new gossip: "now pray tell me, how squares go with you, since last I saw you." In fact, for much of this second dialog Katy now seems to be the older and wiser cousin, telling Frances of her experiences and some new things she and Mr. Roger have invented, including a "method for fucking in front of company:

> Mr. Roger gave me a Visit one Night, as we were dancing with some few of our Neighbors, he being a little flustrated with Wine set himself on a Chair, and whilst others danced, feigned himself a sleep; at last he pulled me to him, and sat me down on his knees. . .with a little Pen-knife he pulled out of his

Twesers [Trousers], he made a hole in [my dress], and thrust his Prick into my Cunt, which I was very glad of; we went leasurely to work, for we durst not be too busie for fear of being caught.[151]

Apparently the 17th century French and English partied harder than we ever do today. But the second dialogue does not just mention these inventive sexual escapades, as the introduction also advertises that it shows, "the curious and pleasing ways, how a man gets a Virgins Maidenhead, it also describes what a perfect Beauty (both Masculine and Feminine) is, and gives instructions, how a Woman must behave her self in the extasie of swiving."[152] Katy recounts—in great detail—the difficulty Roger has in 'relieving' her of her maidenhead. He tries one position after another, adjusting Katy like a doll, but his 'great Tarse' stretches and pains her, almost to the point of fainting. Eventually however, Roger strikes upon the idea of using pomade (hair grease) as a sort of lube, and, adjusting Katy once again, succeeds:

> **Katy:** But he put me in a Hundred postures incunting at every one, shewing me how I must manage my self to get in the Prick farthest, in this I was an apt Schollar, and think I shall not in hast forget my lesson. . . . At last he thought of that, and did nothing else, then he placed me on a Chair, and by the help of the Pomatum got in a little further, but seeing he could do no great good that way, he make me rise, and laid me with all four on the Bed, and having rubbed his Tarse once more with Pomatum [lube], he charged me briskly in the reer.[153]

Incunting—presumably meaning insertion of the penis into the vagina, is a word that seems to have (sadly?) fallen into disuse over the years, but being charged in the 'reer' here does not seem to imply anal intercourse. After a rather exhaustive list of sexual positions they tried over the intervening week, Katy finishes with "And this Cousin, is the plain truth of what hath befallen me since last I saw you, now tell me what is your opinion of it all?" Frances is congratulatory, and says, "Truly you are arrived to such a perfection in the Art of Fucking, that you need no farther instructions. . . . Why I say you have all the Terms of Art as well as my self, and can now without Blushing call Prick, Stones, Bollocks, Cunt, Tarse, and the like names."[154] It is very interesting in the ways that this montage of sexual positions and feelings is similar to a more modern pornographic work—and perhaps that is the point— but at the very least it is a presagement of what is to come.

In the way that Frances accepts and cheers Katy on, it is apparent that she now thinks of her younger cousin as her equal or better, as she can use the language of the whorehouse without being a whore herself. So, if we were to make a brief summary of the history of the obscene from Aretino to Millot, it would be that the trickster-whore has been replaced by the domestic mistress who can call things 'what they are,' and when it is time to go to bed, they are graduates of the 'School of Venus.' This is a far cry from the blushing virgin that women were stereotypically supposed to be on their first night. The women in these dialogues are not some sort of ideal "maiden in the streets/whore in the sheets," they are, in fact, a rather sexist male fantasy that projects the virgin/whore ideals onto a perfect woman. This is why Frances advocates keeping several men on the side as partners—those several men would likely be the young gentlemen who were reading *The School of Venus*. A father or a husband, who had a vested interest in keeping his daughter virginal and his wife from cuckolding him, would have been greatly disturbed by the text. Indeed, these male authorities likely found much to be upset about in this text.

One such problematic passage is where Katy worries what

to do if Mr. Roger makes her pregnant, as she is not married. Frances tells her that her best bet is to get married so she can have as many affairs as she likes, and, at the end of the second dialogue, says that she will find a husband for Katy to marry as soon as possible. The other solution, Frances says:

> **Frances:** [F]irst know that these misfortunes are not very frequent, that we need [not] fear them before they happen. How many pregnant Wenches are there, that daily walk up and down, and by the help of Busques and loose garbs hide their great Bellies till within a Month or two of their times, when by the help of a faithful Friend they slip into the Country, and rid themselves of their Burthen, and shortly after return into the City as pure Virgins as ever? Make the worst of it, 'tis but a little trouble, and who would lose so much fine sport for a little hazard, sometimes we may Fuck two or three years and that never happen[s], and if we would be so base 'tis easie to have Medicines to make us miscarry, but 'tis pity such things should be practiced in this time of Dearth, and want his Majesty hath of able Subjects, in which there are none more likely to do him Service then those which are illegitimate, which are begot in the heat of Leachery.[155]

It is probably pretty easy to figure out what the authorities' reactions to Frances suggestions would be. Abortion and illegitimate children are problematic for any society at any time, but for a European society that was incredibly concerned with legitimacy and purity, Frances' suggestions are deeply disturbing. Additionally, in describing methods of contraception and birth control (a cloth over the head of a penis, *coitus interruptus* or the pull-out method), Frances is taking a position that was the exact opposite of public policy, which was obsessed with increasing the birthrate. As noted before, the governmental reaction of seizure of property, exile, and orders of execution, show just how disturbing it was to them. Still, and despite commands for its total destruction, *The School of Venus* survived and was a major influence on the developing pornographic genre. Less than three years later, another author would put pen to paper and attempt to take on the mantle of Pietro Aretino; Nicolas Chorier.

The Sodatical Satires of Nicolas Chorier

AS I POINTED OUT EARLIER, the erotic book market was becomingly increasingly popular among the upper-class and the newly-literate middle class readers and writers. Much of this has to do with the increasing commodification of the book market. Part of this growth was caused by the attack and counter-attack of the Reformation and Counter-Reformation, but another significant contributor was increasing literacy and decreasing cost of literature. Shifts in political culture are reflected in literature—but they are also determined by the history of the genre. For example, a novel that fits the genre of a 'western' has certain things that apply across every single gle work in that genre—law and order, cowboys, edge of humanity, a desert, etc. However, the genre of western itself has changed as the United States has changed—in the beginning it was very much a pro-cowboy, anti-Indian genre, idolizing the man living on the edge of society. These are the sorts of Louis L'Amour novels that deal with Buffalo Bill, Jesse James, Wyatt Earp, and so on. As the United States evolved politically and culturally, there was a corresponding change in the genre of the western as well—Cormac McCarthy's *No Country for Old Men* and *The Road* are highly different in style and topic from Buffalo Bill. However, they still involve some of the elements of a western—law vs. order, private and personal justice, and living on the frontier or fringes of human society.

These same traditions and developments apply to the

genre of pornography. This is one of the things we will see with the one and only *Maître Advocat* Nicolas Chorier. Why is this obscure French lawyer and historian important for the history of pornography? Well, it turns out that Monsieur Chorier had a secret life. As I noted in the last section on *The School of Venus,* Aretino's *Raigonamenti* had large impact on French (and therefore, European) literature. Specifically, many French authors, such as L'Ange and Millot—or whomever they paid to write—took to copying *Raigonamenti*'s whore dialog format, where two women speak to each other on private and secret matters. In turn, books such as *The School of Venus* influenced later French works and authors. As a result of Chorier and the Millot/L'Ange team, the center of the book trade shifted from Italy to France, and would remain so until the mid-1700s. More to the point, however, there was a common culture of readers and producers of erotic texts, with frequent callbacks, similarities, and allusions to earlier works. Chorier's text is no different.

Nicolas Chorier was born in Dauphine, France, in 1612, and received a doctorate of law in 1639. He made his living mostly as a lawyer, but he also wrote several books on the history and legal practices of France, some of which are still used today, 400 years later. He was described as "a man of cultivated mind, a passionate lover of letters, [and] a first-rate Latinist." However, aside from his 'official' works, he also had a hobby of writing what he referred to as 'Sotadical' verses. The word Sotadical, like the word pornography, is a sort of 'code' word, of course—it comes from the name of the Ancient Greek poet Sotades, who specialized in writing obscene and pederastic (sexual activity between an older man and a younger boy).

In 1660, looking to make a bit of extra money on the side, Chorier secretly published *Aloysiæ Sigeæ Toletanæ satyra sotadica de arcanis amoris et veneris: Aloysia hispanice scripsit: latinitate donavit J. Meursius.* Translated, this means "Luisa Sigea Toledana's Sotadic satire, on the secrets of love and sex. Luisa wrote it in Spanish; it has been translated from Latin by J. Meursius" (Chorier's pseudonym). In going with the general tongue-in-cheek style of erotic novels, he falsely credited the work to Luisa Sigea de Velasco, who was a 16th century female Christian intellectual. The reason for this is partially malicious, as Chorier and many of his contemporaries were critical of women and the idea that women could or should ever be educated. The other reason is that he hoped the Latin text and the fake pseudonym would prevent him from running into any legal issues like Millot and L'Ange had, and this would become a frequently-used device in the decades and centuries that followed. That would have mixed results for him, as we shall see.

In his "Foreword," J. Meursius mocks Luisa Sigea and Spanish culture: "Conspicuous for her genius, learning, and beauty, she was pre-eminently gifted with all those qualities. . .which render honest women so estimable. Instead of making virtue consist in an abject and stupid abasement of reason. . .she believed it was best to devote one's self to liberal studies."[156] Supposedly, Meursius' version of Sigea detested the "dissolute and disgraceful behavior of aristocratic ladies in particular" so she 'decided' to write this Sotadical Satire. And because she detests lying so much, she "employed a rather free style" (which we should read as a 'rather pornographic style'). Besides, Chorier argues, "women are better qualified for this sort of description," because of their better nature and inclinations.[157] This is another reference to how women were generally seen as more sexually aggressive.[158]

The story opens in nearly exactly the same way as *The School of Venus*. While there is a chance that Chorier had read *The School*, as it would have been circulating around France at the time, it is unlikely. If not, then it is evidence for both the continuing popularity of writing in the Aretine style, and for the change from public whore to the private, domestic mistress. It takes place between two women named Ottavia and Tullia, supposedly the names of upper-class aristocrats in Sigea's Spain. Tullia is Ottavia's older married cousin, and the story begins with her telling her how happy she is about Ottavia's upcoming marriage to a man named Caviceo, and is happy that Ottavia will finally get to know the "delights of marriage."

Ottavia agrees, and said that she was "truly surprised by the unwonted fire of his kisses when he made free with me eight days ago...the fool took them against my will, brandishing his glowing tongue between my lips."[159] She goes on to explain that he tried to convince her to have intercourse with him, and when she denied him, he still tried to have his way with her, but she was luckily saved by her mother. Why this is considered a healthy sign of a future relationship, I do not know, but it was apparently considered so. At first it would seem that the plot of *Luisa Sigea* follows the plot of *The School of Venus*—cousin comes to visit, they get to talking about men, and then the older cousin begins to educate the younger one. However, in sharp contrast to the *School of Venus*, this dirty discussion 'naturally' leads to the arousal of both of the girls and they engage in 'tribadism,' or lesbian intercourse:

> **Ottavia:** Hold off, thou art running thy hand over my whole person, thou art now thrusting it lower down. Why art thou fondling my thighs? Ah! ah! ah! Tullia. Pray why art thou fumbling that spot? Nor dost thou remove thy piercing eyes from it.

> **Tullia:** I am viewing this field of Venus with curious longing; it is neither wide nor spacious, but full of the sweetest delights; inexhaustible Venus shall herein waste away the force of thy Mars.[160]

This is actually a remarkable scene, because it is the only erotic text until the 1800s to offer a representation and a defense of female homosexuality. Although lesbians or at least female same-sex desire has undoubtedly been present throughout history (with the terms Sapphist or tribade usually applied), tracking down any sort of information or history of them has been notoriously difficult, as Julie Peakman writes.[161] Unlike male same-sex desire, women tended to escape notice and were able "carry out the most intimate of relationships without raising undue concern from observers. Indeed, passionate female friendships were considered normal right up until the twentieth century. Although occasionally queries hung over certain women with more 'masculine' qualities, little attention was paid to them apart from the odd derogatory remark."[162] Unfortunately, Chorier and others (until *Fanny Hill*) do not mention same-sex male interactions, likely because these tended to be frowned on entirely, but this mention of female same-sex desire and action remains significantly early.

In the scene, Tullia 'deduces' that because Ottavia is 15 she does not know the "delights of Venus" and needs to be instructed. She asks (or more, demands) the right to instruct her in the "ways of Sappho," that is to say, lesbianism. Ottavia consents, and shows her ignorance in this scene:

> **Ottavia:** Enjoy me as much as ever thou mayest, I consent to it. But I am well aware that no pleasure can accrue to thee from a maiden as I am, nor to me from thee either, even though thou really wast as a marvellous garden of all delicacies and attractions.
>
> **Tullia:** Thou hast indeed a garden, wherein Caviceo will feed his spumy mood on the most delicious fruits.
>
> **Ottavia:** I have no garden which thou hast not likewise abounding in the same fruit. Now, what is it thou callest a garden? Where is it situated? What

are these fruits? ... Perhaps thou designates by this word that spot which thou art clutching in thy right hand, teasing with thy fingers and tickling with the ends of thy nails, to excite a desire in me?

Tullia: That's so, cousin; having no experience of it, thou ignorest its use; but I shall try and make thee know it.[163]

After a scene of, er, the sodatical, Tullia lays back and sighs. This is in fact one of the very first scenes of outright lesbianism that we have encountered, as most of the writers we've discussed have simply touched on just heterosexual intercourse. The exception of course is Aretino, but any moments of homosexual intercourse there take place between nuns or priests, in a way of critiquing monastic corruption—this is the first instance of intercourse between the laity. Indeed, it is a very interesting moment, as Chorier has Tullia launch into a defense of lesbianism, which includes the assertion that Italian, Spanish and French women "love one another: and were they not held back by shame, they would all rush headlong one against the other in rut."

Having taken her pleasure of her cousin, Tullia decides to educate her about the anatomy of the male and female body and how intercourse happens between men and women. For example, in talking about the clitoris she says, almost as if quoting from an anatomy book:

Tullia: The Latins and our contemporaries generally call that part of our person, about which we have already spoken, vulva, cunnus, fregna, fica, potto. Vulva, as if they meant valve; cunnus from cuneus, a wedge, because great force must be exerted to drive into it on the first assaults... Into this spot Caviceo will first thrust his huge lance, with all his might; he will in this moment cause thee great suffering, but, shortly after, still greater joys... Thou beholdest its marvellous structure. It first bulges out with a certain protuberance, which a light down covers with thee; and do not fancy it is concealed between the thighs for shame sake, of which it is utterly devoid, but it is set there for use. They style this protuberance the hillock of Venus: whoever has once climbed it, my dear Ottavia, prefers it ever after to the Parnassus, Olympus or the sacred hills... There are two slits, the one under the other, through which this hillock opens to a full coition. They call the first, the large one; the second is the interior one. The former is suitable for bringing forth... the inner one is narrower; I have already stated that the lips which cover the edges of the broader slit are called cadurda. Inside this slit, namely, the more hidden one, there are wings; they are very prominent in me: these they call nymphs... But I have forgotten to speak about the clitoris. This is a membranous body situated almost at the bottom of the pubis, and replaces a kind of cod. It stiffens up, as if it were a cod, at any amorous desire; it inflames rather sensible natured women with so keen an itching that, if excited unto pleasure by drawing the hand near it, they generally spill of their own free will, without awaiting a rider. Of course I have experienced this pretty often whilst Callias is sprinkling me with his lubricities, whilst he is fondling me and toying with the thing itself. A copious dewy sap falls from my garden into his hands, whilst he is playing too freely in these localities.[164]

Or, in discussing male anatomy, she talks about the testicles, describing them as, "two balls, not too small either, not quite round, but extremely hard; the harder they are, the more suited they are for pleasure. Owing to their being two, the Greeks call them "didyms," and many great heroes have borne this name."

These 'lectures' point to a very important difference between modern-day pornography and erotica, which is that pornography from the early modern period until about the 1750s contained much information that we would see as medical or anatomic. Modern pornography, visual or not, does not tend to focus on the operation of the body or how intercourse works—instead it is focused on just the pleasurable aspects of intercourse. Tullia discusses at length how urination works, where the clitoris is and what its function is, and how masturbation works with men and women. Erotic works in this period were as much educational as they were for pleasure or satire, and the educational or anatomical parts are frequently longer and more detailed than the actual scenes of intercourse. Depending on your perspective, this is perhaps a loss: from both news reports and scientific research it is clear that pornography is being used as a form of self-help sex-ed, but the actual anatomy of sex and bodies is not covered in modern pornography. Indeed, scenes and works like this demonstrate a dual purpose of the author in titillation and education, but also the same dual appeal to readers or purchasers.

Indeed, one of the most popular sexual-topic books throughout the early modern and well into the modern era was a combination sexual-advice and obstetrical manual, *Aristotle's Masterpiece*. Despite the name, this work has no real connection to Aristotle besides copping his name in an effort to sound dignified and definitive. As Mary Fissell notes, the work "was first published in London in 1684, [and] it went through hundreds of editions in England and America. It was still for sale, largely unchanged, into the 1930s and beyond."[165] Every single edition of the *Masterpiece* is different

—a vast Frankensteinian amalgamation of sources pasted together from philosophy, midwifery, gossip and erotic texts, serving as a sort of encyclopedia. It was seen as useful to newly-married couples (as a wedding gift) as it was dangerous to six teenage boys that were caught masturbating over its (decidedly rough) illustrations.[166] A similar work, Nicolas Venette's *Tableau de l'amour conjugal* (1686) was also incredibly popular and followed a similar outline, scaffolding, and subsequent history. Both texts tended to begin with a woodcut illustration of a naked woman, and be followed by a racy and suggestive poem. This was a clever (and effective) advertising strategy, as John Cannon recounted in his diary in 1700 when he bought it for a shilling to "pry into the Secrets of Nature especially of the female sex," and demonstrates the and the works of Chorier and L'Ange also play a similar role in their long sex-ed digressions.[167]

To return to our story, Tullia continues her lectures in a new chapter, this one focusing on her first (and marathon) night with her husband, who has to nearly force her to have sex with him. The language is playful and coded:

> Briefly: having placed his leg inside of mine, applying it first as a wedge, he thus made way between my thighs for his whole person. He mounted me, pressing his breast down upon mine; what could I refuse him then? This new and unusual weight inspired me with violent awe. He, while abating with one hand the fury of Priapus, applied the battering-ram to my gates. . . [In another event] "Take away," said I, "this incendiary hand of thine, withdraw; why dost thou excite me?" He was in his glory because I owned I was burning. He snatched my left hand. —"I am lighting this Venereal firebrand for thee," he says, "it will extinguish the fire it has caused." So he orders me to take this firebrand; having become bolder by this time, because my desire had increased, I do take

it.[168]

The Dialogues of Luisa Sigea are also interesting because they serve as a revealing document on how sex and sexuality was approached in a very different way than it is today. In some cases, this can seem downright bizarre to modern readers. For example, the morning following their intercourse, Tullia notes: "My mother ran to Callias' arms: "My son, hast thou fought gallantly? The shouts of my darling Tullia proved that thou wast victorious; I congratulate thee and Tullia on thy victory. Hadst thou not conquered, the bride would remain a widow."[169] Another truly bizarre moment is when Ottavia discusses her mother lifting her nightgown to see the stains on it, and exclaiming, "O daughter! What is that I see! what a rich and inexhaustible fountain of seed Caviceo possesses! Oh! how joyful and fortunate wouldst thou have been, had this flood of seed but watered the inner recesses of thy womb!"[170] Part of this, of course, points to the fantasy of a male writer, but also, it also documents a more casual attitude towards sexual privacy, such as when Tullia is talking to her sister, and her husband says, "I want you to watch, the cruel way in which I treat your sister." He then proceeds to do so, she narrates; "he jumped upon me and drove his huge tool into the sore in my nether mouth. The wounds he had already made bled afresh, and now that they were pricked, I writhed under the smartest pain.--"Ah! my darling Pomponia, help me!" I cried, "fly to my aid!""[171] Even though, yes, this is a sort of fantasy, there is no sense of privacy or the whiff of scandalous transgression that comes with violating privacy in more modern erotica.

Luisa Sigea also reveals the types of foods one should eat to conceive and beliefs about sex that were common: "[my mother] ordered me to eat three conserved nuts which she brought me, and whispered into my ear to prevail on my husband to go and sleep a few hours; his health required sleep and quietness after that wrestling." You can almost feel the

Brian M. Watson

Cosmopolitan or Buzzfeed article that could be written from that. The *Dialogues* can also shine light on what was thought about conception. For example, when Tullia's husband "laid his hand upon my skiff, and even drove his middle finger into it; he found my vulva dry, and not fuddled. "May the Gods be propitious!" he cried; "thou hast undoubtedly conceived, my darling soul, in this onset. This matrix of thine, which is indebted to me for children, has drunk up all thy seed and mine."[172] The fourth dialogue ends with Ottavia thanking Tullia for all of her instruction and her saying that she will look forward to her wedding night, and the fifth is a very long-winded and detailed description of the wedding night in question. The sixth dialogue is another in this tradition, except it involves two men, Rangoni and Lampridio, who are the women's lovers.

Despite all of Chorier's precautions in naming a false author and translator and having it secretly printed with a fictitious date and location, he was not able to escape full suspicion. The book was reported to authorities, an investigation was started, and either the printer confessed or other information led to his door. But unlike Millot and L'Ange, Chorier had taken the caution of writing the text in Latin and assigning it to false author, thus getting it under the protection of "ancient books allowed by elegance and quality of style." If that argument was not enough, the judge and prosecutor Du Gue de Bagnois was one of Chorier's best friends, and chose not to prosecute him. Chorier would thank him for this by dedicating the second edition of the book to him in 1678, and he would live out his life in peace, dying at the ripe old age of 80. Towards the end of his life and the end of the 18th century, he no doubt witnessed the increasing air of liberalism and sexual freedom. In this way, *The School of Venus* and *Luisa Sigea* mark the point where the pendulum began to swing away from religious strictures to a greater period of tolerance. Nowhere was this more so than across the Channel, in England.

The Libertines

THE AUTHOR L.P. HARTLEY once famously wrote, "the past is a foreign country: they do things differently there."[173] The reason this statement has become almost proverbial is because it is accurate—it holds true whether you're talking about military conquests or moral standards, but nowhere is it more accurate than when you're talking about sexuality. It's very hard to peek behind the bedroom doors of our ancestors, but the glimpses and the little details we get reveal a vast gulf from their time to ours. We have already discussed some of these differences and shifts in sexuality and sexual attitudes, such as the fact that women were seen as much more sexually voracious and aggressive than men, or that acts that we would see as public sex weren't really remarkable (or remarked upon) in earlier centuries—even the complete lack of privacy. In fact, these sexual attitudes are very old compared to our contrary modern ones; showing just how the past is a foreign country. But we can trace our way back into the past, to show where things began to shift towards being more recognizably modern: the 18th century.

Perhaps the best way of doing that is to look at the people who were considered debauched and dissolute during their own times, and were remarkably known for it. In other words, it is best for us to look at The Right Honourable John Wilmot, the Earl of Rochester. Over the course of his three decades on earth (he died at the age of 33), John Wilmot was King Charles II's royal pimp, a sexual and theatrical tutor of famous actresses, an utterly unrestrained and unrepentant drunkard, a war hero, a member of the House of Lords, a sheriff, a traitor, a renowned poet, a playwright, and a kidnapper. And he was remarkably self-aware of all of these things—a poem he wrote towards the end of his life reads like the most humorously screwed-up resume:

Rochester: Son of a whore, God damn you, can you
   tell
   A peerless peer the readiest way to hell?
   I've outswilled Bacchus, sworn of my own make
   Oaths [that] would fright Furies, and make Pluto
   quake;
   I've swived [fucked] more whores more ways than
   Sodom's walls
   E'er knew, or the college of Rome's cardinals.
   Broke houses to break chastity, and dyed
   That floor with murder which my lust denied.
   Pox on't, why do I speak of these poor things?
   I've blasphemed God, and libeled kings.
   The readiest way to Hell, Boy, quick, ne'er stir!'

Boy: 'The readiest way [to hell], my Lord's [is] Rochester['s way].[174]

John Wilmot was born in 1647 to Henry, Viscount Wilmot, and Anne St. John. The senior Wilmot was made the Earl of Rochester when John was five, for outstanding service to King Charles II during the English Civil War. His father engineered the escape of Charles II after a disastrous military battle by hiding him in an oak tree. At the age of seven, the young John was privately tutored by the Reverend Francis Giffard, who adopted the usual relationship of a tutor with a young man, which included education and supervision from sunrise to sunset, and according to Rochester's biographer James William Johnson, from the ages of seven to thirteen, "Mr. Giffard used to lie with him in the family, on purpose that he might prevent any ill accidents."[175] Ill accidents, of course, meant masturbation or homosexual contact with young men his age. This was, as Rochester's biographers Green and Johnson note, very common in the 17th century. As historian Lawrence Stone notes, parents were "indifferen[t] to the dangers of adolescent homosexual contact," even when it was well-known that tutor-student sleeping arrangements often lead to sexual activity.[176] But as Johnson notes, "There is no evidence that Francis Giffard engaged in overt sexual behavior with John Wilmot, but Wilmot's adult homosexual interests may have begun in emotions he experienced as a child."[177]

Johnson also convincingly argues throughout his biography that Rochester's strict upbringing by his staunchly Puritan mother, and his half-decade of tutoring by Reverend Giffard, resulted in an overwhelming fear of death that would cause him to turn to alcohol and sex as an escape. Death was universal in 17th century England;

> In addition to unrecorded deaths of relatives, still-births, and infant deaths, four of his close male relatives died before he reached the age of twelve, including two half-brothers and, most importantly, his father. By the time he was twenty, Rochester was the only surviving male heir of his generation of Wilmot's and Lees. His uncertainties and ambivalences about sexuality and money were caught up in his apprehensions about death. Death so filled his mind that, as Dr. Samuel Johnson said, 'the whole of life [was] keeping away the thoughts of it.'[178]

As Rochester approached puberty, he was accepted into Oxford as a student—something that would become very important for his later development. His education at Oxford would give him a great deal of classical knowledge of Greek and Latin texts, which included Horace, Virgil, Epicurus and others. Although there is some debate about how good his Latin and Greek abilities actually were, it does not make that much of a difference, as Rochester lived in time of increasingly available English and French translations. As the English and French reading public increased dramatically throughout the 17th century, printers and booksellers found it increasingly cheap and profitable to make available translations of ancient works. Eventually, this would have consequences for our history of pornography—as copies of ancient works became worthless, other publishers turned to more recent and more scandalous works—but more on that in a later chapter.

Rochester's attendance at Oxford in 1660 was also important for another reason: the English Restoration that resulted in the glorious recrowning of King Charles II after the English Civil War. The effect on the English public at large, and the Oxford student body as well, was like setting off a firework in a crowded movie theater: "Lectures gave way to drunken, bawdy songs. . . . In the weeks following, the academic order was lost in anarchy as carousing, rioting, and whoring students grew increasingly wild and licentious."[179] The 13-year-old Lord Rochester was caught up in this riot and fell in with a group of students who taught him how to masturbate, where the whorehouse was, and likely engaged in same-sex intercourse, all of the worst fears manifested. In fact, Rochester's college was so well-known for homosexuals that parents were warned against sending beautiful sons to Oxford. His college (Wadham) was nicknamed 'Sodom,' and carries that nickname to this day.

After graduation, Wilmot began a Grand Tour of Europe, which no doubt had further debauching effects on his character. The Grand Tour was a significant cultural milestone, in the lives of upper and upper-middle class English men in from the sixteenth to the nineteenth centuries. It was seen as the last step of education or 'finishing,' a threshold between boyhood and manhood. It was generally expected that young man on a Grand Tour would gain some sexual experience, and Paris and Italy were generally viewed by them as the best place to do so. Their families however, generally had an unfavorable attitude towards the sexual exploits of young men: the *Daily Post Boy* claimed that British gentlemen spent all of their time drinking and whoring, and the *London Journal.*, frowning with disapprobation, noted:

stressed the sexual risks presented by women travelling: 'it is highly probable, that by means of our ladies travelling, some of our noble families may be honoured with a French Dancing Master's son for their heirs.' There was a clear sexual allusion in a newspaper comment of 1739: 'I look upon France as the Hotbed to our English Youth, where they are immaturely ripened, and therefore soon become rotten and corrupt at home. . . [Additionally] Italy, and, in particular, Venice, was notorious for prostitution[180]

Truly, it would have been hard to avoid the aggressive and flamboyant Venetian courtesans and prostitutes, not to mention the overtly sexual masques and balls that occurred year-round. Later on his life, Rochester would note that he learned about two important things in his time in Italy: the dildo, and Pietro Aretino. Johnson notes another interesting aspect to their journey:

> Arriving in Italy, Rochester and his guide encountered customs men. Firearms had to be left at town gates, though dagger-wearing was permitted in Naples, Venice, and Milan. They were also searched for any "Prohibited Book," but the worldly bibliophile, Dr. Balfour, soon discovered bribes: "yet there are wayes enough to convey Books, or any other thing of whatsoever Nature. . .which you will easily understand, after your being a while in the Country."[181]

These restrictions were directly tied to the Reformation and the Counter-Reformation. Although we might not consider books to be as dangerous as guns or knives, in the 17th century they were still considered to be very dangerous—more dangerous than a weapon. In some cases, possessing them resulted in death, as we discussed with Pallavicino. Nonetheless, the effects of discovering Aretino for Rochester were immense. Taking all he learned from Aretino's political and social satire, Rochester turned it into beautifully structured poetry that obeyed all the poetic conventions of the day, but none of the moral ones. Upon his return to England, this creativity and unique style turned him into a highly-sought-after writer for speeches and plays. Part of the reason for his success however, was that he was incredibly self-aware, aware enough of his elite cultural and social status to mock himself and his peers as part of the problem.

Upon his return from the Continent, John Wilmot, Lord Rochester turned quickly to marriage, in order to secure his name and connections to English society. However, as with many of his contemporary lords he was in great need of money, so he eventually settled on a girl that was, as Graham Green put it, an 'heiress for sale.'[182] The girl was Elizabeth Mallet; her parents were exceedingly rich and promised a large dowry for their daughter. Setting his eyes on his goal, Rochester wrote many lovey-dovey poems and letters to Miss Mallet, confessing that he was head-over-heels in love with her, and also had King Charles II recommended him to her. Ms. Mallet seemed to delay and hesitate, playing hard to get in Rochester's eyes, and perhaps deliberately—as Amanda Vickery recounts (albeit for a different generation):

> the girl of the period was cynically advised to 'keep herself at a genteel Distance, lest the Conquest afterwards might be reckon'd cheap'. She was continually warned against those 'Easy Compliances' that 'extinguish the Desire of Marriage'. . . Ellen Rothman and Karen Lystra have both argued that it was common for women to secure an engagement, but repeatedly to defer the wedding. Moreover, Lystra found that betrothed women liked to throw several obstacles in a lover's path, eventually orchestrating

some deciding crisis to test the mettle of their men and to reconcile themselves to the enormity of the commitment they had to make.[183]

The Right Honourable Lord Rochester decided to force the moment to its crisis, deciding a more forceful method of action was needed. We have mentioned Samuel Pepys before, but to turn away from his masturbation habits to draw on his account of London gossip, specifically on Rochester's kidnapping of Mallet:

> Here, upon my telling her a story of my Lord Rochester's running away on Friday night last with Mrs. Mallet, the great beauty and fortune of the North, who had supped at White Hall with Mrs. Stewart, and was going home to her lodgings with her grandfather, my Lord Haly, by coach; and was at Charing Cross seized on by both horse and foot men and forcibly taken from him, and put in a coach with six horses and two women provided to receive her, and carried away. Upon immediate pursuit, my Lord of Rochester (for whom the King had spoken to the lady often, but with no success) was taken at Uxbridge; but the lady is not yet heard of, and the King mighty angry, and the Lord sent to the Tower.[184]

Elizabeth Mallet was eventually returned home to her parents, but John Wilmot was jailed. After suffering a month in the Tower of London he would have to write a groveling letter to the King, and volunteer to fight in the navy during the Anglo-Dutch War before the king released him. Against all expectations, Rochester performed admirably and courageously in battle, volunteering for daring exploits against the Dutch and saving fellow nobles from grievous wounds.

When he returned to England in February of 1666, he was greeted with a hero's welcome and awarded by King Charles II with a highly-prized title: Gentleman of the Bedchamber (formerly known as the Groom of the Stool). Rochester and 11 other Gentlemen had on-and-off duties that included dressing and undressing the King, providing a chamber pot and serving his meals, and sometimes sleeping at the foot of the King's bed in exchange for an annual salary of £1,000 (about $106,396/£76,770 today).[185] Rochester also took it upon himself to charm and seduce any virgins the king took a fancy to—and, because the king "preferred sexually experienced women for mistresses, it became the agreeable duty of the seductive Earl to initiate young women into the techniques of love detailed in Ovid's *Ars Amatoria* and depicted in the sixteen Postures of Aretino in preparation for their role" as mistress.[186]

His duties also included sexual escapades alongside the King:

> On December 2, Pepys heard Charles's "silly discourse" about Rochester having his clothes and gold stolen by one wench while he was abed with another. The Earl's clothes turned up later, stuffed in a feather bed, but the gold was "all gone." Rochester turned the tables, according to another story, by accompanying the King in disguise to a brothel and sneaking off his clothes and money while Charles made sport. Trapped, the embarrassed monarch offered to pay for his pleasure with a ring, which was recognized—as was its royal owner. Such farcical doings were widely talked about.[187]

When he was not drunkenly cavorting with the King, Rochester spent his time with several friends in secret society called the 'Ballers'—because they attended balls and dances, not because they were balling out. They were dedicated to such pastimes as "drinking, sexual exhibitions, and dancing naked with the young women in a brothel kept by "Lady" Bennett, the enterprising widow of a baker. One of Henry Savile's letters to Rochester makes it clear the Earl was a mastermind among the Ballers."[188] Somehow, among all this drunkenness, John Wilmot was able to sober up long enough to (re)seduce Elizabeth Mallet and persuade her to elope with him. Although her parents were at first unhappy, they did finally relent and provide the massive dowry that was promised. Although the marriage would be troubled by Rochester's several mistresses and his passing of an STD to Elizabeth, it seemed to be a genuinely happy and trusting one, and his daughter would later recount that her parents were very close.

About this time, Rochester wrote what is often considered to be his obscene masterpiece, and perhaps the greatest obscene poem in the English language; *A Ramble in St. James Park*. The title is a satire of another poem by Edmund Waller, who was attempting to kiss the King's derrière. However, Waller was not the only target. As biographer Johnson notes, *A Ramble* mocks "the entire spectrum of London society, British history, classical mythology, human and animal copulation, the Devil of Christianity, cowards, school-boys, whores, Jesuits, doctors, atheists—and himself." The poem begins simply and abruptly enough with the narrator commenting that "Much wine had passed, with grave discourse / Of who fucks who, and who does worse."[189] However, unsatisfied, he goes out into St. James's Park to check out women and men and to relieve his drunkenness with "lechery [and] to cool my head and fire my heart".[190] Looking over the park, he is greatly amused that it is named after St. James, because it is clearly an unchristian place. Part of what makes the poem such a 'masterpiece' is that Rochester cleverly alternates beautiful description with perverse vulgarity, thus creating two conflicting narratives. The effect is that even though the park is supposed to be 'pure' like the countryside, it is in fact as corrupt as the rest of the city:

> Poor pensive lover, in this place
> **Would frig upon his mother's face;**
> Whence rows of mandrakes tall did rise
> **Whose lewd tops fucked the very skies.**
> Each imitative branch does twine
> **In some loved fold of Aretine,**
> And nightly now beneath their shade
> **Are buggeries, rapes, and incests made.** [191]

The park also functioned as a great leveler of classes, which allows all levels of London society to be mocked:

> Unto this all-sin-sheltering grove
> Whores of the bulk and the alcove,
> Great ladies, chambermaids, and drudges,
> The ragpicker, and heiress trudges.
> Carmen, divines, great lords, and tailors,
> Prentices, poets, pimps, and jailers,
> Footmen, fine fops do here arrive,
> And here promiscuously they swive [fuck].[192]

But suddenly, to Rochester's great dismay, he spots one of his mistresses in the company of "three knights," who, flirting with her, "with wriggling tails made up to her".[193] At first, he seems embarrassed because of "the proud disdain she cast on me," but then he rebels and rages against her: "But mark what creatures women are / How infinitely vile, when fair!"[194] When she leaves on a 'date' with all three gentlemen, the Earl squirms in self-loathing that gives way to anger:

> So a proud bitch does lead about
> Of humble curs the amorous rout,
> Who most obsequiously do hunt
> The savory scent of salt-swoln cunt.
> Some power more patient now relate
> The sense of this surprising fate.
> Gods! that a thing admired by me
> Should fall to so much infamy.

...

> But why am I, of all mankind,
> To so severe a fate designed?
> Ungrateful! Why this treachery
> ...Did ever I refuse to bear
> The meanest part your lust could spare?
> When your lewd cunt came spewing home
> Drenched with the seed of half the town,
> My dram of sperm was [eaten] up after[195]

But the self-loathing and disgust soon turns to anger: "May stinking vapors choke your womb / May your depraved appetite, / Beget such frenzies in your mind / [that you] Turn up your longing arse t' th' air / And perish in a wild despair!"[196] Then, the narrator's anger turns to cold calculation, and he promises to "plague this women and undo her:"

> But my revenge will best be timed
> When she is married that is limed.
> In that most lamentable state
> I'll make her feel my scorn and hate:
> Pelt her with scandals, truth or lies,
> And her poor cur with jealousies,
> Till I have torn him from her breech,
> While she whines like a dog-drawn bitch;
> Loathed and despised, kicked out o' th' Town
> Into some dirty hole alone,
> To chew the cud of misery
> And know she owes it all to me.
> And may no woman better thrive
> That dares prophane[profane] the cunt I swive![197]

The *Ramble* immediately claimed (and deserves) its title as one of the most obscene poems in English. By following the poetic conventions of the day, but wrapping them up in forthright sexuality, it subverts the expectations of the readers from the very first lines. Secondly, there seems to be a very real emotion that cuts across and through the poem, puncturing through the 'sentimental' posturing of the day, making it a satire and mockery of the social conventions and behaviors of the day. The subsequent history of the poem would also demonstrate its continued offensiveness and obscenity, and is perhaps the most famously-censored and suppressed poem in the English language.

For unclear reasons, in the final decade of his life, Rochester would increasingly move away from the former closeness he shared with Charles II. Though he died before a full split happened, a sense of disillusionment and bitterness began to creep over the once-intimate relationship. Regardless of the explanation, a definite division occurred in the mid-to-late-1670s, and would eventually result in Rochester's bitter lampoon, *A Satyre on King Charles II*, and his expulsion from the Court. A contemporary wrote that, "my Lord Rochester fled from Court some time since for delivering (by mistake) into the King's hands a terrible lampoon of his own making against the King, instead of another the king asked him for." We will turn to the poem that Rochester accidentally (or maliciously) gave Charles II in a moment—first we should examine the poem he meant to give to the King, a poem known as *Signor Dildo*.

Signor Dildo was written in 1673 as a biting satire against the women of the King's Court, both mistresses and higher class women like the Duchess of Cleveland. As a result, it starts off with an address to "You Ladyes all of Merry England / Who have been to kisse the Dutchesse's hand," and asks them "Pray did you lately observe in the Show / A Noble Italian call'd Signior Dildo?"[198] Unlike his *Ramble in St James'* the poem jauntily specifies courtly ladies and their relation with 'Signor Dildo:'

> The Countesse of Falmouth, of whom People tell
>> Her Footmen wear Shirts of a Guinea an Ell: [very expensive shirts]
>> Might Save the Expence, if she did but know
>> How Lusty a Swinger is Signior Dildo.

...That Pattern of Virtue, her Grace of Cleaveland,
Has Swallow'd more Pricks, then the Ocean has Sand,
But by Rubbing and Scrubbing, so large it do's grow,
It is fit for just nothing but Signior Dildo. [199]

Signor Dildo is such a good and tireless lover that he unseats many lords and men of the court, whose insecurity Rochester satirizes in the poem by calling them by the name 'Count Cazzo' [Count Prick]. And there was, in fact, a great deal of masculine insecurity surrounding the

> The Dutchesse of Modena, tho' she looks high,
> With such a Gallant is contented to Lye:
> And for fear the English her Secrets shou'd know,
> For a Gentleman Usher took Signior Dildo.
> . . .Doll Howard no longer with his Highness must Range,
> And therefore is profer'd this Civill Exchange:
> Her Tee th being rotten, she Smells best below,
> And needs must be fitted for Signior Dildo.[200]

The poem was immediately popular among the men (and some of the women) of the Court, and garnered Rochester great praise and laughter. One of these must have mentioned it to King Charles II, because on the night of January 20th, after drinking all night with Rochester, he asked for a copy of the poem. Unfortunately for Rochester, when he reached into his pocket to pull out the poem, he accidentally gave the king his brutal *Satyre on Charles II*, which I reproduce here:

> In th' isle of Britain, long since famous grown
> For breeding the best cunts in Christendom,
> There reigns, and oh! long may he reign and thrive,
> The easiest King and best-bred man alive.
> Him no ambition moves to get renown
> Like the French fool, that wanders up and down
> Starving his people, hazarding his crown.
> Peace is his aim, his gentleness is such,
> And love he loves, for he loves fucking much.

Nor are his high desires above his strength:
His scepter and his prick are of a length;
And she may sway the one who plays with th' other,
And make him little wiser than his brother.
Poor Prince! thy prick, like thy buffoons at Court,
Will govern thee because it makes thee sport.
'Tis sure the sauciest prick that e'er did swive,
The proudest, peremptoriest prick alive.
Though safety, law, religion, life lay on 't,
'Twould break through all to make its way to cunt.
Restless he rolls about from whore to whore,
A merry monarch, scandalous and poor.

To Carwell, the most dear of all his dears,
The best relief of his declining years,
Oft he bewails his fortune, and her fate:
To love so well, and be beloved so late.
For though in her he settles well his tarse,
Yet his dull, graceless bollocks hang an arse.
This you'd believe, had I but time to tell ye
The pains it costs to poor, laborious Nelly,
Whilst she employs hands, fingers, mouth, and thighs,
Ere she can raise the member she enjoys.
All monarchs I hate, and the thrones they sit on,
From the hector of France to the cully of Britain.[201]

The poem very clearly paints the King of England as being ruled by his sexual desires; running the risk of losing his crown and starving his people in his ignorance. A closer look at the poem reveals something else, however—Rochester isn't targeting Charles personally and specifically—no, in fact, he is targeting him as *King* Charles II by attacking the symbols of kingship—the scepter, the island, the throne—and how the people are threatened publicly by the king's poor private decisions. This is a classic demonstration of the use of the erotic discourse for both political and social purposes—not as a masturbatory aid. It seems that Rochester had become completely disillusioned by the King, or perhaps he was looking make himself independent from Charles II. Either way, he got it. Charles roared for Wilmot's head, but the owner of that head was smart enough to retire to the country for a few months, until the king forgave him.

This episode kicked off a cycle of mistakes, anger, exile, and forgiveness between Charles and Rochester that would go on until the end of Wilmot's life in 1680, six years later. Another episode in 1676 involved a drunken fight with the night guard that resulted in one of his friends being killed, and Rochester was once again exiled by the king. Unwilling to return to a boring life in the country, Rochester decided to go into hiding by disguising himself a quack doctor named Dr. Bendo. According to a friend, this doctor, "among other practices, made: Judgments upon Moles, Wenns, Warts and natural Marks. . . . And if the modest Lady had any such about her where without blushing she could not well declare them; why the Religious Doctor Bendo would not, for all the world, so much as desire to see it."[202] He would send his 'wife' to look at it instead, who was Rochester himself, disguised as a hunchbacked woman.

According to John Timbs, a contemporary "wryly noted that Rochester's practice was 'not without success,' implying his intercession of himself as surreptitious sperm donor."[203] According to Johnson, the escapade was "in effect, [Rochester] mocking his former faith in the curative powers of physicians by becoming the mountebank, Dr. Alexander Bendo, in July, 1676. He was close to abandoning hope for his own cure [of syphilis]." Indeed, he would die from the disease less than four years later. Perhaps angry and bitter, the Dr. Bendo pamphlets reached rhetorical heights:

> Those that have travell'd in Italy will tell you to what a miracle art does there assist nature in the preservation of beauty; how women of forty bear

the same countenance with those of fifteen; ages are
there no ways distinguish'd by faces: whereas here
in England, look a horse in the mouth, and a woman
in the face, you presently know both their ages
to a year. I will therefore give you such remedies,
that without destroying your complexion (as most
of your paints and daubings do) shall render them
purely fair. . . . I will also cleanse and preserve your
teeth, white and round as pearls, fastening them
that are loose; your gums shall be kept entire and
red as coral, your lips of the same colour, and soft as
you could wish your lawful kisses...[204]

Rochester's Dr. Bendo escapade was not the first or the
last instance of disguising himself for his amusement and the
amusement of others. Graham Greene notes two other humor-
ous episodes worth relating here:
He is said once to have dressed himself as a tinker
and walked to the neighbouring hamlet of Barford
St John. Here, when the people gave him their pots
and pans to mend, he knocked out the bottoms.
They put him in the stocks for it, but he sent a man
with a note addressed to Lord Rochester at Adder-
bury, and presently his coach and four horses drove
into the village, and he was released. The tradition
is a kindly one, for he is said to have sent the villa-
gers new pots and pans.[205]

Another day, he dressed up as a tramp, and:
[M]eeting another tramp, asked him [where] he was
going. The man said that he was going to Lord Rochester's, though it was useless, for he never gave anything [in charity]. The Earl accompanied him and
while the tramp went to the back of the house, he
went to the front and gave orders to his servants

how they were to receive him. They seized him and put him in a barrel of beer, and every time he raised his head Rochester knocked it down again. Presently he was released, given a meal and a new suit of clothes, and told never again to say that Lord Rochester gave nothing away.

Rochester took a life-long interest in theater and in comedy, and was responsible for writing many monologues and performances for the Court. Also, many of the women he 'recruited' and sexually educated for the king were actresses. The most famous of all Charles II's mistresses (Nell Gwyn) was an actress, though it is unclear if Rochester had any relations with her. For these reasons, we finish our discussion of John Wilmot, Earl of Rochester, with his most scandalous play, *The Farce of Sodom, or The Quintessence of Debauchery.*

There is a good deal of argument surrounding the work —many academics and historians have debated over whether Rochester actually wrote *The Farce of Sodom* or not. Greene notes that "Contemporaries were not agreed that the play was by him; Anthony Wood was doubtful. . .Professor Prinz, who shows little hesitation in claiming the poem for Rochester, brings forward no contemporary English authority except the notorious 'Captain' Alexander Smith. *Sodom* differs from Rochester's satires in its air of unreality; it is an obscene fairy story."[206] Johnson, in his biography, argues that there is evidence that Rochester wrote the earliest version of the play. A 1689 version, attributed to "E. of R." and titled '*Sodom and Gomorrah: The Quintessence of Debauchery*,' was destroyed, but a copy which was made for a collector of Rochester's works survived. For these reasons, and for the reasons I described above, I agree that Rochester *did* write *The Farce of Sodom*. Nevertheless, it is somewhat irrelevant exactly who wrote it or when the play was written—I include it here because of its connection with Rochester and it clearly meets with the definition of erotic discourse or obscenity we are working with here.

The dramatis personae or list of actors is as amusing as the rest of the play. The cast includes, with my rough translations of their names:

Dramatis Personae	
BOLLOXIMIAN, *King of Sodom*	Maxima bollocks, huge testicles
CUNTIGRATIA, *His Queen*	Cunt-grace, Her Grace Cunt
PRICKETT, *Young Prince*	Prick
SWIVIA, *Princess*	From 'swive,' to fuck
BUGGERANTHUS, *General*	Bugger-er. (lit. anal-sex-er)
POCKENELLO, *Pimp & the King's Favourite*	The poxed one, with syphilis
BORASTUS, *Buggermaster-general*	Cunning north wind; a bag of hot air
PENE & TOOLY, *Pimps of Honour*	Penis and Tool
LADY OFFICINA, *She-pimp of Honour*	Official Lady
FUCKADILLA, *Maid of Honour*	Self-explanatory.
CUNTICULA, *Maid of Honour*	To drill (into) the 'cunt'
CLITORIS, *Maid of Honour*	Self-explanatory
FLUX, *Physician-in-ordinary*	Another word for dysentery
VIRTUOSO, *Dildo and Merkin maker*	A merkin is a pubic wig

From the very beginning of the *Dramatis Personae*, it is apparent who Rochester's audience would have been, as he uses semi-fudged names that would have been very apparent to audiences with the best of classical education. *The Farce of Sodom* opens in a room described as "an antechamber hung with Aretine Postures," the same kind of *I modi* postures we have already discussed. King Bolloxmian enters the room swearing that "in the zenith of my lust I reign, I drink to swive, and swive to drink again. Let other monarchs who their sceptres bear, to keep their subjects less in love than fear. . . . My pintle [penis] only shall my sceptre be. My laws shall act more pleasure than command, and with my prick I'll govern all the land."[207] This is a clear reference to the *Satyre* on Charles II.

His courtiers Borastus, Pockenello, Pene and Tooly all fall over each other trying to flatter him, one saying that his "royal tarse [penis]" will make him richer than all kings, and the other saying "May your most gracious cods and tarse [testicles and penis] be still / As boundless in your pleasure as your will. . . . May lust incite your prick with flame and sprite, / Ever to fuck with safety and delight."[208] This safety worries the King:

> **Bolloximian:** My prick, Borastus, thy judgement and
>   thy care
>   Requires, in a nice juncture of affair.
>   [My penis requires your advice in these uncertain
>   times]
>   . . .But this advice belongs to you alone
>   Borastus. No longer I my cunts admire,
>   The drudgery has worn out my desire.
>   . . .Henceforth, Borastus, set the nation free.
>   Let conscience have its force of liberty.
>   I do proclaim, that buggery may be used
>   O'er all the land, so cunt be not abused.
>   That's the provision. This shall be your trust.[209]

This, of course, all occurs while the king is having anal

intercourse with all four of the courtiers, one after another. The act even includes an amusing exchange over merkins, or pubic wigs, which were popular among prostitutes at the time—merkins would be worn over the genital area after the hair had been shaved off. They were to prevent pubic lice and to hide the symptoms of syphilis—it is possible that Rochester got syphilis from a prostitute hiding her symptoms. Pockanello declares that merkins should be banned from the court, and Tooly agrees, saying that, "It is not proper that cunt should wear a tower."[210] A tower was a type of tall hairstyle that was popular among upper class women at the time. Pockanello reveals to the king that there is a treasonous plot against him. Pene, he says, has been much too familiar with the King's mistress, Fuckadilla, and he has given her syphilis, and therefore the king is at risk of catching it from her. The king says "Alas, poor Pene! I cannot blame the deed / Where Nature urgeth by impulse of seed," but says he shall punish Pene 'in his fundaments [rear end].' As for the women, he argues that men should henceforth avoid having sex with women, because vaginal intercourse isn't as good as buggery.

The next scene shows the women of the court, who are completely heartbroken and desperate for sex. This scene drips with misogyny, perhaps the most mysognistic of Rochester's scenes (if it was truly by him). Throughout his life, he constantly wavered back and forth between a uniquely feminist attitude for his time, and very misogynistic moods. The queen is so desperate that her periods have "been stopped with grief and care / In all [the King's] pleasures I can have no share." Fuckadilla cries out: "What woman can a standing prick refuse? / When love makes courtship, there it may command. / What soul such generous influence can withstand?"[211] Another one of the queen's women recommend that she should sleep with the general Buggeranthus, and the queen agrees, but then says there is no way she will survive the 12 hours until she sees him next:

> **Officinia**: Sit down and frig [masturbate]
> awhile--'twill ease your pain.
> **Cuntigratia**: I spring a leak. All hands to pump amain!
> [Here the QUEEN, sitting in a chair of state, is frigged
> with a dildo by Lady OFFICINA. And the rest pull out
> their dildos and frig too, in point of honour.] [212]

It is revealed that some of the women haven taken to seducing their relatives, such as Swivia and Prickett in the next
act. I'm not going to focus on this act as much, because it is
likely that it is a later addition not written by Rochester, but
the act amusingly starts like this: "[Six naked women and six
naked men appear, and dance, the men doing obeisance to the
women's cunts, kissing and touching them often, the women
doing ceremonies to the men's pricks, kissing them, dandling
their cods, etc., and so fall to fucking, after which the women
sigh, and the men look simple and sneak off.]"[213] This scene is
amusingly referenced in the 2004 Johnny Depp film *The Libertine*, but was likely never performed.

The queen finally gets the general, Buggeranthus, alone, and
he reports that all the men in the army have taken to anal
intercourse now that it is legal—they no longer have any need
for women. When the queen herself tries to seduce him, he
declines, arguing that "But toils of cunt are more than toils of
war." The queen cries out "Fucking, a toil?! Good lord! You do
mistake."[214] Eventually, the queen goes mad from lack of sex
and kills herself, only to descend on the king as a ghost and say
that she shall have her revenge. The king refuses to go back to
his queen, and:

> [The clouds break up and fiery demons appear in the
> air. They dance and sing:]
>
> **DEMONS**: Frig, swive and dally,
> Kiss, rise up, and rally,
> Curse, blaspheme and swear,
> Here are in the air

> Those will witness bear|
> Fire your bollocks singes,
> Sodom on the hinges.
> Bugger, bugger, bugger.
> All in hugger-mugger,
> Fire does descend.
> 'Tis too late to mend.[215]

Fire and brimstone fills up the sky and the world begins to end, but even then the king declines to change his course. He takes Pockanello and retires to a cave to screw his last moments away. The play, from start to finish, is an inversion and a parody of a Christian morality play. Indeed, in many ways, Rochester presaged de Sade in how he takes a cultural narrative and turns it on its head, which is perhaps a common trend among libertine and erotic works of the error. The play also mocks the King and his court, therefore playing the exact same sort of role that Aretino's poetry and stories did—it combines social, religious and political critique into an erotic format for maximum impact.

Rochester, however, did not get to screw his last moments away. A few years later he fell desperately ill, likely from the symptoms of tertiary syphilis. He was attended to in his deathbed by a priest friend of his mother, Gilbert Burnet. According to a rather self-congratulatory work, Burnet claimed that he managed to get Rochester to renounce libertinism and all of his sins, and presided over the Earl's supposedly very religious final moments. Because the primary source of this deathbed conversion is Burnet himself, there is plenty of argument over whether or not the conversion and the post-death canonization was legitimate. One way or another, on the 26th of July, 1680, John Wilmot passed from this world, preceding his king and pseudo-father by only five years—Charles II would die childless in February of 1685. The age of the libertine court was over, and reformers could begin again.

The Reformers

IF IT WAS NOT APPARENT from the discussion of Lord Rochester, then let me state it clearly: European culture in the late 17th century (1650-1700) was undergoing a dramatic shift in attitudes towards sex and sexual morality. Part of the reason for this is that moral laws began to be questioned and reinterpreted during the European Age of Enlightenment. The Protestant Reformation in England and on the Continent, along with the Catholic Counter-Reformation, had major impacts on education and philosophy, causing a shift from traditional lines of authority such as the church and Christian morality to an emphasis on reason, science, and individualism. In regards to our topic here, both the Bible and the Old Testament began to be questioned. Specifically, the seventh commandment ("thou shalt not commit adultery") and various injunctions, from the Bible and Leviticus, against fornication, whoring, and sexual activity, began to be questioned and reinterpreted.

Scientists and philosophers (in many cases one and the same, as science was still developing as a distinct field) began to question the reasons and purposes behind moral laws handed down by Scripture, especially as early anthropologists and explorers began to uncover (or claim they had) all sorts of different societal configurations from polyandry (one woman and multiple husbands) to brothel-houses containing men. The writer Daniel Defoe, who lived in Rochester's time, commented that "monogamy is a mere church imposition, a piece of priestcraft, unreasonable."[216] A judge who ran in Rochester's and Defoe's circles, Sir John Vaughan, declared that "No copulation of man with any woman, nor an effect of that copulation by generation [children] can be said 'unnatural.'" Even King Charles II said that he "could not think God would make a man miserable [in hell] only for taking a little pleasure out of the way."[217]

And to return to our good friend Lord Rochester, for one last time, Dabhoiwala quotes from him at length in *Origins of Sex*, summing up Wilmot's moral philosophy "in two maxims: that he should do nothing to injure himself, or to hurt another person." He continues to explain Lord Rochester's view that "immorality was no offence to God, for He was too great to hate His creatures, or to punish them," and that "Religion was no more than 'the jugglings of priests'; the Bible and its miracles were but incoherent and unbelievable stories; Christian morality was only hypocrisy, obeyed by 'the rabble world' because they knew no better." His explanation also dives in to sexuality:

> It was absurd to think that humans were fallen, that 'there should be any corruption in the nature of man', or that reason was meant to restrain our physical instincts - the only true 'rules of good and ill' were those provided by our bodily senses, the only real purpose of life, to pursue happiness. It followed that the ideas of monogamy and chastity were 'unreasonable impositions on the freedom of mankind'. On the contrary, sexual pleasure 'was to be indulged as the gratification of our natural appetites. It seemed unreasonable to imagine these were put into a man only to be restrained, or curbed to such a narrowness'.[218]

In his writing and in his poetry, Rochester attacked rationalism, or the belief that Christianity and European culture as a whole (and its laws and norms) had reasonable or rational purposes. To Rochester, the senses, not the intellect, were the greatest ability of mankind. This philosophy would be elaborated on and embraced more fully in the 18th century, especially by the Marquis de Sade (who we will turn to later). This is not to say that society as a whole embraced libertine and 'corrupting' opinions and views—in fact, to quote from

Dabhoiwala: "Although the idea of carnal liberty was articulated at all levels of society, and free unions of various kinds were to be found in many late 18th and 19th century working-class communities, its reasoned justification was pre-eminently associated with gentlemen and noblemen. By contrast, sexual propriety was often held up as a distinguishing feature of middle-class respectability."[219] There were far more libertines as antiheroes or villains in literature and cultural discussions than there were actual libertines—playing much the same role that Bohemians or Beats would: a moral foil for the moral majority to define itself against. It was this middle-class morality that began to emerge and grow in power in the late 17th and early 18th century (1680s-1750s). They were determined to have an impact. The middle classes, more than anyone or anything else, are responsible for the invention of obscenity, the division between 'art' and 'filth,' and the idea of pornography. And by the late 17th century, the middle-class began to reach a critical mass, first in London (which is why it is our focus) and then in other European capitals.

In England, the death of Charles II with no heir meant that his brother James II, a known Catholic, inherited the throne and the kingdom. From the beginning, the fact that James II was Catholic was a worrying sign to the Protestant English Church and the larger English public. Having just survived through the English Civil War, they knew all too well what conflict could result when the king and the state were not aligned in religious harmony. At first, the fact that James II had no male children boded well for the future, as his eldest daughter, Mary, was a Protestant and she would inherit the throne as long as James did not have a male heir. The birth of a son on the tenth of June 1688 spelled doom for any hopes of a Protestant monarch.

Making things worse, James II had not done a good job of relieving the tension. He had both pushed for more tolerant laws for Catholics, and had put Catholics in charge of various

military positions. Growing increasingly distressed, a group
of powerful English nobles and figures came together in a secret organization that went by the odd and slightly amusing
name of the Kit-Cat Club. They reached out to James' daughter
Mary and her husband, William of Orange, and invited them
to take the throne from James II. This 'taking of the throne'
was a resounding success, and became referred to as the Glorious Revolution, resulting in the reign of William and Mary. .
The Kit-Cat Club was so successful in its purpose of seeing a on
the throne of England that it managed to upend the entirety of
the European world in a Glorious Revolution—without a single shot fired—and to this day retain their own special room in
the National Portrait Gallery.

Clubs and clubby organizations quickly became an influential force in seventeenth century England (and indeed elsewhere). And who could blame them? The seventeenth century
was largely a creation of that most influential clubs, the Kit-
Cat Club. Clubs rapidly emerged as the most uniquely British institutions. There were many as 25,000 different clubs
and societies of 130 different types that were having regular
meetings and events throughout England and her colonies.[220]
The clubs ranged from the regional and ethnic to medical and
musical societies, professional ones, prosecutional groups,
scientific 'academies,' and dozens of others, and members ran
the motley from upper class to upper-lower class and middle
class. Wherever they came from or their purposes for belong-
ing to the club they were all bound together by the idea of
'clubness' in which societal, religious or personal grievances
or differences should be subsumed into the larger group. The
idea of clubs, in the words of Peter Clark increasingly pene-
trated every nook and cranny of British social and cultural
life:

> Almost every group or institution, past and present,
> was reincarnated in associational terms: King Ar-
> thur's knights were described as the 'original club

of Round Table Troopers', while Edinburgh town council was denounced as the 'land-market club'. Increasingly, voluntary associations were not so much perceived as miniature exemplars of national society; rather, national society itself was viewed as an untidy aggregation of voluntary societies. Even heaven was visualized in terms of one large friendly society.[221]

The reasons for this cultural movement are multifarious, but the biggest seems to have been population. London in particular and Britain in general saw explosive growth, even when measured against the explosive growth that Europe saw as a whole during this era. Demographic growth was incredibly high in the bigger British towns, with London's population accelerating and then doubling in the seventeenth centuries and then growing more than 40% between the 1650 and 1700. Other British provincial towns and capitals, such as Edinburgh, also grew at a rapid clip until they were eclipsed by the rise of major manufacturing centers such as Manchester or Glasgow. By 1700, London was far larger in population than cities like Venice, Rome, Amsterdam, and Vienna, and the only one that came close in population was Paris, although it fell behind year by year.[222] Amidst all this growth, a growth that required more than 8,000 new immigrants a year, there was a growing sense of alienation and loneliness amongst the crowd. Every day, newly minted city folk would see more faces and people and hear more voices and languages than their ancestors had in their entire lives:. The effect could be mind-boggling and overwhelming, and increasingly led to a sense of frustration:

The American John Dickinson echoed this dismay: 'I found myself in a social wilderness . . . as in the strangest forest . . . I was surrounded with noise, dirt and business . . . [and] the vast extent of the city.'

> Attempting to meet people without prior arrange-
> ment was difficult. 'How provoking', William John-
> stone Temple moaned, 'to take a long walk and then
> not find the people you want ... Everyone is indiffer-
> ent to another'.[223]

Despite living in a world different than their ancestors, this new generation still needed the same things their ancestors did—community, friendship, and purpose—and turned to clubs as a way to fill this gap.

One such club was the Society for the Reformation of Manners, the first major and important anti-vice society. The Society was formed by a group of religious reformers and churchmen who embraced the arrival of the Glorious Revo-lution as "visible evidence of God's concern to save England and restore her civil and religious life to the glories of former times." Having been disturbed and alienated by the perceived indulgence and lax morality of Kings Charles and James, its leaders sought reconciliation with the monarchy in order to create a new social order of "Church and state working har-moniously together in the maintenance of a society charac-terized by uniformity of belief and obedience to authority." In fact, the idealized England they spoke about in sermons, pamphlets, and reports was a "hierarchical society whose levels were linked by deferential obligations (subject to ruler, man to master, child to parent)."[224] Included in their ideals were strict rules against "unchecked or corrupt manners such as blasphemy, drunkenness, prostitution or Sabbath-break-ing," which they saw as contributing to the downfall of soci-ety, as well as the bonds of family and community. In the view of the Society for the Reformation of Manners, bad manners, more than anything else, threatened to destroy England.

However, the leaders of the organization were aware that they did not have any sort of political power or authority to enforce laws or morality on the English public. Authority in this era came down from the king and the Parliament, and if some random group or club were to just go out in the street and try to forcefully reform society, they could, and would, be executed for trying to assume power that belonged to the monarch. So, they hit on a clever legal strategy that would be copied by many anti-vice societies; they decided to seek support from Queen Mary—who obliged by writing *A Letter: for the Suppressing of Prophanes and Debauchery*, which would go on to be the basis for King William's *Proclamation for Preventing and Punishing Immorality and Prophanenefs* in 1697. In it, she called for enforcement of "those Laws which have been made, and are still in force against the Profanation of the Lord's Day, Drunkenness, Profane Swearing and Cursing, and all other Lewd, Enormous, and Disorderly Practices."[225]

Pioneers in their field, the Society for the Reformation of Manners understood Mary's letter as a sincere expression of royal support, and they used it to help erect "an umbrella of royal patronage" over their actions. This would be a strategy that the Proclamation Society and the Society for the Suppression of Vice would follow. The Manners Society proceeded to set up what can only be described as an elaborate network of informers. In their case, life imitated philosophy, and their hierarchical dream became manifest. Consisting of four levels of membership, it began with the 'First Society' for the original founders, "persons of eminency in the law, members of Parliament, justices of the peace" and preeminent Londoners.[226] In other words, the first society recruited members in positions of power or wealth to support their mission, much as a modern lobbyist group might do. The Second Society focused on "suppressing lewdness and sexual license, swearing, drunkenness and profanations of the Lord's Day...[and on] the publication of the names of convicted offenders, called the Black Roll."[227] The Black Roll was a an innovative technique: the wrongdoers that were captured and fined by the Manners Society would find their names listed on the Black Lists (which were posted in public places) until they paid their fines and had their names removed—it was a campaign of public shaming. This strategy illustrates two separate points: first, that the Reformation Society was still depending on the public shaming strategies of church courts and non-urban communities to be effective in an urban environment (more on this later), and second, the group seemed to think that enough people would be able to read and comprehend the Black Rolls—thus meaning that literacy was increasingly widespread.

The 'Third Society' was the strong-arm of the movement. It consisted of constables and guards, who split London up into patrol zones and precincts and coordinated amongst themselves—it was perhaps the earliest attempt at a citywide police force. Fourth Society was a group of about 150-200 'trained' informers, who the other three levels depended on. These informers were provided with blank warrants to fill out and provide to the police as they came across 'issues.'[228] By the end of 1714, there existed 39 smaller chapters of the parent society, established throughout the United Kingdom. These informers, unpaid at first, became increasingly professional, and would cause a lot of tension among the upper and middle-class supporters, especially those in the legal profession. Indeed, the use of informers would eventually lead to the group's downfall, but more on that in a moment.

The system seemed to be very effective at targeting and prosecution—from its founding in 1688, the Manners Society operated for almost 30 years, until 1715. At first, they were overwhelmingly successful—their 'Black Rolls' show 1240 convictions for the year 1700, 1259 in 1701, 1186 in 1702, and so on. In fact, one member, Josiah Woodward, noted that there were, within the first 11 years, duplicate or copy-cat groups founded in the cities of Coventry, Chester, Gloucester, Hull, Leicester, Liverpool, Newcastle, Nottingham, and Shrewsbury, Bristol, Derby, Canterbury, Leeds,

Norwich, Northampton, Portsmouth, Reading, Wigan, Warrington, and York. Even cities in other countries had them, including America, Belgium, Denmark, Germany, Holland, Jamaica, Switzerland and Sweden.[229]

This would seem to suggest that the Manners Society was quite successful in driving down London's immorality, and that this was be a truly remarkable point in history. This, though, would be a misunderstanding of the Society's main goal, which was a complete and total reformation; they wanted to "affect a moral and spiritual reformation in both public and private life and to enforce laws against vice and dissolute behavior."[230] They were not interested in the reform of individual people, but instead with complete and total reformation of the manners of the English public, to the point where they could dissolve the Society.

In that case, looking at the numbers again reveals that in 1702, for example, the Society saw 858 individuals prosecuted, but with a total of 1186 convictions, which meant that over a quarter of the convicts were recidivists, arrested again for the same crime. In many cases, the same individuals would appear in front of the court ten or more times in a year. This meant that they were failing to reform the English public. Furthermore, later years, such as 1708, saw as many as 3299 prosecutions—if anything, the number was going up. London was getting more immoral by the year, and the world was collapsing into sin and lechery.

One reason for the increasing numbers was a result of their religious passion. The Society for the Reformation of Manners became responsible for policing the sex lives and activities of everyone in the capital. The sexual policing that used to be seen as the task of the state began to be outsourced to this socio-sexual proto-police. Not only did they try to shut down purveyors of dirty works and texts, they also tried to go after brothel houses and homosexuals. According to Dabhoiwala, in 1693 the Society was responsible for 25% of all prosecutions for homosexuality, but by 1703 they prosecuted nearly 85% of them.[231] As Andrew Craig argues in his PhD. dissertation, this to a certain extent explains their publishing of a 'Black Roll' of prosecuted and convicted women. While the Black Roll/List might have been massively effective at behavior reform in a small community, it would register as little more than a blip in London, where Craig notes that many of the names are likely not real, but may be "common aliases like 'Mary Smith' whose omnipresence in the Black Lists made her the most durable whore in the metropolis."[232]

Despite their early and numerous successes, the Society began to receive heavy criticism over their use of informers, especially when a 1706 scandal revealed that some magistrates were simply extorting nightwalkers for money, and not reporting the fines. They were mocked and scorned for going after poor street-walkers, not upper class corrupters of morality. In his *Reformation of Manners: A Satyre*, Daniel Defoe mocked the group:

Ye Hypocrites, reform your Magistrates. . .
And poor Street Whores in Bridewel feel their Fate,
While Harlot M--n rides in a Coach of State. . .
The Mercenary Scouts in every Street,
Bring all that have no Money to your feet,
And if you lash a Strumpet of the Town,
She only smarts for want of half a Crown:
Your Annual Lists of Criminals appear,
But no Sir Harry or Sir Charles is there.[233]

Members of the Manners Society believed that their work would defend both religion and the English state from the onslaught of Hell, but many of their critics, especially the religious ones, felt that their campaign was far too secular and non-religious. A Jacobean preacher noted that they should be targeting "the greater men [because they are] more distasteful and foul are their voluptuous actions," and they deserved to be punished more than the poor, who did not understand their crimes: "merely to punish 'little sinners' but not 'the whore-master of quality' was hence ineffective, offensive to God, and distasteful to the world."[234] On top of all of this, the lower class and common people named on the Black Lists began to take aggressive action against the reformers. In 1702 and 1709, constables were stabbed to death while trying to arrest streetwalkers, and a couple years later, an entire group of con-stables were "dreadfully maimed, and one mortally wounded, by ruffians aided by 40 soldiers of the guards, who entered into a combination to protect the women." The same year, there was an incident where a thousand sailors attacked the local police and released some popular prostitutes who were on their way to jail. Faramerz Dabhoiwala notes that:

> In 1709, the trial of three soldiers. . .turned into a major debate about whether an officer could law-fully arrest a prostitute if she was only soliciting, rather than actually having sex. Before 1688 this would have been an inconceivable question: no one would have doubted that common whores could be summarily punished, But the actions of the soci-eties made it for the first time a matter of serious de-bate how far the law should be stretched to correct the morals even of harlots and scoundrels. . .legal opinion was increasingly sceptical. 'What!' ex-claimed the Lord Chief Justice, Sir John Holt [said it]. . .'must not a woman, tho' she be lewd, have the liberty to walk quietly about the streets? . . . Why, a light woman hath a right of liberty as well as an-other to walk about the streets.' It was insupport-able that 'the liberty of the subject shall depend upon the good opinion of the constable'; to arrest a woman 'upon a bare suspicion that she was lewd. . .is not that against Magna Carta?'

To summarize: by 1725, The Society for the Reformation

of Manners was facing criticism from the upper and middle classes in the form of writers, lawyers and social critics; their own brethren in the form of churchmen; and they were being assaulted by the lower classes in the streets. Despite all this, they remained remarkably enthusiastic about trying to reform England and the English people. Then the death blow came. The high court in Westminster ruled that the Society's use of warrants and informers against sexual offenders was "irregular and illegal," which destroyed their operations. It seems the group continued to meet on and off until the 1750s, but their prosecuting campaign was finished.[235]

Even today, it is striking how complex an operation the Reformation Society was, and how much time, money, and legal work went into a herculean attempt to reform the manners of London and the country as a whole. This would be the last attempt at complete and total societal reformation by private and religious groups—no other group would undertake this sort of project, something that makes it remarkable to this day. The Manners Society failed for a variety of reasons, all of which were instructive to later groups. First and foremost, it took on an absurdly broad task in trying to prosecute every manners violation from minor swearing to the bigger crimes like brothel-keeping. In their eyes, even minor swearing represented bad manners that could endanger the English state. Later societies tended to be much more focused and specific. Second, a turbulent political environment was made even more so by their diverse religious membership—which ranged from Anglican to nonconformist—and that made them badly suited to the political engagement and lobbying that later groups would do.

Finally, as cities developed in Europe—especially the cities of London and Paris—it became increasingly hard to enforce sexual norms and behavior. This was the reason for the Society, but they fell ill to the disease they were trying to cure. The Society was an obsolete construction of an earlier time—before the mid-seventeenth century or so, sexuality and sexual identity was largely controlled and supported by the village or town community. People who fell out of line from what was seen as correct or right were often beaten, humiliated or even tried by their local communities. As Stone puts it:

> During the late sixteenth and early seventeenth centuries, this intrusive scrutiny actually intensified due to the rise of ethical Puritanism and the increased activity of the Church courts in controlling personal morality. Everyone gossiped freely about the most intimate details of domestic relations, and did not hesitate to denounce violations of community norms to an archdeacon's visitation enquiry, so that people were constantly testifying in court about the alleged moral peccadilloes of their neighbours.[236]

Aside from church courts, and indeed some of the court's sentences were town humiliations. One such sentence or community punishment might be the use of the cucking/ducking stool where the cuckold or the woman accused of being too dominant and controlling or argumentative would be ducked in the water. The 1615 ballad Cucking of a Scold recounts one such event:

> Then was the Scold herself,
>> In a wheelbarrow brought,
>> Stripped naked to the smock,
>> As in that case she ought:
>> Neats tongues about her neck
>> Were hung in open show;
>> And thus unto the cucking stool
>> This famous scold did go.[237]

The other form of community punishment might be the *charivari* or Skimmington ride, which would include an impromptu town parade of people banging on pots and pans

Brian M. Watson

and singing rowdy and lewd ballads—sometimes to force an unmarried couple to wed, sometimes to humiliate a man who couldn't control his wife, sometimes in the case of older widows remarrying. It was a form of social control. As one historian puts it:

> Both the state and the community relied on this collective opinion to ensure social order: hence the importance of one's 'good name and fame' in determining guilt and innocence in both civil and criminal trials/ the courts' use of 'shame' punishments - the pillory, stocks, cucking stool and public whipping - to solicit community participation in the public destruction of the reputations of those convicted of certain crimes.[238]

This moral order held more or less true until the founding of Society. The difference is that by the seventeenth century, the amount of community control over sexuality had begun to collapse. During this time, male clubs and ideas of masculinity, and indeed, acceptable behavior and tastes were undergoing a dramatic transformation—the elite libertinism where a man's success and prowess was tied heavily to his sexual(ity), ability, and honor was under decline.[239] By mid-to-late nineteenth century it was seen as boorish, immature, and uncivilized to boast of sexual conquest—the cult of domesticity and virtuous self-control held increasing sway, and a man's honor and, more importantly, his credit and chances for advancement became increasingly dependent on his public behavior.[240] As Erin Mackie puts it:

> Guided by codes of polite civility and restraint, eschewing personal violence for the arbitration of the law, oriented toward the family in an increasingly paternalistic role, purchasing his status as much, if not more, through the demonstration of moral virtues as through that of inherited honor, and gen-

dered unequivocally as a male heterosexual, the modern English gentleman has been cited in contemporary masculinity studies as the first type of "hegemonic masculinity." In contemporary eighteenth century scholarship, he is identified as the embodiment of the ideals emergent on the cultural negotiations following the political settlement of 1689.[241]

But this is not the last word that the Society for the Reformation of Manners will have in our story. One of their last acts turned out to be one of their biggest.

5

1690 – 1740 : Curlicisms

The Unspeakable Curll

T HE FINAL YEAR FOR of the Society for the Reformation of Manners was 1725, because their use of warrants and informers against sexual offenders was ruled "irregular and illegal." Unbeknownst to them, the target of one of their final campaigns would end up affecting the entirety of European literature, and would kick off the modern understanding of pornography and obscenity. This was the trial of bookseller and publisher Edmund Curll.

In August of 1724, the tri-weekly newspaper *Flying Post* asked, "Why is poor Curll hunted down by the Society for Reformation of Manners for his unprofitable starving Bawdry?"[242] As it turned out, Edmund Curll had made himself a target of the Society when he published a pamphlet titled *Heydegger's Letter to the Bishop of London*, which contained, among other things, a short poem defending masquerades. The topic of masquerades had long been a touchy subject with the Society, and especially with the then-Bishop of London, Edmund Gibson, who was being mocked by Curll's pamphlet. A few months earlier, on January 6th of 1724, Gibson had preached a sermon to the Society where he "inveighed against masquerades for the opportunity they offered to lascivious persons of both sexes."[243] Masquerades, Gibson argued, gave both sexes "the freedom of profane discourse, wanton behavior, and lascivious practices without the least fear of being discovered." Although it was the defense of the masquerade that got Curll in the targets of the English legal system, a very different sort of offense would land Curll in jail, court, and then the pillory.[244]

But to begin at the beginning: Who was Edmund Curll? Despite his importance to the story of obscenity and legal history, very little is known about his early years. According to biographers Paul Baines and Pat Rogers, Curll was likely born on the 14th of July, 1683, somewhere outside of London—the precise location is unclear, as both Edmund and Curll were very popular names at the time. Nothing is known about his childhood, but he was definitely apprenticed around 1679, at the age of 14, to various booksellers, until he found himself in the employ of Richard Smith around 1698 or '99. As Baines and Rogers note, the 17th century publishing industry was different then, and printers and booksellers had started to diverge into separate professions:

> The functions of printer and bookseller, once more or less united in the same individual, had for some time become separated into specialized professions, though there were individuals who continued both to print and to sell. The booksellers, to the annoyance of the printers, had long since gained the upper hand in all economic aspects of the trade as a whole. And just as there were specialisms within the mechanical processes of book-production—typefounders, compositors, press-men, correctors, printer's devils, engravers, and bookbinders —so there were different kinds of bookseller, from the 'mercuries' and hawkers who sold ballads on the

Brian M. Watson

street, through the auctioneers and the keepers of bookstalls in St Paul's Churchyard and elsewhere, to those with retail premises and those who operated wholesale businesses[245]

Curll's importance though, comes from his "innovative exploitation of now familiar techniques of publicity." In his 40 years of publishing (1706-1746), Curll's brash personality and aggressive style gave him a name and made him infamous. As Ralph Strauss documented in his 1927 biography of Curll, and perhaps, my favorite character description ever:

There was never a man that was called by so many names. There was never a man who succeeded in irritating almost beyond endurance so many of his betters. And nothing could make him see the 'error' of his ways: he just continued to irritate. If, for instance, objection was raised to some book of his of the bawdier kind, it would likely as not be followed by another even more scandalously improper. If a furious author declared that a book of his, published by Curll, was wholly unauthorized, he would probably find that a 'Second Volume' of his work was being advertised as 'Corrected by the Author Himself.[246]

Often, Curll went too far, and he would run into an absurd series of misadventures:

He was given an 'emetick' on a celebrated occasion by Pope, he was beaten by Westminster schoolboys, he was several times imprisoned, and once he stood in the pillory. Actions were brought against him in the Courts, he was almost annually lampooned, and word was even coined from his name to describe the regrettable methods of business. Pachydermatously, Curll continued to exist.[247]

Several historians have argued (convincingly) that the book was the first thing to become a consumer good—that is, the book market was the first market to become capitalist. If that is the case, Curll was the first blatant and unreserved capitalist. He would publish literally anything with the faintest whiff or hint of scandal surrounding it. Indeed, one of the first books he published was *The Works of the Right Honourable the late Earl of Rochester*, in 1707. Nor was he afraid to steal from others or republish things as his own. Until April of 1710, it was perfectly legal for him to do so—there was no such thing as copyright law, or any sort of law addressing what was appropriate and legal to publish.

Adrian Johns' *Piracy: The Intellectual Property Wars* does an excellent job of documenting the ins and outs of copyright history and, as he notes, the 1662 Licensing of the Press Act (passed under the demands of Rochester's Charles II), forbade anything "contrary to good life or good manners," but it was much more specifically targeted at "heretical, schismatical, blasphemous, seditious, and treasonable books, pamphlets, and papers," not at obscenity or erotica.[248] It was also different from modern copyright in the sense that it was the publishers who owned the work, not the authors. The 1662 act was renewed in 1685, and finally expired in 1692 when the House of Commons refused to renew it. The result of the refusal created a situation in which there existed no copyright or control method for the book trade. The business of publishing, and the profits to be made, exploded almost instantaneously as everyone tried to turn profits on anything they could publish, whether previously published, private, or obscene. If these "pyratical publishers" (in the words of Alexander Pope) had a pirate-king, it was Edmund Curll, known as the 'unspeakable Curll' by his enemies. Curll was unabashedly capitalist and opportunistic, profiting off of scandal and misfortune, and using every chance at publicity.

On October 24th of 1724, the *Whitehall Evening Post* reported that "the Printers and Publishers of several obscene Books and Pamphlets, tending to encourage Vice and Immorality have been taken into Custody by Warrants."[249] Curll was among their number, and he was accused of the printing of *A Treatise of Flogging* and *Venus in the Cloister*. Upset at being accused of "vice," Curll responded with *The Humble Representation of Edmund Curll, Bookseller and Stationer of London, concerning Five Books, complained to of the Secretary of State* (Evidently, our modern book titles are not what they used to be). Curll's response was to note that the *Treatise* was, of course, a "medical work, translated from the Latin—a really learned dissertation which...should not be criticized by a layman."[250] The book itself is quite curious, drawing on fake medicine, anatomy, and descriptions that are borderline pornographic. It claims to describe how flagellation is used by monks for spiritual and medical purposes. We will return to this text later on.

Why is it so important? Because in 1725, Edmund Curll was arrested by the government for being a "Printer and Publisher of several obscene Books and Pamphlets." The result of the trial, which would take over three years of argument and counter-argument, was the creation of a new legal category, obscene libel, which had not existed previously. Prior to 1728, the judgment of libel usually only applied to seditious libel (printed calls to overthrow the king or threats against the government), or blasphemous libel (slander against the church or blatant atheism). The biggest issue for the government in passing judgment on Curll was that there was no concept of obscenity for 'degrading the manners of the public.'

The Cloister of Venus

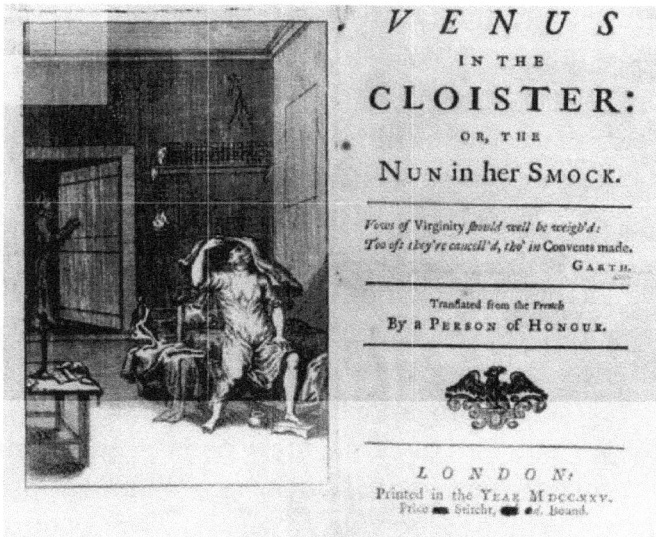

Figure 6: Frontispiece and title page of Venus in the Cloister.

THE OTHER BOOK that Curll was accused of publishing was *Venus in the Cloister*, which is a much more infamous work and frequently considered representative of early 18th century pornography. It is also an example of how Aretine-style cultural criticism fused with the developing pornographic genre. In our theme of 'dirty French novels,' *Venus in the Cloister* was originally written in 1683 by Jean Barrin, who was the French Catholic vicar-general of Nantes. Interestingly, it was republished in 1692 by Henry Rhodes, but he was not prosecuted nor fined for the text, unlike Curll three decades later.

Curll's (1725) English edition was translated by a "Person of Honour" from the French 'original,' written by the pseudonymic 'Abbe du Prat.' It contained five dialogues, combined with footnotes and a new introduction. The introduction claims that the "Duchess of ******" ordered the translation, which is, in fact, an attempt to cast a veil of legitimacy over the text. The introduction also claims that, contrary to what you might think, silly reader, it is a *moral* text, not a lewd one:

"he that rightly comprehends the Morality of this Discourse shall never repent the reading of it [and the discourses are] full of Sharpness and Morality."[251]

Amusingly, the footnotes throughout the text try to provide the reader with a moralistic and 'correct' reading, though that too flounders when a character refers to an Italian book on kissing. This book, according to the footnotes, has (handily enough) "now been translated into English and printed for Mr. Curll over against Catherine-Street in the Strand."[252] (So get your copy today!) As noted, Curll's 1725 English edition added two dialogues to the existing three of the original work. The first was actually from another French book called *Noveau Contes*, by Jean de La Fontaine, and the second seems like it was directly inspired by Curll's other publications on the use of whipping in the bedroom. As a result, there is quite a dramatic shift in tone, character, and subject matter, so I will be dealing with only the first three dialogues.

As is usual, the dialogues take place between two women, one older and more experienced, and one younger and more innocent. In this case, the story begins with an elder nun, Sister Angelica (though as her age is 20, hardly 'elder'), walking into the bedroom of a 16-year-old novice nun, Sister Agnes. Agnes cries out, "Ah Lard! Sister Angelica, for heaven's Sake do not come into our Cell; I am not visible [decent] at present. Ought you to surprize People in the Condition I am in? I thought I had shut the door."[253] Angelica responds "Be quiet, my dear, what is it gives thee this Alarm? The mighty Crime of seeing thee shift thy self [seeing you in a nightgown], or [the crime of] doing something somewhat more refreshing? Good Friends ought to conceal nothing from one another."[254] It seems that Angelica has caught Agnes masturbating, though there is no explicit detail of this.

Angelica is not shocked at all—in fact, she thinks it 'quite good' that Agnes is 'abusing' herself in this way. She says that Agnes has no reason at all to be embarrassed or upset, that it is perfectly natural, and that Angelica herself wishes to en-gage' with Agnes: "Thou hast reason, my Child, to talk after this Manner; and though I had not all the Affection for thee, a tender Heart is sensible of. . . . Let me embrace thee that our Hearts may talk to each other in the Tumult of our Kisses!"[255] Agnes, however, is utterly shocked at Angelica's sudden be-havior change, and she rebuffs the seduction attempt with, "Ah Lud! How you squeeze me in your Arms; Don't you see I am naked to my Smock? Ah! you have set me all on Fire!"[256]

Not understanding why she is being rejected, Angelica tries to charm Agnes. Agnes tries to play dumb, thinking that An-gelica could not have seen her:

Angelica: Ah! how does that Vermillion, which at this instant animates thee, augment the brilliancy of thy Beauty? That Fire which sparkles in thy Eyes, how amiable does it make thee? . . . must a young Creature so accomplished be thus reserved? No, no, my Child, I'll make thee acquainted with my most secret Actions, and give thee the Conduct of a sage and prudent Religious; I do not mean that austere and scrupulous sageness which is the Child of Fast-ing, and discovers its self in Hair and Sackcloth. . .

Agnes: My amorous Inclination! Certainly my Physi-ognomy [face] must be very deceitful, or you do not perfectly understand the Rules of that Art. There is nothing touches me less than that Passion; and since the three Years that I have been in Religion it has not given me the least Inquietude.

Angelica: That I doubt very much, and if thou wouldst speak with greater Sincerity thou wouldst own that I have spoke nothing but the Truth. What, can a young Girl of sixteen, of so lively a Wit, and

a Body so well formed as thine, be cold and insensible? No, I cannot persuade my self to think so: Every
thing thou dost, however so negligent it is, convinces me of the contrary, and that Je ne sais quoi
that I saw through the Crevice of the Door before I
came in, convinces me that thou art a Dissembler
[liar].

Agnes: Ah dear! I am undone! . . . But pray what did
you perceive thro' the Crevice?

Angelica: Thou perfectly tirest me with this Conduct. . . . Why I saw thee in an Action, in which I
will serve thee my self, if thou wilt, and in which
my Hand shall now perform that Office which thine
did just now so charitably to another part of thy
Body. . . . Thou wouldst not believe that such holy
Souls were capable of employing themselves in such
profane Exercises. . .Ah Lard! in what good Plight
thou art! what delicate proportion of Shape! Let me
__[257]

Conveniently (for the readers), Sister Angelica suddenly
realizes why she is being rejected—Agnes has no knowledge of
sex or sexuality (much like conveniently-innocent Katy and
conveniently-innocent Ottavia). So, she decides that she must
teach the young nun "a great many Things of which thou art
ignorant," and change her entire worldview, replacing it with
the 'wise' teachings of a 'Jesuit' and her own philosophies.
Agnes agrees (of course), "Do me the Favour, Sister Angelica,
to give me a perfect Idea of this good Conduct; believe me
entirely disposed to hear you, and suffer my self to be per-
suaded by your Reasonings, when I cannot refute them by
stronger."[258] And so the first and quite long dialogue begins
—it is so long, the two nuns must have missed all of their

sleep for that night. Angelica begins her dialogue, saying that "I shall teach thee in a few Words, what a Reverend Father Jesuit, who had a particular Affection for me, told me at the Time when he endeavoured to open my Understanding, and make me capable of the present Speculations," and indeed, this Reverent Father did, uh, endeavor to open Angelica with his well-reasoned philosophy, which I quote from below at:

> As all your Happiness. . .depends upon a certain Knowledge of the religious State you have now embraced. . .you must take Notice that Religion. . .is composed of two Bodies, one of which is purely celestial and supernatural, the other terrestrial and corruptible, which is only the invention of Men. One is political, the other mystical with Reference to Christ, who is the Head of the true Church. One is permanent, because it consists in the Word of God, which is unalterable and eternal; and the other subject to an infinity of Changes, in as much as it depends on the Word of Man, which is finite and fallible.

> This being supposed, we must separate these two Bodies, and make a just Distinction between them, in order to know to what we are obliged; and to do this well is no small Difficulty. . . . In obeying the Commands of God, we must consider whether his Will be written with his own Finger, or proceeds from the Mouth of his Son; or whether only from the Voice of the People: So that Sister Angelica may without Scruple. . .[dispose with the] Vows and Promises which she indiscreetly made between the Hands of Men, and resume the same Liberty she was in before her Engagement[259]

To summarize, Angelica's philosophy argues that religion is composed of "two Bodies, one of which is purely celestial and supernatural, the other terrestrial and corruptible, which is only the invention of Men." The former is 'Mystical and Permanent,' as it is directly related to Christ and Heaven. The latter, Angelica terms 'Policy,' as they are the rules and regulations of the church and state. Angelica considers these rules and laws to be feeble and wrong as they "cast poor Soul[s] into Despair" and, as they were "indiscreetly made between the Hands of Men," Agnes should "dispense with the Laws, Customs, and Manners" which she submitted herself to at her entrance into the convent, and explore her sexuality in order to commune with God (and, one would assume, with Angelica). What is more, both Angelica and Agnes have been put into the nunnery by their family against their will. Angelica seems to state very angrily that, "That Cloisters are the Common-Sewers, whereinto Policy discharges itself of its Ordures!"[260] Which is to say that the useless people in society are cast into monasteries or nunneries to get rid of them.

Having appropriately educated Agnes, Angelica makes her move again:

> **Agnes:** Take away your Hand, I beseech you, from that Place, if you would not blow up a Fire not easily to be extinguished. I must own my Weakness, I am a Girl the most sensible you ever knew; and that which would not cause in any other the least Emotion, very often puts me entirely into the utmost Disorder.

> **Angelica:** So! then thou are not so cold as thou wouldst have persuaded me at the beginning of our Discourse! and I believe thou wilt act thy Part as well as any one I know when I shall have put thee into the Hands of five or six good Friers.[261]

The second dialogue takes place eight days later, when the previously-innocent novice Agnes meets up again with Angelica. The pair have been separated while Angelica was in a spiritual retreat, and Agnes was getting into more temporal adventures. Agnes says that she is "quite ashamed to appear before [Angelica]. I fancy to myself that you know already the most minute Particular that hath happened to me in your Absence." But Angelica denies knowing anything about the past two weeks, and commands Agnes: "thou wilt begin to make me a faithful Recital of thy Adventures."[262]

Agnes describes how she began to meet the Confessor that Angelica recommended to her in a 'Parlor' made for confession. The translator offers this handy note to describe what she means:

> *Parlour, is a Room (of which there are several in every Nunnery) into which the Nuns come to talk with Strangers: It is divided in the Middle by an Iron Grate, and contrived so that those in one Parlour cannot hear what is said in another. Strangers come into it through a Gallery, having first received a Key from the Mother Portress.[263]

As Angelica advised her in the first dialogue, Agnes made a "semblance of being somewhat shy and ignorant, giving very serious Answers to the Civilities he shewed me," in order to create the impression that she is sweet and innocent; a certain level of duplicity considering the stories Angelica had told her. In some ways, the transformation from representing women in erotic works as the *manipulators* to the *manipulated* keys us into some of the ways the gender dynamics of the seventeenth and eighteenth centuries were changing. It also points to the fact that the likely readers of these texts were young men.

Brian M. Watson

Agnes' pretended innocence did in "no ways discourage him; on the contrary. . .I don't know what you told him of me, but I found he made very considerable Advances for a first Visit." In fact, he goes so far as to show her "three Letters from our Abbess, which convinced me that whatever I did was no more than treading in her Steps." With this sort of endorsement, Agnes "could not help bestowing on him some small Favours."[264] But, there is still the problem of that pesky metal grate between the two of them:

> I represented to him, that the Grate was an insurmountable Obstacle, and that of Necessity he ought to content himself with some Toyings, for that it was impossible for him to advance any farther. But he soon convinced me, that he was more knowing than I, and shewed me two Boards, which he removed, one on his side, and the other on mine, which opened a Passage [he called] The Streights of Gibralter; and told him, that he ought by no Means to venture the Passage, without being furnished with all the Things necessary, especially if he designed to stop at Hercules's Pillars. In short, after several Disputes and Contests on both sides, the Abbé passed the Streights, and arrived at the Port, where he was well received. But this was not without some Pain and Difficulty, and that too after his assuring me, that his Entrance should not be attended with any bad Consequences. I permitted him to sojourn there so long as might make him happy. [265]

This is a rather amusing passage—the understanding of which hinges on the understanding of the Pillars of Hercules/Straights of Gibraltar metaphor. Which, if it is not clear, compares the legs and genitals of a woman to the entrance to the Mediterranean Sea. Regardless, Angelica is absolutely delighted and says, "I plainly see he pleased thee. He is well made, and a beautiful young Fellow. For my part, I call him nothing else but my large white Thing.*" The little asterisk there is from the translator who says that the "large white Thing" alludes to "the white Habit those Fathers wear." This is clearly incorrect—Angelica is referring to a *very* different 'large white thing,' but the translator is trying to create a moralistic reading of a non-moralistic text to avoid prosecution or a worse fate. Nevertheless, the strategy failed.

There is another interesting moment when the 'moralistic notes' try to present a reading of the story that is clearly incorrect to reality of the story. Later on in the second dialogue, Agnes notes that:

His Entertainment and little Toyings, pleased me infinitely, and I had no Difficulty of granting him the Passage which I so much disputed with the Abbé. I only represented to him, that he had Cause to fear lest the Fooleries that passed between us two, be not attended with a third. I understand you, replied he, and drew at the same time out of his Pocket, a little Book, which he gave me, written in French, called, *Remedést doux & faciles contre l'embonpoint dangereux.*

[translator note] † The Title of this Book is one of those double Entendres, which cannot be translated. . . Those who understand French will know the Author's Meaning.[266]

The title of the book when translated into English is "Sweet and Easy Remedies against Dangerous Fatness" (or as Bradford Mudge translates it, 'A Sweet and Easy Remedy for the Dangerous Plumpness'). The little book she is speaking about is actually a simple guide to abortion. Thus, though there is a slight double entendre on the word 'plumpness,' the translator's real reason for not translating the title is to avoid *directly* discussing abortion—a definite no-no for the time—but indirect mention seems to have been deemed acceptable to Curll and others.

A final place where the translator notes break the illusion of the moralistic reading is when Agnes is listing a series of books she received from her lovers. A note attached to one of these books handily offers that "It is now translated into English and printed for Mr. Curll over against Catherine Street in the Strand." This is not the only place where the characters reference books—books are heaped on top of books in *Venus in the Cloister*. At one point, Agnes even recommends an entire catalogue of what presumes to be some of the erotic and semi-erotic works that would have been available for a discerning purchaser:

> *Fruitful Chastity*. A Curious Novel.
> *The Passport of the Jesuits*. A Gallant Piece.
> *The Prison enlightened*: or, *The Opening of the Little Wicket*, with Figures.
> *The Journal of the* Feuillantines.
> *The Prowess of the Knights of S.* Laurence.
> *The Rules and Statutes of* C****** Abbey.
> *A Collection of Remedies against* l'Embonpoint d'angereux. *Composed for the Commodity of the Nuns of St. George.*
> *The Extreme Unction of dying Virginity.*
> *The Apostolical* Orvietan, *Composed by the Four Orders Mendicant*, ex precepto sanctissimi.
> *The Cut—A———se of the Friers.*
> *The Pastime of the Abbés.*
> *The* Carthusian's *Battle.*
> *The Fruits of the Unitive Life.*

This particular list of books is fictitious, each one being a joke in itself—but there are several very real erotic texts mentioned in throughout the remaining dialogues, and they include works such as *The School of Venus*, and Chorier's *Luisa Sigea*, both of which we have discussed previously. According to Peter Wagner, this piling on of books shows that *"In Venus in the Cloister*, sex has become a religion. . .the new faith, sexual pleasure, is set down in the books Agnes receives from her abbe, all of them obscene or pornographic."[267] Although I might not go so far as to say that sexual pleasure was a 'new' religion, Wagner is correct in his observation that works like *Venus in the Cloister*, and *The School of Venus* mark the transition of the erotic novel into the obscene—mark the transition from primarily social critique to increasingly more erotic works meant to be used (or, in the case of Pepys, definitely used) as masturbatory aids. Regardless, for a book that would help create 'obscene libel,' *Venus in the Cloister* does not get particularly raunchy when compared to both earlier and later works of obscenity and pornography. Nor is it as descriptive about actual sex acts as *The Dialogues of Luisa Sigea* or *The School of Venus*. In fact, this would cause some problems for the judges sitting in trial against Curll.

Curll's Veneral Trial

VENUS IN THE CLOISTER is a difficult work to categorize, as it is a work that combines earlier forms of cultural and religious criticism with forms of pornography that were just beginning to take shape. When Curll republished the 1683 work, the Society for the Reformation of Manners made an official complaint, and Curll was taken in for questioning. As Curll's biographer, Ralph Strauss, says, "Authority had good reason not to desire harsh measures, yet it seemed impossible to do nothing at all. But what exactly could be done? A police prosecution, such as would happen to-day, had not yet been invented."[268] They charged him with libel.

Of course, Curll's prosecution didn't come out of anywhere—by the time Curll was taken in by the authorities, he

had already racked up a series of literary cimes and misde-
meanors. Both in 1716 and 1721 he had been brought before
the House of Lords, reprimanded, and forced to kneel before
the bar in punishment—first for publishing the accounts of
a Jacobite, and then for publishing the private works of the
Duke of Buckingham, which was considered an assault on the
Lord's privilege. As Rogers and Baines put it "besides this,
he [had] endured treasury prosecutions, Chancery suits, private lawsuits, and even communal punishment, when he was
tossed in a blanket at Westminster School. More recently,
Curll had been taken up in May 1724 for publishing a libelous
pamphlet called *Heydegger's Letter to the Bishop of London*."[269]
In another article, they write, correctly that "we must not
think of the charges laid against Curll as suddenly appearing
in a vacuum. He was a prime suspect for many literary misde-
meanors, though not always the right victim."[270] Part of the
reason for Curll's constant trips to courtrooms was a publication strategy, as he seemed to have hit on the truth that drama
and scandal would drive book sales. The other part of that
truth however is that the books that cause drama and scandal
also carry the most risk.

Curll appeared in front of the King's Bench, the highest
court at the time in England. He pleaded not guilty, arguing
that the first work he had been indicted on, A *Treatise of Flogging* (about using whips in the bedroom), was a 'medical text'
and therefore not subject to the usual standards of propriety.
As far as *Venus in the Cloister* went, Curll's lawyer argued that
there was no evidence that Curll had published the text because his name was not on the cover—an argument that was
pretty unconvincing. Furthermore, he argued that it was "a
Satirical Piece exposing the Intrigues of the Nunes and Fr-
yars done out of French" and furthermore there was "no Law
prohibiting the Translations of Books either out of Latin or
French or any other Language, neither we can presume can
such Transactions be deemed Libels."[271] Curll's lawyer was

correct, as there was no legal definition of obscene libel before his client went on trial—the creation of obscene libel was a result of Curll's trial.

Neither argument was particularly persuasive, and Curll was quickly found guilty of publishing the two books. The judgment however, was stopped on jurisdictional grounds. All of the judges agreed that Curll's publication should be prosecuted, but in the words of Justice Fortescue, "I own this is a great offence; but I know of no law by which we can punish it. Common law is common usage, and where there is no law there can be no transgression." [272] In previous centuries and years, what would have normally happened is that Curll would have been referred to church courts. Church courts are not very familiar to modern people, as they no longer have the power or the authority that they used to have, but they carried far more power and authority in the seventeenth century. Beginning around the year 1100, church courts were established by the Catholic Church to punish civil crimes such as adultery, fornication, prostitution and bawdiness. And in fact, sexual and marital cases accounted for 60-90% of all cases depending on the year.[273] They operated side-by-side with secular courts (which focused on things such as assault, fraud, murder, etc.), but church court punishments included things such as atonement for sins, pilgrimages, or payment of fines. More commonly, however, they were publicly beaten and humiliated by the entire community of a town or village.

However, after the Reformation, these sorts of punishments began to be mocked and were seen as too weak. Faramerz Dabhoiwala recounts: "Their 'toyish censures' (as a Puritan manifesto of 1572 put it) did nothing to reduce immorality; the main point of their proceedings seemed to be to milk people for legal fees."[274] The dislike of church courts was strengthened by their use in England to persecute Puritan ministers and parishioners for "non-conformity." The church courts were not only "corrupt and ineffective, it now seemed, they also unjustly persecuted godly men and women for following their consciences."[275] This pushed Protestants to move policing of morality to the civil government, and the result was that, "Bills for the stricter punishment of sexual offences were introduced in almost every parliament of the early seventeenth century: in 1601, 1604, 1606-7, 1614, 1621, 1626, 1628, and 1629 [and beyond]."[276]

So, when Curll's lawyer moved to have judgment removed or arrested on jurisdictional grounds, saying that Curll should face a church court instead of a state one, he was inadvertently (or purposefully) walking into this power struggle between the church and the state—secular courts were beginning to take over punishment for moral and sexual offenses, in a way that they had not before. This is a theme that is repeated throughout the centuries that this book documents—religious groups lobbying and pressuring the civil government to police morality. It's a theme that we see even today, in the 21st century, when the governments of the United Kingdom, India, or Australia are pressured into blocking pornography to protect children, or where the government of Germany orders that adult eBooks can only be sold after ten pm.

Making the issue even more complicated was the fact that *Venus in the Cloister* was not regarded as a particularly obscene book, as even Curll's lawyer argued. Justice John Fortescue commented that, "I thought [*Venus* was] published on Purpose to expose the Romish Priests, the Father Confessors, and the Popish religion." These sorts of religious propaganda were largely tolerated, if not encouraged, because Catholics were seen as a religious and a political threat. Historian Julie Peakman points out in *Mighty Lewd Books* that, "Importation of Catholic books was forbidden. Caches of illicit Catholic books were searched for and destroyed by government pursuivants [agents], and the burning of such books was an officially condoned demonstration against their distribution. Anti-religious texts perceived to threaten the established Church of England were also prosecuted."

It took nearly three years for the Justices to come to a conclusion. Indeed, the decision took so long that Curll would likely have escaped punishment had he not kept up his controversial publishing habits—while on bail in 1725 he advertised his intention to publish a controversial and blasphemous religious tract by William Staunton.[277] The final decision was that because *Venus in the Cloister* and *A Treatise on Flogging* were books sold in a public book market, they should be punished by the temporal (secular courts): "The Spiritual Courts punish only personal spiritual defamation by words; if it is reduced to writing, it is a temporal offence."[278] Justice Fortescue noted that Curll had not 'libeled' any one specific person, stating that "This [judgement] is for printing bawdy stuff, that reflects on no person: and a libel must be against some particular person or persons, or against the government.

It is stuff not fit to be mentioned publicly."[279] *Venus in the Cloister* did not "name" actual persons, but only filthy ideas and images.

In order to make the case that they had the power to punish Curll, the Court drew on a previous case that involved the confidantes and fellow 'Ballers' of our friend, the Earl of Rochester. In 1663, Rochester's close friends (and 'Ballers'), Sirs Buckhurst and Sedley, got rip-roaringly drunk at the Cock Tavern in London. In the spirit of all drunk people who want an audience, they moved out onto the tavern's balcony, which attracted a crowd of passers-by, whereupon Sir Sedley stripped naked and began parodying a sermon, mocking Christianity, and some reports suggest he urinated on the spectators. The pissed-off (and pissed-on) crowd drove them indoors with a rain of bottles. Sedley was subsequently brought before the King's Bench and fined 2,000 pounds. How does this serve as a precedent for the judgment against Curll? The Court argued that in punishing Sedley, it had acted as guardians of London's moral well-being. According to Justice Reynolds, by this standard, Curll's case "is surely worse than sir Charles Sedley's case, who only exposed himself to the people then present [naked], who might [choose] whether they would look upon him or not; whereas this book goes all over the kingdom."[280] In a roundabout way, Curll's publication of *Venus in the Cloister* was the equivalent of urinating on the reading public of London.

The decision handed down was that Curll's book was libel, punishable by the temporal courts, and that Curll had broken the peace. As peace was part of the king's "government and that peace may be broken in many instances without an actual force. 1. If it be an act against the constitution or civil Government; 2. If it be against religion; and, 3.If against morality."[281] The third point, though pornography would seem to match the definition of being "against morality," still referred to Christian morality, as the explanation made clear: "Christianity is part of the law, and why not morality too?" Unfortunately for Curll, Christian morality—the body of 'Policy'—was specifically targeted by *Venus in the Cloister*, therefore guaranteeing his punishment. The fact that the genre of pornography was just beginning to take shape proved to be the key argument that saved Curll from a worse fate at the hands of the Kings Bench.

His punishment was not overwhelming, but still significant—a fine of 100£ and a day in the pillory. Although this new category of obscene libel would eventually lead to the creation of pornography, it was still attached to Christian and religious morality, not the 'public morals' that porn would offend against—the court saw no distinction between political, religious, or obscene libel. The fact that Curll targeted Christianity's doctrines was the key that led to his conviction; not the supposed obscenity of *Venus in the Cloister*. This idea is supported by the fact that the next person convicted of obscene libel was John Wilkes, who libeled the church and a bishop in his *Essay on Women*. If obscene libel just required sexy writing, then John Cleland would have been convicted for *Fanny Hill* two decades later, which he was not.

In the end, however, Curll managed to escape what could have been a very bad day in the pillory—people were known to have been stoned to death in an hour on the pillory. He cleverly managed to avoid being pelted to death by having friends give audience members a pamphlet that said, "the man before you is there for defending the memory of the deceased Queen Anne," who was well loved by the English population. I'll let Curll's biographer Ralph Strauss close us out:

> The crowd came to look and to jeer, and possibly throw a few eggs. One man exercised his privilege and threw an egg. He was nearly lynched. The others smiled and grumbled at Governmental stupidity.... In any case, 'he was treated with great Civility by the Populace,' and when he was released he seems to have been lifted on to the shoulders of an admiring crowd and taken away to a tavern and [had] as many drinks as even he wanted.[282]

Doctors and Lawyers and Farmers, oh my!

BEFORE WE TURN TO PART THREE, and begin our climb into the apex of our history, let's stay with Curll for one more moment, as his creativity and importance for the history of pornography cannot be understated. One of the genres he pioneered, that would carry throughout the 18th and into the 19th century was medical pornography. The already-mentioned book, *A Treatise on the Use of Flogging*, was the best known of his works. The *Treatise* is quite curious, drawing on fake medicine, anatomy, and the borderline pornographic. It

claims to be a series of letters between Johann Heinrich Meibom (M.D.) and Thomas Bartholin (M.D.), written to Chris-
tianus Cassius, Bishop of Luebeck (in Germany), describing
how flagellation is used by monks for spiritual and medical
purposes.

In the introduction, the author of the book (perhaps Curll
himself) notes that "Books which treat upon subjects of this
curious nature, [are] being liable to the censure of the [unjust],"
and argues that "The author himself was a man of great reputation, an eminent physician. . .[and if he had] foreseen any ill
effects from a treatise of this sort, he would hardly have risked
his fame and practice by suffering it to be published. A bishop
desired him to write it," so therefore he did. It is not the author nor the translator that is lewd or pornographic; "the fault
is not in the subject matter, but the inclination of the reader,
that makes these pieces offensive."[283]

A rather amusing turn of phrase, isn't that? It's not the
whipping and the moaning that makes this book bad, it's the
reader's dirty filthy mind that does—cleanse your mind, o
hypocrite lecteur! But still, like *Venus in the Cloister*, the *Treatise*
is not all that pornographic or obscene—for the most part it
talks about how you can use flogging to prevent people who
"dissemble diseases," i.e. hypochondriacs. The cure is partly
in the method however, if someone gets tied up and beaten
for being sick, they might find themselves suddenly feeling
better. 'Meibom' writes that there is much to recommend it
for a physician, comparing the harsh methods described to a
doctor restraining a frenzied patient, or a father punishing his
son; both acts done in the recipient's best interest. He adds
that, "if they should neglect them and suffer them to perish,
that false clemency is rather a cruelty. . . . I have observed that
boys, and men too, have been cured of pissing in bed by whipping." Perhaps the most scandalous paragraph in the *Treatise*
is:

But what you could not so readily believe upon

my affirmation was, that there are persons who are stimulated to venery [horniness] by strokes of the rod, and worked into a flame of lust by blows; and that the part which distinguishes us to be men, should be raised by the charm of invigorating lashes[284]

Medical and pseudo-medical pornography were a profitable business for publishers before, during, and after Curll (as we have already addressed in discussing *Aristotles Masterpiece*), and they remained so even with the introduction of photography, as some of the first photographs of naked women were also used in anatomy textbooks. Indeed, these sorts of works were still being produced a century later when John Joseph Stockdale wrote *On Diseases of the Generative System* in 1811, and quickly found himself in a court case against the British Parliament— *Stockdale v. Hansard*. Wagner also makes the point that medical and para-medical pornography played an important role in first categorizing and identifying (and then abnormalizing) homosexuals, transsexuals, and hermaphrodites.[285] Curll however, took the existing format and put a curious twist or curl upon it, with the *Merryland* series.

After his trial for obscene libel, Curll stopped producing religious obscenity and blasphemy, but he definitely did not disappear off the face of the earth (or fall out of the history books; he continues to crop up in a variety of places.) He continued in the publishing business for the next 20 years until his death in 1747. During that time, he continued to publish any and every author with the whiff of a scandal about them, including Delariver Manley. After more than 30 years in business with some success, Curll managed to have one last spectacular success with the *Merryland* series. The series were a parody of adventure stories that were so popular at the time such as *Robinson Crusoe*, the writings of Captain John Smith, or those of Marco Polo. Instead of describing the ins and outs and the hard life of being on a desert island, dramatic tales of being saved by native 'princesses,' or the wonders and marvels of faraway lands, the *Merryland* series uses the same sort of reporting voice to describe what at first seems like a strange new land, but is actually a description of a woman's body.

Curll appears to have paid a certain Thomas Stretzer, about whom nothing is known, to write the book. According to Paul Blaines, Stretzer obviously "possessed some technical competence as a writer, with a good grounding in the classics, and a broad range of reading in contemporary literature and the sciences,"[286] but otherwise there is nothing to go off. Stretzer's *Merryland* was probably inspired by an earlier work titled *The Present State of Betty-land* (1684), but it is a unique work. Julie Peakman seems to think that the *Merryland* style of books were marketed to middle and upper-middle class men and women, and the author agrees with them, as he notes in a sequel that, "some of the Fair-Sex, as well as the Men, have freely testified their Approbation of this pretty Pamphlet".

Although the name of *Merryland* was a pun on the recently-established American colony (and later state), 'Maryland,' the central image of the series, the female body as a fertile land, is probably as old as the idea of 'mother nature.' Women become the earth itself in the descriptions of *Merryland*—pregnancy becomes a gigantic growing mountain, vaginas become deep caves, breasts become hills, and so on:

> MERRYLAND is a Part of that vast Continent called by the Dutch Geographers, the Vroislandtscap [female landscape]; it is situate in a low Part of the Continent, bounded on the upper Side, or to the Northward, by the little Mountain called MNSVNRS [Mons Veneris/pubic mound], on the East and West by COXASIN and COXADEXT [left and right hips], and on the South or lower Part it lies open to the TERRA FIRMA....[287]

At the End of the great Canal toward the Terra Firma, are two Forts called LBA [labia], between which every one must necessarily pass, that goes up the Country, there being no other Road. The Fortifications are not very strong, tho' they have Curtains, Hornworks, and Ramparts; they have indeed sometimes defended the Pass a pretty while, but were seldom or never known to hold out long against a close and vigorous Attack....

Near these Forts is the Metropolis, called CLTRS [clitoris]; it is a pleasant Place, much delighted in by the Queens of MERRYLAND, and is their chief Palace, or rather Pleasure Seat; it was at first but small, but the Pleasure some of the Queens have found in it, has occasion'd their extending its Bounds considerably. [288]

But the extended metaphor/analogy does not stop there—the work goes on to describe, in various chapters, the 'Air, River, and Soils,' 'The Ancient and Modern Inhabitants and their Customs,' 'The Products and Commodities,' the government, religion, and language of the fictional country. For example, in describing the main river of Merryland, the author notes that it "takes its Rise from a large Reservoir or Lake in the Neighbourhood called VSCA [latin for bladder]." He continues the metaphors with:

There is a spacious [vaginal] CANAL runs through the midst of this Country, from one End almost to the other; it is so deep that Authors affirm it has no Bottom... All the superfluous Moisture of the Country is drained off through this Canal, and it is likewise the Conveyance of all Provisions to the upper Part of MERRYLAND; all the 'Seed' sowed in that Country is conveyed this Way to the Great Store-

> house at the upper End of it; and in short, there is
> no Commodity imported into MERRYLAND, but by
> this Road; so that you may easily conceive it to be a
> Place of great Traffic[289]

A place of great traffic, of course, because it appears that he is describing the body of a prostitute. When the author goes on to describe the air and climate of Merryland, he refers to the danger of sexually-transmitted diseases—the most common of which was syphilis, which could eventually result in the death of the infected, like the Earl of Rochester:

> The Air in MERRYLAND is very different, being
> in some Provinces perfectly pure and healthy, in
> others extreamly gross and pestilential; for the
> most part it may be said to be like the Air in
> Holland, "generally thick and moist, by reason of
> the frequent Fogs which arise from its Lakes and
> Canals,". . . The Climate is generally warm, and
> sometimes so very hot, that Strangers inconsid-
> erately coming into it, have suffered exceedingly;
> many have lost their Lives by it, some break out into
> Sores and Ulcers difficult to be cured; and others, if
> they escape with their Lives, have lost a Member.
> [290]

Crabs, another sexually transmitted disease, was also known of, and seen as nearly universal. The author notes that *Merryland* has "Crabs in plenty on its Banks." But both syphilis and crabs could be avoided with the right education:

> This dangerous Heat of the Climate, with all its
> dreadful Concomitants, is not so very terrible, but
> it may be guarded against by taking proper Pre-
> cautions, and People might venture into it without
> much Hazard, even at the worst Seasons, and in the
> most unhealthy Provinces. . .[if they are] careful al-

ways to wear proper Cloathing. . .made of an extraordinary fine thin Substance, and contrived so as to
be all of one Piece, and without a Seam, only about
the Bottom it is generally bound round with a scar-
let Ribbon for Ornament.[291]

What the author is referring to is, of course, condoms. In
their earliest forms, condoms tended to be made of linen, silk,
or in some cases, sheep-gut, and have a ribbon at the bottom
for tying it to the penis. It is in the 18th century that references to condoms begin to appear more frequently. Casanova,
for one, referred to them as 'English Overcoats,' but found
them 'nasty, disgusting and scandalous.' One woman "complained that she did not like '*ce petite personnage*' [the little
character, aka penis] so much when it was covered."[292] The
Merryland author comments that: "Some people invent[ed]
Means of preventing the Seed taking Root. . .but such Practices
are only used by Stealth, and not openly approved of; it is
looked on as bad Practice, and we are told it was formerly punished with Death."[293]

Regardless of the disapproval, Curll still managed to find
room for a commercial opportunity and published a *Merryland* sequel, *The Potent Ally: or Succours from Merryland*, which
discussed contraceptives.

Although the entire text is very tongue-in-cheek, there is
one scene that is especially amusing and significant. While
discussing the frequent 'visitors to Merryland,' it seems that
either Curll or Stretzer makes a reference to Curll's obscenity trial. The narrator comments that there are many soldiers
and sailors to be seen among the people of Merryland (among
the prostitutes), but as to the clerical visitors, "I am not able
to gratify [the Reader's] Curiosity [in regards to] the Clergy
[as they] endeavour to keep it a secret as much as possible
among themselves, being a Mystery they think improper to be
divulged among the Laity; and tho' I could mention some par-

ticulars on this Subject, which have accidentally come to my Knowledge, I must desire to be excused, being very unwilling to give Offence to [that] Body of Men"[294] The fact that Curll was not punished or prosecuted for this book, even though it was quite successful, further demonstrates that as long as authors steered clear of religious or political critique (as Curll/Stretzer did in not mentioning if there were Clergy in Merryland), then the law would steer clear of them.

Merryland also spends a good deal of time expressing opinions on various topics. For example, the narrator discusses anal sex by introducing the landmark, "The Antipodes to MERRYLAND is by some said to be that prominent Part of the Continent called PDX [podex, Latin for anus], known in High Dutch by the Name of der Arsz-back." Then adds their opinion that, "there are some People who very preposterously (as I think) give the Preference to the PDX: the Italian Geographers...some of the Dutch...and of late Years a few in Great Britain have appeared not altogether averse to it."[295] This is a confirmation of the English stereotype that the Italians are well-known homosexuals, which comes primarily from the works of Aretino, as he was a well-known bisexual. The comment that a few Englishmen have lately "appeared not altogether averse to it," suggests a concern that the morals and manners of the English populace were shifting in a dangerous way. This idea is confirmed when the author turns to discussing marriage in Merryland, using the analogy of land tenure. While there are many different "kinds of Tenures in MERRYLAND," the 'Lease for Life' is the most common, 'tho not perhaps the best Tenure, is the most encouraged by Law." First the author describes how a marriage would have been negotiated in the 1600s and 1700s:

> When a Man resolves to take a Spot in MERRYLAND by this Tenure, he makes the best Agreement he can with the Proprietor of the Farm, and the Terms being concluded on, publick Notice is given, that he

designs speedily to enter into Possession, that any Person, who has just Objection to it, may forbid it before it is too late.[296]

The regular objections being that the man is infertile (incapable of manuring his Farm), or that he was already married to another women (having already another Farm on his Hands), and so on. The narrator also makes note of the new custom of getting a marriage license: "they sometimes purchase a License, which dispenses with the Ceremony of giving publick Notice." And then, if everything checks out, the man can proceed to a ritual to 'take control' of his 'farm.' The reason I touch on this final bit is because during the mid-1700s, when Stretzer was writing and Curll was publishing, there were a great deal of dramatic cultural shifts around the institution and regulations of marriage; shifts that have great impact on our story here. These shifts, that would cause obscenity and sex to become 'dangerous' and 'bad,' carry us into the

PART III: CLIMAX
(1741-1857)

6

1740 —1800: The Society for the Suppression of Fannies

Marriages, Privacies, Sexualities

T HE ROLE OF FAMILY, SEX, AND MARRIAGE prior to the Renaissance and the Reformation were dramatically different from the types of society that developed afterwards, and incredibly alien and removed from our current situation. Until the 16th century, the home the home lacked the boundaries we are familiar with today know. Lawrence Stone characterizes it this way: "[I]t was open to support, advice, investigation and interference from outside, from neighbors and from kin; and internal privacy was nonexistent."[297]

Stone, of course, has received a great deal of recent criticism for taking his argument perhaps a bit too far, but this characterization remains essentially right—the prereformation household was a much more open institution than we would be familiar with today. Marriage, too, was a very different intuition—as Martin Ingram observes, "essentially marriage was 'till death us do part'. Indeed in 1500 in the whole of western Europe, divorce in the modern sense – the dissolution of a valid union with the right to remarry – was anathema."[298] As we've already discussed, Protestants critiqued the idea of marriage as a sacrament and allowed more grounds for divorce than the Catholic Church had (incest, forced unions, or inability to consummate), but still retained an essentially conservative position.

For the most part, among the lower, middle and much of the upper classes, marriages were rarely forcefully arranged. Instead, marriages usually involved trying to get the consent of every involved party within a rational negotiation, with more or less groups involved the further up or down the social scale one was. Although, as David Kertzer points out, parents still controlled the places and situations that young people met and interacted in, thereby controlling and policing their behavior and possible outcomes. Sexual passion and love were seen as a negative, not a positive, indicator for the success of the marriage as a whole—in general, uncontrolled passion was seen as a destructive force to be controlled and dissipated if possible. To a contemporary of Shakespeare, the tragedy of Romeo and Juliet was not so much that they were star-crossed lovers, but that they violated the norms and rules of their society to go against family wishes and common sense.

In many cases, the negotiations that took place before a marriage were seen and treated much like a private contract between two families exchanging property. For example, they often contained protections for the bride in the case of the death of, or divorce by, the husband. However, for those without property, a marriage became more of a private contract between two individuals like it is today. Regardless of how a marriage was established, its norms, boundaries and expected behavior was still strongly enforced by the larger community's sense of what was right and wrong.[299]

The unpropertied classes often tried to avoid a church ceremony as it was seen as unnecessary and expensive, "especially since divorce by mutual consent followed by remarriage was still widely practiced."[300] Eventually, even the lower classes were also increasingly forced to have a public church ceremonies. The definition of what an appropriate marriage was developed rather slowly, but eventually it came to a five-step process:

1) A contract between the families for financial arrangements and exchanges of property (in cases where there were finances or property to be exchanged).

2) The spousals—the exchange of promises spoken between the husband and wife in front of witnesses.

3) The proclamation of banns for three weeks prior to the marriage. The banns were a loud public announcement on behalf of the marrying couple for three weeks prior to the marriage, to allow people to dispute or contradict it.

4) The wedding in, and the blessing of, the church (when the wedding actually took place in a church).

5) Sexual Consummation. Legally speaking, anyhow —surviving evidence shows sexual consummation happened among the lower classes before the marriage in many cases.

It was this process of Lease for Life that the author of *Merryland* was commenting on. To him, these leases were dangerous because of infertility or incompatibility: "these long Leases have been the Ruin of many a substantial Farmer, for People are too apt to engage in a hurry, without due Consideration of the Consequence, or competent Knowledge of the Goodness of the Farm, which frequently proves to be a stubborn Soil, and makes the poor Farmer soon repent his Bargain; but there is no Remedy, the Man is bound, and must drudge on for Life."[301] Furthermore, infidelity could be an issue. In the case of the man, it didn't meet with as much disapproval: "they become ill Husbands, growing quite indolent and negligent of their Farm; and tho' they cannot throw up their Leases, they will let their Farms lie fallow, and clandestinely take another that is more agreeable to them." But husbands were cautioned to watch out for female adultery: "it is a difficult Matter to fence or enclose [women] so securely, [because] the neighbors, who are very apt to watch all Opportunities, may easily break into them."[302]

Much of this is old material for us, and has already been discussed, but there were several changes in family life and marriage that occurred in the late 17th century that moved it to a more recognizably modern shape. For example, parents began to allow their children increased freedom in choosing an appropriate spouse without oversight or express consent. The idea of soulmates and marriages for love alone were increasingly propagated throughout society by religious reformers such as the Society for the Reformation of Manners, because they thought it would prevent adultery and prostitution. The most profound change in family life however was the change in attitudes towards children over the course of the eighteenth and nineteenth century. Part of this shift came from the increasing identification of children as a special group, separate from adults, and the building up of their own institutions and culture such as schools or children's literature.[303]

Furthermore, adults increasingly tried to protect children from the knowledge and danger of death, and as health and successful medical outcomes increased, this became easier. Of course, the idea of children as a special status group needing particular protection started to develop all the way back in the Renaissance (if not earlier) with the philosophy of humanism, but from the 1500s onward, an increasingly larger proportion of children began to be educated. Many of these schools were church sponsored or affiliated. In England, this meant they were often controlled by the Anglican Church; in northern Germany by the Lutheran Church; and in France in Italy, the Catholic Church. But all three shared the Renaissance ideal of the purity and innocence of the child. Due to the Reformation and the Counter-Reformation, there developed a "deadly fear of the liability of children to corruption and sin."[304] The threat of religious, intellectual, and political chaos set off by the Reformation "induced moral theologians. . .to agree that the only hope of preserving social order was to concentrate on the right disciplining and education of children."[305] Thus, in a particularly convoluted way, one could argue the rise of flogging and spanking at home and in school became a sign of increasing respect and love of children.

Another manifestation of the increasing concern for children in the 1700s was the explosion of worry over the spiritual and physical dangers of masturbation and sexuality. This had been a concern for a while, but in 1710, an anonymous publication titled *ONANIA OR, the Heinous Sin OF Self-Pollution, AND All its Frightful Consequences* was published by a clergyman. It was an amazingly resounding success, posting sales numbers that would still be good today. By 1760, 50 years later, 38,000 copies had been sold in nearly 20 English editions, and it had rapidly been translated into French, German, Italian and Dutch. It was wildly successful in those editions as well, despite—or perhaps because of—its overwhelming moralizing and rather unlikely tales of resulting disease:

> IN [boys] it has been the Cause of fainting Fits and Epilepsies; in others of Consumptions; and many Young Men who were strong and lusty before they gave themselves over to this vice, have been worn out by it. . . . In Women SELF-POLLUTION if fre-

quently practis'd. . .makes 'em look pale, swarthy and haggard. It frequently is the Cause of Hysterick Fits, and sometimes, by draining away all the radical Moisture, Consumption.[306]

By the late 1700s, the tract and its ideas had convinced even legitimate scientists and doctors. One such doctor, the internationally celebrated Dr. Samuel-Auguste Tissot, gave the masturbation problem medical recognition. He cited cases of "masturbating youths - and maidens - falling victims to lassitude, epilepsy, convulsions, boils, disorders of the digestive, respiratory or nervous systems, and even death."[307] This support from a respected authority began: "a growing onslaught on masturbation in the late eighteenth and nineteenth centuries, which has been compared by one scholar with the witchcraft persecutions of the sixteenth century or with modern anti-semitism."

Although we will deal with this in later chapters, the *Onania* tract was the very first one to identify and specifically target 'evil books' as a cause for masturbation:

> SELF-POLLUTION is a Sin, not only against Nature, but a Sin, that perverts and extinguishes Nature, and he who is guilty of it, is labouring at the Destruction of his Kind, and in a manner strikes at the Creation it self. . .I Shall not here meddle with the Causes of Uncleanness in general, such as Ill Books, Bad Companions, Love-Stories, Lascivious Discourses, and other Provocatives to Lust and Wantonness

This is one point where the cultural tide began to turn against 'ill books,' but it would not reach peak fever until the mid-nineteenth century. The second thing of note in this section is the fact that there is a definite and final shift away from religious discourse to medicalized language. The success of the tract and the works that followed it meant that its argument that immoral actions had material, measurable, and biological impacts serves as the transition point from the power of religious discourse to the power of popular, professionalized, medical discourse. Doctors took up the cry of moralized danger and developed theories of *spermatorrhea* and perversion, which convinced the public and empowered the newly-developing and professionalizing field of medicine. The medicalized porn of Curll becomes hysterical medical tracts that declare physical effects of immorality.

One reason for the sudden rise in concern over masturbation came from the fact that children and adults now had privacy to do the things they wanted to do. Whereas houses prior to the mid-1500s had been designed as a series of connecting rooms which you had to walk through to get anywhere (for example, to get to the toilet in the middle of the night you might have to go through several other bedrooms), houses in the late 1600s onward utilized corridors and hallways, which were built with privacy in mind. Rooms now branched off from central corridors that people could walk through.[308] However, these innovations only applied to the upper and well-to-do middle classes, who could afford to purchase multiple rooms or have their houses redesigned. Up until the middle of the 1800s it was still common for the lower classes to share a bed amongst an entire family. As Beth Bailey observes

> Children commonly slept in the same room as their parents unless the family had uncommon wealth; when families were poor or winters were cold enough, the whole family might share one bed. There was no privacy for marital relations; children heard and saw adults having sex. Animals, too, were a source of sexual knowledge. Children saw animals copulating and giving birth; few adults saw any need

to protect children from such observations.[309]

For example, in Essex, court records recount a man having intercourse with a girl while her sister was in the same bed, and of a case in which the girl's mother was in the same bed. Another example is found in the diaries of Francis Place, who slept in the same bed as his brother alongside that of his parents for most of his young life. When he grew up and got married, for the first ten years of his married life he and his wife lived, slept and worked in the same room, during which time conceived and raised three children.

There also began to be other outward indicators of distinction between the middle/upper classes and the lower classes. This was in the rise and perpetuation of 'manners,' which very clearly marked off the uneducated lower classes from those taught proper manners. This included such things as the substitution of forks for fingers in eating, as previously forks had been seen as suspect and possibly devilish. Other manners, such as "supply by the host of separate plates and utensils for each course, the substitution of handkerchiefs for fingers or clothes for nose-blowing, the control of spitting, the wearing of nightclothes, the introduction of washbasins, portable bathtubs and soap, the substitution of wigs [and merkins] for lice-ridden natural hair" were also developed and encouraged during this century in every European home that wanted to seem 'civilized.'[310] To Stone, the motive behind all of these 'refinements of manners' is clear:

> It was a desire to separate one's body and its juices and odours from contact with other people, to achieve privacy in many aspects of one's personal activities, and generally to avoid giving offence to the 'delicacy' of others. The odour of stale sweat, which had been taken for granted for millennia, was now beginning to be thought offensive. . .[and finally] sexual activity and excretion became more

---

Brian M. Watson

private.[311]

These 18th century shifts in culture, and the development of separate behavior for public and private life, combined with fears over masturbation and arguments for protecting the children, would eventually manifest in the regulation of obscenity and pornography. First in the book market, and then later in photography and film regulation. The first salvo in the reformation of the book market came from truly unexpected source—Samuel Richardson and his novel *Pamela or, Virtue Rewarded*, in 1740.

Cultivating the Principles of Virtue and Religion

SAMUEL RICHARDSON (1689-1761) was a tremendously successful English printer before he ever began writing moralistic tales. Born in Derbyshire to parents that were relatively middle-class, Richardson would go on to become one of the most famous novelists in the world. Although his father wanted him to become a clergyman, the family could not afford to send him to theology school, so his father asked him to choose his own career. The young Richardson picked printing as his career path, largely because he enjoyed reading as a child. As was usual, he was apprenticed as a young boy to a master printer known as John Wilde, and he dedicated himself to his apprenticeship with great fervor and talent. This ended up catching the eye of Wilde's daughter, Martha, and by 1721 they had married and started their own printing shop in London. In their ten years of marriage, he would have five sons and one daughter with Martha, but by 1731 they had all died, along with Martha—a demonstration of just how common it was for death to carry off entire families. Richardson was obviously devastated, and it is reflected in his later work, but he threw himself into his work as a distraction. A year later, he married Elizabeth Leake, and they would go on to have four daughters together, all of whom survived, and one son, who died after a year.

Among all these events, he also found time to begin his own writing career. In 1733 he wrote a sort of self-help advice guide in the style of Donald Trump for apprentices that wanted to be as successful as him—the key was to be ascetic and pure, denying oneself all the pleasures (and corrupting influences) of theaters, taverns, and gambling. The dangers associated with these institutions—the same institutions the Society for the Reformation of Manners took issue with—was always foremost in his mind and his writing, and would go on to inform the rest of his writing. In 1739, a friend asked him to write "a little volume of Letters, in a common style, on such subjects as might be of use to those country readers, who were unable to [compose them] for themselves."[312] As historian Susan Whyman puts it, these letters were "written in the form of mini-narratives about ordinary events," which allowed common people to copy them and adapt them to their own situations.[313] One of these letters was from a "young servant girl in danger of amorous advances from her master. This gave Richardson an idea for a book and he unexpectedly created *Pamela* in two months, writing at a furious pace."[314] And because he was a master printer, he had all of the contacts and connections that a successful printer would, and used these to great profit.

From the beginning to the end of Richardson's novel it is very clear that he had ulterior motives in writing and publishing it. Indeed, the title page speaks for itself:

> PAMELA : or, Virtue Rewarded. In a SERIES of Familiar Letters from a Beautiful Young Damsel, To her PARENTS. Now first Published In order to cultivate the Principles of Virtue and Religion in the Minds of the Youth of Both Sexes. A Narrative which has its Foundation in TRUTH and NATURE; and at the same

time that it agreeably entertains, by a Variety of
curious and affecting Incidents, is entirely divested
of all those Images, which, in too many Pieces calculated for Amusement only, tend to inflame the
Minds they should instruct.[315]

This broadside against the perceived immorality of literary culture is carried into the Preface, where Richardson
argues that his goals are "to Divert and Entertain, and at the
same time to Instruct, and Improve the Minds of the Youth of
both Sexes. . .to set forth in the most exemplary Lights, the
Parental, the Filial, and the Social Duties, and that from low
to high Life. . .to give practical Examples, worthy to be followed in the most critical and affecting Cases, by the modest
Virgin, the chaste Bride, and the obliging Wife."[316] If Richardson sounds a bit defensive here, he had good reason to be—he
knew that a certain scene in the book caused a small amount
of controversy among the reading public of France and England.

As Bradford Mudge puts it, the introductory pages prepared
the reader for "an entirely new genre-- the moral romance
novel in which good triumphs over evil and all conflicts
disappear into the happily-ever-after of the marriage ceremony."[317] The scandals, heroic adventures, and sinners are replaced by, "the perfect, normal, British marriage, predicated
of course on an ideal femininity finding at once true love,
the perfect mate, and lots of money," or as Erin Syke Mackie
might put it, the novel killed the rake, highwayman and pir-
ate-star.[318]

To a modern reader the plot of *Pamela* is so moralistic and
predictable as to be boring, but that is only because we have
had the benefit of nearly three centuries experience with the
romance novel and its formulaic plot, still followed to the letter by modern authors such as Nora Roberts or Susan Mallery.
However, in Richardson's day, *Pamela* was a "vigorous attempt

to reform the romance novel that had been popularized [by women.] [It] attempted to redefine the romance novel to make it at once more realistic and more moral."[319] Yet, in taking an attractive young heroine from the 'real world' and "exposing her to possible and plausible adventures lively enough to 'catch young and airy Minds, and when Passions run high in them, to shew how they might be directed to laudable Meanings and Purposes," Richardson hit upon something new, the perfect combination for his age and its gradually expanding reading public—he produced an entirely new genre of writing.[320]

There is no room or reason to examine the entirety of *Pamela's* plot at length here—a spoiler-filled summary will have to suffice. *Pamela* concerns a girl (obviously) named Pamela Andrews, who is a servant of a certain 'Lady B.' After the death of Lady B, her son, Mr. B, begins to take notice of Pamela and starts a ridiculous seduction campaign—at one point he jumps out of a closet while she is undressing for bed and tries to seduce her, only to be rejected. Pamela considers leaving his service to maintain her virtue, but the rapacious Mr. B catches word of this and takes her prisoner in another house, far away from any help. She is imprisoned by the horrible Mrs. Jewkes, whom she suspects of the worst possible trait: "for my master, bad as I have thought him, is not half so bad as this woman—To be sure she must be an atheist!"[321]

As Bradford Mudge has argued demonstrated conclusively in a recent article, "*Pamela* is unrelenting in its celebration of female chastity, for example, its narrative energy is utterly dependent on voyeurism and the ongoing threat of rape."[322] Indeed, the novel meets its ultimate emotional climax when Mr. B has Mrs. Jewkes (representing the whore) hold Pamela (the virgin) down for an attempted rape, whereupon she faints dead away, resisting the advances of the evil man and cutting off the narration. Curiously, she notes later on that she "cannot answer for the liberties taken with her in her deplorable

State of Death," but conveniently the episode causes Mr. B to repent and to "realize" that he cannot take her by force.[323] He decides he must marry her, leaving her chastity intact and rewarding her for her virtue. The novel ends safely in a socially-acceptable middle-class marriage, where the rapacity of the aristocracy has been tamed by the virtues of the working class. It is a testament to the cultural conflict over the shifting nature of marriage that the final major conflict in the book is between Mr. B and his sister, Lady Danvers, who has been fighting for an aristocratic marriage for her brother. As final evidence of his reformation, he casts Lady Danvers out and marries Pamela for love.

Despite (or perhaps, because of) the fact that *Pamela's* plot is more than a little scandalous—with its kidnapping and attempted rape of a 15-year-old—the book became immensely popular. It was the sort of novel that set a type for everything following it; there is a distinct before and after in the history of books, and also in the history of British — and European— morals. Dabhoiwala notes that the impact of Richardson's "portrayal of male rapacity and female seduction was enormous—not just on English attitudes in the later 18th and 19th centuries, but on literate culture across the whole of the western world."[324] *Pamela* was also perhaps the first major cultural marketing phenomenon—there were *Pamela* prints and paintings, *Pamela* playing cards and fans, and there were both encouraging and angry reactions.[325] One contemporary pamphleteer remarked upon this, nothing that there were in "particular among the ladies two different parties, *Pamelists* and *Antipamelists*," who disagreed as to "whether the young virgin was an example for ladies to follow. . .or. . .a hypocritical crafty girl. . .who understands the art of bringing a man to her lure."[326] These Pamelists and Antipamelists let their opinions be known; within a year of *Pamela's* publication, there appeared positive reactions (*Pamela Commedia, Pamela's Conduct in High Life*), and negative (*Pamela Censured, The True*

Anti-Pamela). Henry Fielding's anti-Pamela had a particularly amusing title: *Shamela — An Apology for the Life of Mrs. Shamela Andrews: In which, the many notorious Falsehoods and Misrepresentations of a Book called Pamela are exposed and refuted; and all the matchless arts of that young Politician set in a true and just Light.*[327] Two other works can also be characterized as reactions to *Pamela*, and as it happens, they are the two most notorious works of pornography to originate out of the 18th century: *Fanny Hill, or Memoirs of a Woman of Pleasure* (1748), and *Justine or, The Misfortunes of Virtue* (1791).

Fanny Hill: "The Most Depraved Fantasy of a Feverish Mind"

IF YOU WERE TO ASK someone to name a work of classic erotica or pornography, chances are they might come up with *Fanny Hill*, which is an indicator of just how popular and enduring the work is, since it was published in 1748; over 250 years ago. Much in the same way that *Pamela* set the typology for all novels to follow, *Fanny Hill* set the typology for all erotic works to follow, and it set that bar high. From its first-page promise of "Truth! stark, naked, truth!" to its closing pages, it does not fail to live up to the subtitle 'Memoirs of Woman of Pleasure.'

The author of what is arguably the first pornographic novel in English and in Europe was John Cleland (1709-1789), the son of William, a civil servant and an officer in the British Army, and Lucy Cleland. The young Cleland grew up in a wealthy household and attended the prestigious Westminster school until 1723, when he was expelled for reasons that are unclear. He went on to serve in the British East India Company in Bombay, India, until 1740, when he returned home to his father's deathbed. When his mother took control of the Cleland estate, she chose not to support him, and he ran up high debts trying to find a new career in London. In 1748, at the age of 40, he was thrown into debtor's prison for failing to pay his debts, and he wrote the work that became known as *Fanny Hill* in an attempt to pay off his debts. The fact that he thought a pornographic novel could pay off his debt goes to show just how successful Edmund Curll had been in making sexy material commercial.

There is evidence to suggest that Cleland's original idea for *Fanny Hill* dates as far back as 1730, as there are records of it being read at a secret Scottish erotic book club called 'The Most Ancient and Most Puissant Order of the Beggar's Benison and Merryland' (the very same Merryland!). Their records read:

> 1737. St. Andrew's Day. 24 met, 3 tested and enrolled. All frigged [all 24 masturbated]. The Dr. expatiated. Two nymphs, 18 and 19, exhibited as heretofore. Rules were submitted by Mr. Lumsdaine for future adoption. Fanny Hill was read. Tempest. Broke up at 3 o'clock a.m.[328]

More than casual fans of John Cleland will note that this is quite remarkable—this is nearly a decade before the (public) publication of *Fanny Hill*, and Cleland was in India at the time, a mystery which remains somewhat curious—the likely answer being that this was an early draft for private circulation, which was common for erotic texts in the 18th century. Cleland's connection with one of the Benison members named Robert Cleland is tantalizing—but as of yet unexplained. But in the course of a couple months in debtor's prison, Cleland hammered out the fine details of the cast and plot, and wrote a second volume to accompany it—all for the desperately low pay of £21. Either way, *Fanny Hill* could not have existed in the form and format it exists today if it were not for the publication of *Pamela* in 1740—Cleland's novel was both a satire against and an imitation of Richardson's work.

Figure 7. First episode of Hogarth's A Harlot's Progress

The other source that Cleland is indebted to is *A Harlot's Progress*, a series of six moralistic engravings by William Hogarth that tell a story, much in the same way of his other artwork, such as *A Rake's Progress* or *The Four Stages of Cruelty*, did. Hogarth's moralistic tales were both wildly popular and wildly mocked during Cleland's lifetime. In the first scene, the main character, Moll Hackabout, arrives in London. She is being inspected by a brothel-keeper named Elizabeth Needham, who is covered in pox-scars, and wants to sell Moll as a prostitute. By the second scene, Moll has become a kept woman (mistress) of a wealthy Jewish merchant. Everything about her screams pretentious; she keeps an Indian serving boy and a monkey. The apartment is decorated with paintings that symbolize her promiscuous state. In the third scene, everything has begun to fall apart, Moll has gone from kept woman to common prostitute. Her bed is her only major piece of furniture and a policeman is coming through the door with three armed bailiffs to arrest her. The fourth scene shows Moll slaving away in Bridewell, a prison that attempted to reform prostitutes, and by the fifth scene she is dying of syphilis. The sixth and final scene of *A Harlot's Progress* shows the ultimate conclusion to Moll's scandalous life, her early death, dying son, and scavengers stealing all of her possessions.

John Cleland's *Fanny Hill* however, is a sort of 'alternate history' of Hogarth's *Harlot's Progress* and Richardson's *Pamela*. Fanny is described similarly to Pamela, having a "foundation in virtue [created by] a total ignorance of vice, and the shy timidity general to our sex."[329] Having lost both of her parents, a distant friend recommends she go to London to make her fortune. On the way to London, the friend amusingly sums up the plot of *Pamela*:

[S]he told me, after her manner and style, as how several maids out of the country had made themselves and all their kin for ever: that by preserving their VIRTUE, some had taken so with their masters, that they had married them, and kept them coaches, and lived vastly grand and happy; and some, may–hap, came to be Duchesses; luck was all, and why not I, as well as another?[330]

Finally, as in the first scene of *Harlot's Progress*, Fanny arrives in London, is ditched by her friend, and makes her way to a job office all alone, where a woman picks her up as a servant. This woman, Mrs. Brown, is a brothel-keeper and a procuress, a woman who obtains other women for prostitution. Although this scene of an innocent maid being seduced into the life of a prostitute may be hyperbole, it was one that was frequently referenced in literature and by moralists of the time. It also ignores female autonomy and women who chose themselves to belong to the *demi-monde*. Fanny is of course too innocent to realize what is happening at the house, but soon enough she is seduced and educated by Phoebe, her bedfellow (as it was common to share beds in this era). Phoebe, who has been selected by Mrs. Brown as Fanny's "tutoress-elect, to whose care and instructions I was affectionately recommended," is very forward with her.[331] Fanny's description of this night shows her innocence and seduction at the hands of the Phoebe, who:

> [T]urned to me, embraced and kiss'd me with great eagerness. This was new, this was odd; but imputing it to nothing but pure kindness, which, for aught I knew, it might be the London way to express in that manner, I was determin'd not to be behind hand with her, and returned her the kiss and embrace, with all the fervour that perfect innocence knew.
>
> Encouraged by this, her hands became extremely free, and wander'd over my whole body, with touches, squeezes, pressures, that rather warm'd and surpriz'd me with their novelty, than they either shock'd or alarm'd me. . .her lascivious touches had lighted up a new fire that wanton'd through all my veins. . .I was transported, confused, and out of myself; feelings so new were too much for me.[332]

It seems to Fanny that she is really to be a maid, as Mrs. Brown did "not care that I should be seen or talked to by any, either of her customers," but really she was doing business behind Fanny's back, securing a good price for her virginity. Indeed, Mrs. Brown finds someone willing to pay a high price, though he is described as terribly ugly.

Up until this point, the plot of *Fanny Hill* reads like a combination of Hogarth's and Richardson's work, as it has all of the symbolic characters and plot elements: A powerless girl forced to work for a living, kidnapped and imprisoned at 15 by a brothel madam, who has her virginity sold to the affluent "Lord B" and has her attempted rape assisted by a whorish older woman. Even the Lord B seems to be Cleland's wink at Richardson's 'Mr. B.' Luckily for Fanny, the man fails to have sex with her as he is unable to perform and she manages to escape. This having been her first experience with men, she was horrified and disturbed, to the point of being sick.

However, Phoebe takes very good 'care' of Fanny; she recovers her health and begins to interact with the other women, whose conversations begin to corrupt her:

> Conversation. . .in that house, to corrupt[ed] my native purity, which had taken no root in education; whilst not the inflammable principal of pleasure, so easily fired at my age, made strange work within me, and all the modesty I was brought up in the habit, not the instruction of, began to melt away like dew before the sun's heat; not to mention that I made a vice of necessity, from the constant fears I had of being turn'd out to starve.[333]

These conversations, along with Phoebe's "talents in giving me the first tinctures of pleasure...explain'd to me all the mysteries of Venus. But I could not long remain in such a house as that, without being an eye–witness of more than I could conceive from her descriptions." Peeking through holes in the wall one day (these convenient holes and cracks in walls go all the way back to Pietro Aretino), she sees a couple having intercourse:

> [T]he sound and sight of which thrill'd to the very soul of me, and made every vein of my body circu-

> late liquid fires: the emotion grew so violent that it
> almost intercepted my respiration. Prepared then,
> and disposed as I was by the discourse of my com-
> panions, and Phoebe's minute detail of everything,
> no wonder that such a sight gave the last dying blow
> to my native innocence. [334]

In a probably too-neat (and most likely intentional) parallel to Pietro Aretino's Nanna, Fanny is overcome by this experience and it leads to her masturbation, , "I stole my hand up my petticoats, and with fingers all on fire, seized, and yet more inflamed that center of all my senses. . .and following mechanically the example of Phoebe's manual operation. . .brought on at last the critical extasy."[335] This is the moment where she discovers sexual pleasure and begins to look out for herself. Immediately thereafter, in a twist that is perhaps the most un-realistic in the novel, Fanny meets and falls in love with a man named Charles. Indeed, her description of him is so over-the-top and idealized it could have come straight out of *Pamela*:

> But when I drew nearer, to view the sleeping one,
> heavens! What a sight! No! no term of years, no turn
> of fortune could ever erase the lightning–like im-
> pression his form made on me. . .a fair stripling,
> between eighteen and nineteen. . .a face on which
> all the roseate bloom of youth and all the manly
> graces conspired to fix my eyes and heart. . .his eyes,
> closed in sleep, displayed the meeting edges of their
> lids beautifully bordered with long eyelashes; over
> which no pencil could have described two more
> regular arches than those that grac'd his forehead,
> which was high, perfectly white and smooth. Then
> a pair of vermilion lips, pouting and swelling to the
> touch, as if a bee had freshly stung them[336]

Charles is also struck by her beauty, and helps her escape

from the brothel. As historian Peter Wagner puts it in his *Eros Revived*, "Fanny has found her true love in a brothel; but she must leave the world of prostitution for this love to develop in a place more acceptable for a middle-class audience. Hence Charles deflowers Fanny not in a bawdy-house, but in a public house, where both become aware of their love for each other."[337] And even Fanny's description of his penis is over-the-top and almost comical in its baroqueness:

> [I fixed] my eyes on that terrible machine, which had, not long before, with such fury broke into, torn, and almost ruin'd those soft, tender parts of mine that had not yet done smarting with the effects of its rage; but behold it now! crest fall'n, reclining its half–capt vermilion head over one of his thighs, quiet, pliant, and to all appearance incapable of the mischiefs and cruelty it had committed. Then the beautiful growth of the hair, in short and soft curls round its root, its whiteness, branch'd veins, the supple softness of the shaft, as it lay foreshort'd, roll'd and shrunk up into a squab thickness, languid, and borne up from between his thighs by its globular appendage, that wondrous treasure–bag of nature's sweets, which, rivell'd round, and purs'd up in the only wrinkles that are known to please, perfected the prospect, and all together formed the most interesting moving picture in nature, and surely infinitely superior to those nudities furnish'd by the painters, statuaries, or any art, which are purchas'd at immense prices...[338]

This romantic idyll cannot last, however, and Charles suddenly disappears—much to the dismay of Fanny, who is pregnant, and miscarries the baby. Then, to make matters worse, the evil landlady of the public house sets on her, demanding money or the use of her body for prostitution:

In this situation I sat near half an hour, swallow'd up in grief and despair, when my landlady came in. . .telling me she had brought a very honourable gentleman to drink tea with me, who would give me the best advice how to get rid of all my troubles. Upon which, without waiting for a reply, she goes out, and returns with this very honourable gentleman, whose very honourable procuress she had been, on this as well as other occasions.[339]

This is the point where Cleland's satire of Richardson's *Pamela* is at its best, and indeed, his novel is much more realistic; this 'honorable gentleman' places his hand on Fanny's breast, and she faints dead away. . .awakening to find him not repentant, but "buried in me."[340] These experiences teach Fanny that money is the most important thing to secure her happiness. So she thereafter becomes the 'kept mistress' of this man, Mr. H, managing to go 'up a level' in whoredom. According to an anonymous pamphlet published in 1758 there were various levels of "Whores in the Metropolis," from highest to lowest:

> **Women of Fashion**, who intrigue (An upper class woman who has affairs)
> **Demi-Reps** (married women who had sexual affairs)
> **Good-natured Girls** (Talented women such as actresses)
> **Kept Mistresses** (Women 'kept' by upper class men)
> **Ladies of Pleasure** -- (who live in a 'genteel brothel house,' for upper class men)
> **Whores** (who live in an infamous 'bawdy house,' for lower class men)
> **Park-Walkers**
> **Street-Walkers**
> **Bunters** (someone who picks rags off the street, a destitute prostitute)
> **Bulk-mongers** (a prostitute who plies her trade from

the benches below shop fronts)[341]

By becoming the 'kept mistress' of Mr. H, Fanny went from being a 'whore' to being a 'Kept Mistress' and achieved a greater level of prestige and income for herself. She does not remain Mr. H's kept mistress for long, however, mainly because she refuses to give in to the double standards for men and women of the time. When Fanny catches Mr. H with a maid, she is so outraged that she immediately seduces Mr. H's footman Will to get her revenge. Even though society would have seen it as normal for Mr. H have both a kept mistress and to have sex with other, lower class women, like maids, Fanny is still upset and retaliates. In the end, Mr. H eventually discovers Fanny and Will in the act, and throws her out on the streets.

By this point however, Fanny is in a much more comfortable financial position and has much greater knowledge, so she is able to get a position as a Lady of Pleasure, in an upper-class brothel house, owned by a Mrs. Cole. In this establishment she undergoes—and recounts in great detail—many sexual adventures including flagellation, sadomasochistic sex, orgies and so on, before being reunited with Charles at the end of the novel. In many cases, these stories seem like outright plagiarizing from earlier sources such as the Boccaccio or Chorier, which I suppose shows how desperate Cleland was to make that £21. Each of these episodes are purely sexual, and the concluding narratives of the story could be reduced to a series of sexual positions and activities, much like a modern pornographic film.

The end of *Fanny Hill* arrives soon after this laundry-list of sexventures in a *deus ex machina* fashion. Sufficiently well-off, Fanny leaves Mrs. Cole's brothel and takes a "pleasant convenient house at Marylebone. . .which I furnish'd neatly and modestly. There, with a reserve of eight hundred pounds [I lived] under the new character of a young gentle–woman whose husband was gone to sea."[342] One day, when walking in the countryside, Fanny sees a "well-dressed elderly gentle-man, who, attack'd with a sudden fit, was so much overcome as to be forc'd to give way to it and sit down at the foot of a tree, where he seemed suffocating with the severity of it. . .I flew on the instant to his relief, and using the rote of practice I had observ'd on the like occasion, I loosened his cravat and clapped him on the back," and saved him.[343] As it turns out, he is wealthy and has a good reputation, and takes her up as a mistress out of gratitude.

When he dies, he leaves his entire fortune to her, and "after acquitting myself of my duty towards my deceas'd benefactor, and paying him a tribute of unfeign'd sorrow," Fanny looks upon her prospects. She was still "in the full bloom and pride of youth (for I was not yet nineteen) [and] at the head of so large a fortune." Soon thereafter, she meets up again with Charles, her one true love. Charles, as it turns out, was kidnapped by his father when his father learned that he was consorting with a common woman. Furthermore, he was now destitute, having lost all of his wealth and he says that he "had it not in his power to make [Fanny] as happy as he could wish." But no fear!—for Fanny reveals to him that she is now fabulously wealthy and they can live in happiness.

Fanny's rise from nothing to the height of success is in many ways a 'moralistic' satire or a lesson in virtue. At least, according to Fanny; she says that she got "snug into port, where, in the bosom of virtue, I gather'd the only uncorrupt sweets." She is aware of the irony of that statement in light of her past:

> You laugh, perhaps, at this tail-piece of morality, extracted from me by the force of truth, resulting from compar'd experiences: you think it, no doubt, out of place, out of character; possibly too you may look on it as the paltry finesse of one who seeks to mask a devotee to Vice under a rag of a veil, impudently smuggled from the shrine of Virtue. . .[but] if you do me justice, you will esteem me perfectly

consistent in the incense I burn to Virtue. If I have
painted Vice in all its gayest colours, if I have deck'd
it with flowers, it has been solely in order to make
the worthier, the solemner sacrifice of it, to Virtue.
[344]

Indeed, Cleland was perhaps painting vice in very gay
colors when he described—in great detail—a homosexual encounter between two men. Even though she describes the encounter as reprehensible, disgusting and criminal, and the rest
of Cleland's book downplays lesbianism and prizes heterosexuality, the scene itself set off warning bells, and it is likely
that Cleland went 'too far.' The scene in question:

Slipping, then, aside the young lad's shirt, and tucking it
up under his clothes behind, he shewed to the open air those
globular fleshy eminences that compose the Mount Peasants
of Rome, and which now, with all the narrow vale that inter-
sects them, stood displayed and exposed to his attack; nor
could I without a shudder behold the dispositions he made for
it. First, then, moistening well with spittle his instrument, obviously to make it glib, he pointed, he introduced it, as I could
plainly discern, not only from its direction and my losing
sight of it, but by the writhing, twisting and soft murmured
complaints of the young sufferer; but at length, the first straits
of entrance being pretty well go through, every thing seemed
to move and go pretty currently on, as on a carpet road, without much rub or resistance...

The criminal scene they acted, I had the patience to
see to an end, purely that I might gather more facts
and certainty against them in my design to do their
deserts instant justice; and accordingly, when they
had re-adjusted themselves; and were preparing to
go out, burning as I was with rage and indignation,
I jumped down from the chair, in order to raise the
house upon them...these unsexed, male misses.

A 'criminal scene!' what a major shift in addressing homo-sexual intercourse from Aretino to Chorier to Cleland. In-creasingly so, the anxiety about male homosexual encoun-ters, specifically the encounters between younger and older men, was a greater and greater cultural worry, and, as we shall see, it carries us straight into the 20th century, through the Victorian era, and becomes one of the great battles of the 1900s. As Peter Wagner puts it, Cleland "broke one of the major 18th century sexual taboos. . .and when he was prosecuted for writing the novel. . .the passage about the homosexuals was at the center of the debate."[345] Further evi-dence for this comes from the fact that when Cleland created a censored edition in 1750 he did not include this passage, but when a piratical publisher with the extremely odd name of Drybutter reinserted the scene in 1757, he was put in the pil-lory. The scene never again appeared in modern editions.

Even though *Fanny Hill* ends within the confines of a safe, middle-class marriage, and Fanny becomes 'virtuous' at the end of the book, the work and its author were not seen as virtuous. In fact, they were seen as quite the opposite—Cle-land was first threatened with prosecution in November of 1749 and forced to pay fines, and then on March eighth of the following year, God himself prosecuted Cleland—at least, according to the Bishop of London. Bishop Thomas Sherlock, reacting to a series of earthquakes in London, wrote *A Letter on Occasion of the Earthquakes in 1750*, addressed to the people of London. In it, he declared that it was his "heart's desire and prayer to God. . .that you may be saved" from the "un-natural lewdnefs" England was immersed in, and he targeted *Fanny Hill* specifically as an "open insult on religion and good manners."[346] Cleland was again brought on trial, where he dis-avowed the book and wished it would be forgotten—and even "with God in his side, the Bishop of London could not bring about a prosecution for a literary crime whose status as a crime was culturally undefined."[347]

This is the importance of Cleland and *Fanny Hill*: it marked, for the first time, a type of erotic work that removed the social, moral and religious criticism that had been overtly present in earlier works and texts. It made sex and sexual escapades the forefront and sole purpose. In Cleland's work, pornography and sex become an aim in themselves, rather than a way to focus a social critique—porn for porn's sake. *Fanny Hill* is the first example of how pornography would develop and take off as a genre in the nineteenth century. The Bishop's failure to have Cleland prosecuted or satisfactorily punished was an example of a cultural crossroads, but in this case, it illustrated a gap, a weakness in the armor, between political and religious forces that usually worked in tandem. Cleland unwittingly walked into the same debate between religious and secular power that Curll had. However, as Cleland did not engage in the libels or cultural criticism that had doomed others, and just wrote erotica, the political powers-that-be did not necessarily see *Fanny Hill* as 'disturbing the King's peace.' Religious figures, however, saw Fanny as an 'open insult,' and their failure to get Cleland thrown in jail would eventually lead to the politically-oriented Society for the Suppression of Vice. This is a group which will be discussed in the next section, but it is enough right now to say that it was a religiously-organized and motivated group that used political methods to force the government to pass the Obscene Publications Act in 1857.

Unlike the unrepentant Curll, Cleland was duly chastised, and his next two books—*Memoirs of a Coxcomb* (1751), and the three-volume *The Woman of Honour* (1768)—did not even risk straying over the lines that *Fanny Hill* had crossed. Even if he had thought of writing a more pornographic novel for 1768's *Woman of Honour*, he would have been sharply reminded of the dangers of such a move by the 1763 conviction of John Wilkes for writing a dirty poem. Furthermore, towards the end of his life, in 1789, Cleland would find himself living in an era of changing mores and norms. Richardson's *Pamela*, which had been praised from the pulpit and "said to do more good than twenty sermons," became known as a scandalous work; in 1815 "a young lady looked over the shoulder of Charles Lamb as he was reading this same *Pamela*. She retreated very soon... [and] there was 'a blush between them.'"[348]

The Terrible Mistake of Virtue

FINALLY, WE COME to possibly the most infamous figure in our Annals of Pornographie—Donatien Alphonse François, the Divine Marquis—better known as the Marquis de Sade. This is what I mean when I call the 18th century the Golden Age for obscenity—the two figures of Cleland and de Sade (and a host of other writers and artists, major and minor) tower over this century and cast their shadow over the succeeding centuries. It would be hard to imagine how the genre of obscenity would develop into the genre of 'pornography' without these two. Their two most famous works, *Fanny Hill* and *Justine* were satires and reactions against the ridiculous optimism and moralism of *Pamela*. In their direct or indirect critiques of that book, they were also critiques of novelistic realism (*Fanny Hill*) or critiques of the philosophy of optimism and morality that created it (*Justine* and all of de Sade's other works).

This is not because the two authors and their texts used the same strategies, but because they did not. Cleland managed to survive prosecution and hard times at the hands of the English state by stripping his book of social, religious and political criticism. The closest he comes to it is in describing a homosexual act as reprehensible—a common view for his time. Cleland made pornography *stripped of* cultural criticism. The Marquis de Sade, however, made societal criticism *dressed in* pornography. While Cleland layered sexual act upon sexual act in the baroque explosion of *Fanny Hill*, de Sade wrote endless reams of books, plays and essays of critique upon every possible topic, but all originating from a single impulse: negation. In negating everything, the works of de Sade tear down sexual morality, religious decrees, the laws of the state and church, and even God himself. In doing this, de Sade marks both the pinnacle and the ultimate culmination of the combined cultural criticism/eroticism trend that we have traced from Aretino and through the rest. Future authors in the field of pornography would follow the style and strategy of Cleland, not de Sade. De Sade is the logical extension of and the destructor of the form. There has never really been anyone else like de Sade.

But we get ahead of ourselves. First, let's discuss the biography and the (hi)story of a man that spent nearly half his life imprisoned for his sins. Donatien Alphonse François de Sade, known as the Marquis de Sade, was born in 1740, to the Comte (Count) de Sade, who was a lord in Provence. The de Sade family line went back centuries; one of his ancestors was Laura de Noves, who Petrarch wrote his love poems to, thus kick starting Renaissance poetry and inspiring Boccaccio—things come full circle. Additionally, he was the only child in a large household, so he was absolutely fawned over. According to John Phillips, he was more or less raised by his father and his uncle, Abbé Jacques François de Sade, both of whom were well-known libertines. We have discussed libertines before, when we talked about Rochester, but as always, the French took the philosophy to an extreme level. By the time of de Sade's birth, 'libertine,' had come to mean that a person had an excessive and unfettered sex life, was frequently atheist, and attacked social and religious morals. As Phillips notes, the two men that raised Donatien were extreme libertines:

> [T]he lustful Abbé enjoyed liaisons with a number of society women and even visited some of the more notorious Parisian bordellos, while the bisexual Count was on one occasion arrested for accosting a young man in the Tuileries Gardens. At the same time, both were highly cultured men. Sade's father

was a close friend of Voltaire's and himself wrote verses, while Donatien's uncle in particular had a fine and extensive library which, alongside the classic authors, included all the major works of contemporary Enlightenment philosophy as well as a fair sample of erotic writings.[349]

Indeed, as a result of their education and care, de Sade would achieve the heights of both libertinism and cultural refinement.

Like Rochester, de Sade enlisted in the military after his education, to fight in the Seven Years' War, and he apparently distinguished himself over the course of the next few years as a great fighter against the British and a heroic figure under fire. Immediately after the war, however, he turned to more enjoyable pursuits like visiting plays and operas, seducing actresses, and running up incredible debts. Again, in striking similarity to Rochester, he was forced to marry a woman from a rich family who wanted to marry into the nobility; she was Renée-Pélagie de Montreuil. De Sade and Renée-Pélagie would have two sons and a daughter, and the de Sade family line survives to this day; the current descendant has done much to redeem his infamous name.

However, very shortly after the wedding, de Sade was arrested and thrown into jail for the first of many times. The reason, as it turned out, was that he had hired a prostitute named Jeanne Testard for a night of debauchery, but had shocked her sensibilities when he talked about, among other things, "masturbating into chalices and thrusting communion hosts into women's vaginas, and had then frightened her with whips and other weapons into committing a number of similar sacrilegious acts," with the exception of anal sex, as it was punishable by death in Paris.[350] He was imprisoned for a few months before being released, but the lesson did not stick, and a few years later he found himself in jail again for kidnapping a

36-year-old beggar named Rose Keller. According to trial transcripts, de Sade had spent the night subjecting her to whippings and pouring hot wax on her body before she jumped out a second story window and escaped to the police.[351] He was commanded to leave Paris and never return, but the stricture did not hold.

The Marquis took this in stride, but it wasn't very long until he landed himself in another scandal. Travelling to Marseilles with his valet to borrow money from a contact, de Sade promptly spent some of it in hiring four prostitutes for a night of debauchery. In addition to "acts of flagellation and sodomy," he also gave the women an 'aphrodisiac' which was intended "to cause flatulence, the effects of which Sade found particularly arousing. One of the girls became ill and complained to the authorities that Sade had tried to poison her." A warrant was soon issued for his arrest, but when the police arrived, they had already fled, "accompanied this time by the ravishing Anne-Prospère." Despite his wife's efforts to bribe the prostitutes to drop the charges, de Sade and his valet, Latour, were convicted and sentenced to death *in absentia.*[352]

The 'ravishing Anne-Prospère' that Phillips mentions was, in fact, his wife's sister. De Sade was undeniably attracted to her, as she "represented to de Sade all the taboos that his fictional characters would take such pleasure in breaking; virginity, incest and religion."[353] These were the biggest taboos that were assaulted in his works as manifestations of religious and social control, which de Sade loathed. Unfortunately for de Sade, Anne-Prospère's understandably upset mother succeeded in obtaining a *lettre de cachet* (which permitted arrest without a trial) against her son-in-law. After a series of cat-and-mouse escapes, Donatien was eventually thrown in the Bastille for 13 years, from 1777 to 1784.

It is impossible to deny the effects which that imprisonment had on the Marquis, indeed, if it were not for his access to pen and paper during his long periods of imprisonment, it is unlikely that he would have become a major writer in his lifetime. It seems like he turned all of his sexual energy and enthusiasm towards writing; by the end of his first period of imprisonment in 1788, he was able to list eight novels and short story volumes, two volumes of essays, twenty plays, and sixteen novellas. Of course, only a few of these survived the storming of the Bastille that kicked off the French Revolution —something, by the way, which the Marquis de Sade had a hand in instigating:

> In the months and weeks immediately preceding the storming of the Bastille on 14 July 1789, crowds of increasingly restive Parisians were in the habit of gathering underneath its walls. Sade quickly saw that the present unrest offered his best chance of freedom in 13 years and, improvising a megaphone from a long metal funnel that he used to empty his slops into the moat, he bellowed to the throngs below that the guards were about to cut the prisoners' throats. This provocative act immediately got Sade moved to the lunatic asylum at Charenton, a few miles south of Paris, where he could do no more harm. Ten days after the funnel incident, however, the citizens of Paris took his advice and invaded the fortress, murdering the governor.[354]

When he was released from prison, he managed to find work for a time with the Revolutionary government in several official positions, despite being an aristocrat. He eventually fell out of favor when he spoke against the death penalty and was imprisoned again for another year, barely managing to escape from being guillotined due to a clerical error. His name appeared on a list of men to be executed one day, but when he was called, he didn't say 'here!' (*ici!*), and was marked down as having disappeared. He also wrote his three most famous obscene works during this period: *Philosophy in the Bedroom, Justine,* and *Juliette.* Like Cleland, he was totally bankrupt, and had been forced to sell his castle in Lacoste just to support himself; he hoped that the obscene novels would sell enough to support him, and perhaps they did for a time, as *Justine* became a bestseller.

As some critics have pointed out, it is interesting that we know the Marquis as a pornographic writer first and foremost when in fact most of his works were not obscene or pornographic—out of the nearly 60 works he wrote, only four of them fall under the obscene: *120 Days of Sodom, Philosophy in the Bedroom, Justine,* and *Juliette.* Granted, if we're talking about sales numbers instead of total books, The Marquis is indeed a pornographic writer, as his 'dirty' books were insanely popular during his lifetime. When deciding which text to discuss here, it was easy to exclude *120 Days of Sodom*, as de Sade never managed to finish it—the scroll it was written on was looted when Parisians stormed the Bastille at the start of the French Revolution. It was not uncovered until 1904 by a German doctor named Iwan Bloch. It was written as a sort of catalog of every possible sexual depravity nearly 90 years before Richard von Krafft-Ebing would attempt the same thing in his field of 'sexology.' As a result, it is a rather brutal and uninspiring slog. *Juliette* also had to be rejected because of the insane length of the text—when combined with its prequel, it runs nonstop through 14 volumes, or 1300 pages; longer than *War and Peace.* Even a summary of it would probably take a book in and of itself. This leaves us with *Justine* or *Philosophy in the Bedroom*, of which *Justine* is the obvious choice, because of its impact and influence.

Originally, *Justine* was supposed to be a short story or novella called *Les infortunes de la vertu* (The Misfortunes of Virtue) and it was to be in the same sort of theme of Voltaire's *Candide* —showing how ridiculous and absurd it was to be virtuous in a world full of vice and exploitation. This first draft was written over the course of a two-week period when he was in the

Bastille, and largely lacked the obscenity or aggressive athe-ism that the two later versions did. However, he kept working on it and revising it, and in a reaction against the moralistic trend kicked off by *Pamela*, the text was eventually expanded into a full-length novel called *Justine, ou Les Malheurs de la vertu (Justine, or the Misfortunes of Virtue)*. It was published in 1791, a year after he was released from prison by the Revolutionary government. Although both titles translate to 'misfortunes of virtue' in English, the two words in French, *infortunes* and *malheurs*, are somewhat different. John Philips explains that:

> [W]hile Infortunes [the first story] connotes the un-fortunate fate suffered by virtue through no fault of its own, the ambiguity of Malheurs – ill-luck but also misery, the opposite of bonheur – seems to imply that virtue is itself a wretched state, and so anyone embracing it has only herself to blame. The juxtaposition of the heroine's name – Justine ou les Malheurs de la vertu – personalises the abstract title of the first version, focusing our attention on Justine as the source of her own misery.[355]

Bankrupt after being released from prison, de Sade likely wrote Justine as a way to make a quick buck and support him-self and his partner, Marie-Constance Quesnet. Cleland and de Sade thus prove that the greatest sex writing comes out of financial desperation. In a letter to his lawyer, de Sade wrote that his novel was being printed, but that it was "one too im-moral to send to a man as pious and as decent as you. I needed money, my publisher asked me for something quite spicy, and I made him [a book] capable of corrupting the devil. . . . Burn it and do not read it if by chance it falls into your hands: I re-nounce it."[356]

Even if this unlikely story is true and the editor had pres-sured de Sade for a 'spicy' novel, de Sade delivered tremendously, and the book became an explosive bestseller for the publisher, running through five editions in a decade, which says a lot about the literary tastes of the public of the bloody French Revolution. As with Cleland, de Sade never saw much of the money that greatly enriched his publisher. Even worse for de Sade, it made him a target of the authorities. When Napoleon took charge of France, he ordered de Sade's arrest, saying (anecdotally) that *Justine* was "the most abominable book ever engendered by the most depraved imagination."[357] According to the police reports, he was caught literally red-handed in his publisher's office, with a copy of *Justine's* sequel, *Juliette,* in his hands. He spent the rest of his life in jail—in "a sense then, de Sade fell victim to his own creation."

The three different versions of *Justine* all revolve around the same idea—Justine's (unreasonable) obsession with Christianity and virtue results in nothing but misfortune, and she is taken advantage of financially, socially, and sexually, by everyone she meets. She is framed for murder and robbery, raped, robbed, cast into the woods, chewed up by dogs, forced to work as a slave, and meets a number of other grisly misfortunes. Phillips comments that "Justine was originally conceived as a satire, attacking the corruption of contemporary institutions, including the judiciary, banking, and the bourgeois-dominated world of finances in general and, above all, the Catholic Church, with divine providence being the principal religious target."[358] In each of these episodes, de Sade attempts and succeeds to outdo himself, piling obscenity on top of obscenities.

In de Sade's forward to *Justine,* he says that his intention in the book is to show the world 'upside down,' to show a world where vice is rewarded and virtue is punished:

> [I will] present Vice triumphant and Virtue a victim of its sacrifices, to exhibit a wretched creature wandering from one misery to the next; the toy of villainy; the target of every debauch; exposed

to the most barbarous, the most monstrous ca-
prices; driven witless by the most brazen, the
most specious sophistries; prey to the most cun-
ning seductions, the most irresistible subornations;
for defense against so many disappointments, so
much bane and pestilence, to repulse such a quan-
tity of corruption having nothing but a sensitive
soul, a mind naturally formed, and considerable
courage: briefly, to employ the boldest scenes, the
most extraordinary situations, the most dreadful
maxims, the most energetic brush strokes, with the
sole object of obtaining from all this one of the sub-
limest parables ever penned for human edification.
[359]

In order to do this, *Justine* sets up a sort of 'ideal' scientific experiment between two sisters, Juliette and Justine, who are 15
and 12, respectively. These two sisters "received the best education; daughter[s] of a very rich Parisian banker, [they] had
been brought up. . .in one of the capital's most celebrated ab-
beys where, until the ages of twelve and fifteen years, the one
and the other of the two sisters had been denied no counsels,
no masters, no books, and no polite talents."[360] As a result, the
two girls are the very pinnacle of refinement and culture, the
ideal subjects for Sade's 'experiment.'

Suddenly, disaster strikes the idyllic situation; their father
is bankrupted, dies of grief, and is soon after followed by
their mother, leaving the girls alone and without any support.
Two distant relatives decide what should be done with them:
"No one caring to be burdened with them, the convent's door
was opened, their dowry was put into their hands, and they
were left at liberty to become what they wished." It becomes
quickly obvious which two different paths the sisters will
take:

Juliette spent a minute, perhaps two, wiping away

> Justine's tears, then, observing it was in vain, she fell
> to scolding instead of comforting her; she rebuked
> Justine for her sensitiveness; she told her, with a
> philosophic acuity far beyond her years, that in this
> world one must not be afflicted save by what affects
> one personally; that it was possible to find in oneself
> physical sensations of a sufficiently voluptuous pi-
> quancy to extinguish all the moral affections whose
> shock could be painful; that it was all the more es-
> sential so to proceed, since true wisdom consists in-
> finitely more in doubling the sum of one's pleasures
> than in increasing the sum of one's pains.[361]

Juliette is the ideal manifestation of vice, the pinnacle of corruption. She is de Sade's perfect libertine, and you can hear the
philosophies of de Sade and his friends in her lecture to her
younger sister. To Juliette, the future is clear: she points out
to her sister that they are young and have fine figures, so they
would not die of hunger. She gives the example of a neighbor's
daughter who escaped her family and was, "presently very
royally maintained and far happier, doubtless, than if she had
remained at home with her family." Juliette further cautions
Justine that she should, "take good care to avoid believing it is
marriage that renders a girl happy...instead of which, were she
to surrender herself to libertinage, she might always be able to
protect herself against her lovers' moods, or be comforted by
their number."[362]

Justine however, represents the school of thought that is
the opposite of de Sade's libertine philosophy, and as the representative of virtue on earth, she is horrified and terrified at
her sister's plans. She declares that she "preferred death to ig-
nominy [and] adamantly refused to take up lodging with her
[when] she saw Juliette bent upon conduct that caused her to
shudder."[363] Juliette, only interested in herself, simply shrugs
and, "the two girls separated without exchanging any prom-

ises to see each another again."[364] We learn at the end of the novel (or in the 14-volume *Juliette*) that the older sister goes on to become a tremendously wealthy and powerful woman who consorts (and cavorts) with kings, lords, and popes.

What would happen to Justine though? After the two sisters part, Justine decides to go see a woman she remembered fondly from her childhood, her mother's dressmaker. She finds the woman, tells the story of her misfortune, and asks for work, but the dressmaker barely recognizes her, and Justine is turned away rudely.

> "Oh Heaven!" cries the poor little creature, "must my initial steps in this world be so quickly stamped with ill-fortune? That woman once loved me; why does she cast me away today? Alas! 'tis because I am poor and an orphan, because I have no more means and people are not esteemed save in reason of the aid and benefits one imagines may be had of them."[365]

You can almost feel the Marquis sneering as he writes Justine's overly-sentimental dialogue. Because she is so religious, her next step is to go to a priest, because—surely—a priest would help her out of charity and his heart. She begs of him to help her, but his answer was that, "the parish was heavily loaded; that it could not easily take new charges unto its bosom, but that if Justine wished to serve him, if she were prepared for hard toil, there would always be a crust of bread in his kitchen for her." Then he gave her a kiss which "bespoke rather too much worldliness for a man of the church, and Justine, who had understood only too well, thrust him away."[366]

She briefly manages to find employment as a servant in the house of a loanshark. This loanshark, the Monsieur Harpin, tries to get Justine to steal a jewelry box filled with treasure from his neighbors. When she naturally refuses, Harpin just steals the box himself and hides it beneath her bed. The robbed neighbor raises the police, they search the building, find it, and throw her into jail. The evidence against her is too great and no one listens to her pleas of innocence, so she is sentenced to be executed. Although it may seem harsh, execution was the usual punishment for crime during the 18th century; both robbers and murderers were treated the same, as there were no long-term prisons. Having been personally rejected both by religion and society, Justine languishes in jail and comes within two days of being executed, before another prisoner, Madame Dubois, engineers a prison break. Dubois, like everyone else Justine meets, only helps the 'poor miserable creature' because she sees that the girl can be profitable. As soon as the pair are free, Dubois tries to recruit Justine into her band of highwaymen and murderers, arguing that:

> [T]he callousness of the Rich legitimates the bad conduct of the Poor. . . . Nature has caused us all to be equals born, Thérèse; if fate is pleased to upset the primary scheme of the general law, it is up to us to correct its caprices and through our skill to repair the usurpations of the strongest. I love to hear these rich ones, these titled ones, these magistrates and these priests, I love to see them preach virtue to us. It is not very difficult to forswear theft when one has three or four times what one needs to live; it is not very necessary to plot murder when one is surrounded by nothing but adulators and thralls unto whom one's will is law.[367]

Justine tries to refuse until she is nearly raped by the entire gang of men. She then reluctantly consents, but must give every one of them blowjobs or handjobs in order to convince them of her sincerity. She comments that "at least my honor was respected even though my modesty assuredly was not." [368]

Immediately after this first sex scene, the highwaymen fall

upon three travelers and murder them for their gold and possessions. While they are counting up their spoils, one of the men in the gang comments that it made no sense to kill three people for such a small sum, but Madame Dubois disputes this (and one hears Sade's hatred of the death penalty and full-throated atheism in her argument). She argues that the law is to blame, because "so long as thieves are hanged like murderers, thefts shall never be committed without assassinations. The two misdeeds are punished equally; why then abstain from the second when it may cover up the first?"[369] When the ever-vigilant and virtuous Justine disputes this, and says that such logic will lead to the thieves killing each other in the night for greater profit, Sade's voice enters the highwaymen themselves, and they begin to argue with her like learned philosophers:

> Your objections. . .are sophistries; our criminal fraternities are not by any means sustained by Virtue; rather by self-interest, egoism, selfishness; this eulogy of Virtue, which you have fabricated out of a false hypothesis, miscarries; it is not at all owing to virtuousness that, believing myself, let us suppose, the strongest of the band, I do not use a dagger on my comrades in order to appropriate their shares, it is because, thereupon finding myself all alone, I would deprive myself of the means which assure me the fortune I expect to have with their help; similarly, this is the single motive which restrains them from lifting their arms against me. Now this motive, as you, Thérèse, perfectly well observe, is purely selfish, and has not even the least appearance of virtue; he who wishes to struggle alone against society's interests must, you say, expect to perish; will he not much more certainly perish if, to enable him to exist therein, he has nothing but his misery and is abandoned by others? What one terms the interest of society is simply the mass of individual interests

unified.[370]

You begin to see why de Sade was so popular among the revolutionaries—until he was not. As is probably apparent from my tone, I find the reading, digestion and documentation of de Sade to be somewhat of a slog, as I characterized *120 Days,* above. To some extent, this is an intentional poling up of criticism on top of bitterness on top of eroticism that is just the style of de Sade—but to another extent, I feel, it is due to the fact that he spent so much of his life confined by society, the state, and then his family. To build an monumental pornographic Babel in hopes of toppling them all down was de Sade's one potential escape.

Shortly thereafter, the highwaymen capture a young noble in the woods and imprison him, thinking they can ransom him for more money. Heroically, Justine risks her life and what little money she has to rescue him and get him home. As de Sade points out she is not *completely* pure, as she has the ulterior motive of hoping this young nobleman can save her from the life of poverty and endangerment to her virtue she has found herself in. The young man, far from being grateful, sees through Justine's charity and regards this as her trying to get something for nothing. When they go down a path in the woods the trope of 'falling unconscious at sexual danger' from *Pamela* and *Fanny Hill* reappears:

> "We have arrived, whore," the villain replied, toppling me with a blow of his cane brought down upon my head; I fell unconscious. . . . Oh, Madame, I have no idea what that man afterward said or did; but the state I was in when I returned to my senses advised me only too well to what point I had been his victim. It was darkest night when I awoke; I was at the foot of a tree, away from any road, injured, bleeding. . .dishonored, Madame; such had been the reward of all I had just done for the unlucky man;

and carrying infamy to its ultimate degree, the wretch, after having done to me all he had wished, after having abused me in every manner, even in that which most outrages Nature, had taken my purse. . .containing the same money I had so generously offered him.[371]

Utterly lost and with no money or supplies, Justine stumbles around in the woods and comes across a couple of men having homosexual intercourse. To sum up the small bit of plot that de Sade jams in between the paragraphs of sexual detail and cultural criticism, two men are Monsieur de Bressac and his servant. They move to kill her, but after she begs and pleads with them, they decide she will be useful to them as a personal servant to de Bressac's aunt. Justine manages to find happiness and comfort in this position for a few years, but unable to help herself, she falls in love with de Bressac and tries to save him from his sinful homosexual inclinations. The young man, however, defends his inclinations with a passion that would not be out of place today:

Do not suppose, [Justine], we are made like other men; 'tis an entirely different structure we have; and, in creating us, Heaven has ornamented the altars at which our Celadons sacrifice with that very same sensitive membrane which lines your temple of Venus. . .but we have in addition to them our own, and it is this delicious combination which makes us of all men on earth the most sensitive to pleasure, the best created to experience it; it is this enchanting combination which renders our tastes incorrigible, which would turn us into enthusiasts and frenetics were one to have the stupidity to punish us. . .which makes us worship, unto the grave itself, the charming God who enthralls us.[372]

And, less than a page later, de Bressac extends this critique of society to religion, picking up exactly where the highwaymen left off. He asks how religion can merit any sort of respect: "mysteries which cause reason to shudder, dogmas which outrage Nature, grotesque ceremonies which simply inspire derision and disgust. . . . What is [Jesus] but a leprous Jew who, born of a slut and a soldier in the world's meanest stews, dared fob himself off for the spokesman of him who, they say, created the universe!" He goes on to proclaim that, "I should prefer to die a thousand deaths rather than believe [religion]. When atheism will wish for martyrs, let it designate them; my blood is ready to be shed." This idyll comes to a close when de Bressac uses Justine's love of him in attempting to coerce her to poison his aunt, with the goal of inheriting the estate and her money. Justine pretends to be taken in by him and agrees to help him, only to turn around and confess directly to his intended target. He poisons the aunt anyhow, inherits another 80,000 from a dying uncle, and has Justine chewed up by his dogs and dumped into the woods, proving that vice is always rewarded and virtue always punished.

It seems that these episodes are meant to show that if the virtuous were really virtuous, they wouldn't be duplicitous like Justine is here—de Sade is saying that they get off on being self-serving and holier than thou, and indeed the young nobleman calls Justine out for this when she begs them to remember what she did for him in saving his life: "Why, you bitch, what were you doing when you came to help me—wasn't it to satisfy an impulse of your own heart! Didn't satisfying it give you pleasure! How in hell can you ask me to ask me to be grateful to you for the pleasure you give yourself!?. . .if you saved me, you did it to satisfy and enjoy your own sentiment—I owe you nothing!"[373] Charity, the Sadean world argues, is nothing more than masturbation. Justine's misfortunes aren't even close to over yet. In the next chapter she stumbles her way into a nearby town and befriends a surgeon named Rodin, who treats her dog bite injuries. He lives with his young daughter and he runs a school for poor children with her. When they take Justine in, it seems that something good has finally happened to her. Unhappily, misfortune is lurking in the shadows, and soon rears its ugly head: Justine learns that the good doctor sexually abuses both the schoolchildren and his daughter, and has plans to dissect the daughter alive on the night of her 15th birthday in the name of science:

> Anatomy will never reach its ultimate state of perfection until an examination has been performed upon the vaginal canal of a fourteen- or fifteen-year-old child who has expired from a cruel death. . . . The same holds true, "for the hymeneal membrane; we must, of course, find a young girl for the dissection. What the deuce is there to be seen after the age of puberty? Nothing; the menstrual discharges rupture the hymen, and all research is necessarily inexact. . . . I find it odious that futile considerations check the progress of science; did great men ever allow themselves to be enslaved by such contemptible chains.[374]

When Justine tries to rescue the daughter horrible fate she is to face, she is caught, branded on the shoulder as a criminal, and dumped in the woods again, alone.

Figure 8: Engraving from 1797 Dutch Edition of Justine

The next *Justine* episode, at the Sainte-Marie-des-Bois monastery, is probably the point in the novel that reaches the
greatest Sadean height and absurdity. Justine travels to southern France, begging for bread along the way. One woman mentions the fact that there is a monastery nearby that could
help her, and it "inflames her zeal" to find her way into the
hands of God again. She shows up on the doorstep and is
taken in by Dom Sévérino, who, after sussing out that she is
completely alone in the world with no one to miss her, takes

her into the basement beneath the monastery for 'shelter.' As you're probably guessing by now, Dom Séverino gives Justine anything but shelter. In fact, shoving her into a secret room, he announces "Gentlemen. . .allow me to present you with one of the veritable wonders of the world, a saint who at the same time carries on her shoulder the brand of a whore!" The men proceed to use her in an endless orgy sprawling over the course of several pages, and then engage with the other eight girls held captive there. The next day, Justine begs a monk to tell her how they can engage in such depraved acts in a house of God, which results in another round of philosophizing and societal critique:

> First, you are surprised at the filth we wallow in; and second, wonder how we can get such keen volup-tuous pleasures out of ferocity and somebody else's suffering. Let us analyze it all and you will see how simple it is. You say that only nasty and horrible things give us pleasure. But it's only your own im-agination thinks them nasty and horrible; ours may be different and that's what counts. . . . One's tastes, one's character and temperament is given to him in his mother's womb and nothing later can change it, education nor anything else. A good man or a villain was born such. . . . When anatomy is really perfected, it will be clearly shown that all morality is essen-tially physical. What then will become of your laws, ethics, religion, gibbets, paradise, God and hell, when it is shown that a particular organization of nerves, a peculiar chemical reaction in the body, a certain degree of sourness in the blood makes a man what is, for better or worse?[375]

What indeed, will become of us all when neurobiology and anatomy figures out everything about us?

From this point on in the book, the same cycle of escape,

brutal exploitation, and philosophizing repeats over and over, so in the interest of time, I will quote Justine's own summary of the events so it is possible to see the rest of the events that lie in store for the reader of *Justine*:

> [Afterwards] I attempt to preserve a woman from her husband's fury, the cruel one wishes to put me to death by draining away my blood drop by drop. I wish to relieve a poor woman, she robs me. I give aid to a man whom adversaries have struck down and left unconscious, the thankless creature makes me turn a wheel like an animal; he hangs me for his pleasure's sake; all fortune's blessings accrue to him, and I come within an ace of dying on the gallows for having been compelled to work for him.... I risk my life in a fire in order to snatch a child, who does not belong to me, from the flames; the infant's mother accuses and launches legal proceedings against me.... I implore the protection of a man whose life and fortune I once saved; I dare expect gratitude from him, he lures me to his house, he submits me to horrors, and there I find the iniquitous judge upon whom my case depends; both abuse me, both outrage me, both accelerate my doom; fortune overwhelms them with favors, I hasten on to death. [376]

After misadventure and misadventure, Justine is finally rescued from death row by her sister, Juliette, who has become tremendously wealthy and powerful through sex, murder, and libertinism. Juliette brings Justine to her mansion, and tries to treat her well, but at this point, even God has had enough of de Sade's character. A summer storm descends upon Justine, "as if Nature were wearied out of patience with what she has wrought," and strikes her down in symbolic, if implausible, detail: "a blazing thunderbolt reaches her where she stands in the middle of the room. . .[enters] her right breast, found the heart, and after having consumed her chest and face, burst out through her belly."[377]

This is the end of Justine and her misfortunes. And upon being arrested as the writer of *Justine*, the Marquis de Sade saw the end of his fortunes and misfortunes—he would spend the rest of his days in an insane asylum in Charenton until his death in 1814. The way that de Sade is critiquing state, society and the church should be obvious from the twists and turns that his narrative takes, meeting an institution (friendship, the church, family) and having it exploit and punish Justine. This, of course, is not the place to take a deep dive into the Marquis' psychology, but it is very obvious that he was not a happy man for most of his life and that he took out a lot of it in his writing. And in doing so, he also proved the case that that sort of critique landed an author in jail or in an asylum for obscenity or insanity. Significantly, shortly before de Sade's death Etienne-Gabriel Peignot defined 'pornography' in 1806 in *Dictionnaire critique, littéraire et bibliographique des principaux livres condamnés au feu, supprimés ou censurés*, "for the first time as the category of books repressed for moral, rather than religious or political, reasons – and cited Sade's *Justine* as a particularly reprehensible example."[378] By the 1830s, Amy Wynngard argues, "pornography became a distinct genre of its own, no longer associated with subversive philosophy and politics."[379] This is a characterization that I would agree with, plus or minus a decade or so—de Sade's death also marked the death of a type of erotic satire and critique that we have followed from Aretino onwards. By the 19th century erotic and obscene discourse becomes pornographic.

7

1800 — 1900: The Birth of Pornography

Declarations and Proclamations

WITH THE DEATH of John Cleland in 1789 and the Marquis de Sade in 1814, we now enter the next chapter in our history. The half-century between 1800 and 1850 created modern understandings of pornography as *sexual* obscenity first and foremost, in contrast to political, social, or religious criticism dressed up in sexy clothes. This conception began in England, America and France, and then spread out through other Western countries before being filtered out through the rest of the world through their colonies. The Marquis was, in many ways, the last person who worked the latter format into its highest art form, but it was John Cleland who recognized the way of the future; by stripping *Fanny Hill* of all social, political, and religious critique, he managed to escape prosecution and punishment by the government, despite the cries and aggravation of the Bishop of London.

As discussed in the chapter on Edmund Curll, there was, in the late 1600s, a gap opening up between the powers of church and state that the British government in particular was eager to claim for themselves, and succeeded in doing do. By the mid-1700s, the fact that the Bishop of London could not have Cleland prosecuted or satisfactorily punished illustrated that this gap had widened so far that the church and state were no longer working in tandem. The reaction of the moral reformers in England and elsewhere was to turn away from supporting church courts and to self-organize. The impulse began to be to utilize the power of the state to punish morality-breakers such as prostitutes, pornographers, beggars, and alcoholics. For many years, they were successful in doing this —Curll's prosecution is a perfect example of this strategy— but eventually the strategy began to fail, as a new sort of sexual morality developed. By the 1800s these moral reformers would succeed in getting a totally new system of enforcing what they saw as correct and proper public behavior: the police.

The work of the Scottish philosopher, David Hume, in *A Treatise of Human Nature* (1739) and *An Enquiry Concerning the Principles of Morals* (1751), did much to aid this by arguing that chastity was not a normal human emotion, but instead a social and artificial one, "invented primarily for men to feel secure that their children. . .are really their own. . .confinement of the appetite is not natural." As Faramerz Dabhoiwala puts it in his *Origins of Sex*:

> By 1750 there had thus emerged a fairly well-developed doctrine of sexual liberty - not merely a rejection of existing laws, but a new way of conceiving of the boundaries between permissible and impermissible behaviour, derived from different premises. It usually relied, implicitly or explicitly [on the fact that] behaviour was natural (and, it usually followed, harmless to the individual). In reality this was, of course, not an objective but a culturally determined definition. Conduct deemed to be 'un-

natural', such as sodomy or masturbation, did not meet its test, but otherwise what one did with one's own body was a private matter.[380]

As Cleland did not engage in any obscene libel, in *Fanny Hill*, and presented male masturbation and homosexuality as disgusting, the political powers-that-be did not necessarily see the work as 'disturbing the King's peace,' and therefore did not prosecute Cleland for obscene libel. Religious figures, however, saw *Fanny* as an 'open insult,' and their failure to achieve prosecution led ultimately to their organization of two political action campaigns—The Proclamation Society, and the Society for the Suppression of Vice. These groups, which were based somewhat on the Society for the Reformation of Manners, and who were also religiously organized, used political methods and lobbying to achieve their goal; legal recognition of the 'menace' posed by pornographic works. Without their vociferous campaigning, there would not have been sexual obscenity laws.

This becomes readily apparent when one considers that the next Bishop of London, Beilby Porteus, and his close friend, William Wilberforce (the famous evangelical anti-slavery campaigner) convinced the incoming King George III to issue the *Royal Proclamation For the Encouragement of Piety and Virtue, and for the Preventing and Punishing of Vice, Profaneness and Immorality* in 1787. The *Proclamation* begins with alarm bells and klaxon calls:

Whereas We cannot but observe, with inexpressible Concern, the rapid Progress of Impiety and Licentiousness, and that Deluge of Profaneness, Immorality, and every Kind of Vice, which, to the Scandal of our Holt Religion. . . . We therefore esteeming it Our indispensable Duty to exert the Authority committed to Us, for the Suppression of these spreading Evils, fearing lest they should provoke God's Wrath

and Indignation against Us. . .Issue this, Our Royal
Proclamation.[381]

As one of George III's first acts as King, the *Proclamation*
"enjoin[ed] and prohibit[ed] all Our loving Subjects, of what
Degree or Quality so ever" from playing at dice, cards, and
games on Sunday; commanded them to attend church; called
on police and judges to enforce laws against drunkenness,
blasphemy, swearing and cursing, and to break up gambling
houses, dirty shows, and brothels. So far, this is nearly identical to Queen Anne's *Proclamation*, but the unique and new
part was: "Also [you should] suppress all loose and licentious Prints, Books, and Publications, dispersing Poison to the
Minds of the Young and Unwary, and to punish the Publishers
and Vendors thereof."[382]

This was the very first time 'prints, books, and publications'
were singled out because of their sexual nature instead of
their critique of religion, society, or politics. Earlier *Proclam-
ations* by King George I and Queen Anne did not target books,
prints, or publications in the way George III's did. This novelty
is undoubtedly attributable to the influence of Wilberforce,
who once famously stated that "God Almighty has set before
me two great objects, the suppression of the slave trade and
the reformation of manners."[383] Almost as if to take credit,
Wilberforce established the Proclamation Society immediately after the *Proclamation* was issued.

This Proclamation Society was set up in order to, quite
literally, proclaim and enforce the *Proclamation*; they announced that they had been "formed for the purpose of enforcing the proclamation against vice and immorality, which
his Majesty's provident care for the public welfare prompted
him to issue."[384] Wilberforce argued in his writings that the
"Attorney-General and Secretary of State. . .are too much
cramped by their political relations to discharge [their] duties with effect; yet some official check on vice is absolutely

needed."[385] Wilberforce's (slightly disingenuous) comments help explain why the Proclamation Society (and later the Society for the Suppression of Vice) became so obsessed with prosecution—he is essentially arguing that the government was 'too busy' and unconcerned with vice enforcement. In reality, it is much more likely that the government was simply not interested in the expenditures or exertions necessary to launch a campaign against vice, nor they did not feel that it was particularly necessary, and so left it to private individuals, who formed societies. The Society for the Suppression of Vice would note that "the exertions of an individual may doubtless produce very excellent effects within the sphere in which they may operate," but they would not be enough, and the "only effectual barrier. . . which can be opposed to the overwhelming tide of corruption which threatens our repose, is the united efforts of individuals combining in one extensive and firm association, the virtue, wisdom, and energy of each." [386]

The Proclamation Society managed to be an ineffectual barrier for a few years, prosecuting a John Morgan in 1788 for publishing *The Battles of Venus: A Descriptive Dissertation on the Various Modes of Enjoyment* (1760?), and Lewis McDonald for our previously-discussed *School of Venus* (1680). A third and a fourth prosecution were brought against a James Hodges in 1780 for his publication of Cleland's *Fanny Hill* and *A Dialogue between a Married Lady and a Maid*, published in 1740, which was an abridged version of the *Dialogues of Luisa Sigea.*

The Battles of Venus is the only one we haven't touched on yet, but it wasn't particularly obscene, even by Proclamation Society standards—it is much more likely that Morgan, a hard-pressed and poor printer was an easy target. Its full title was *The Battles of Venus: A Descriptive Dissertation on the Various Modes of Enjoyment: Comprising Philosophical Discussions of the most interesting and affecting Questions. Demonstrative that the loosest Thoughts and Sensations may be conveyed without an Expression verging on Immodesty*, and it claimed to be translated from the works of Voltaire. The book proposed that there were 'degrees of pleasure' that could be obtained with sex It follows the post-Cleland strategy of avoiding any mention of homosexuality and political/religious critique. If there is a novelty to the book it is perhaps it's advice on where and how to 'enjoy a woman

> It must be confessed that, besides the pleasure of novelty and variety, the breast and belly of the woman are not unenjoyed by the roving and pressure of the man's hands; and moreover there are certainly two additional gratifications not known in the former instance, namely, the feeling of her plump, warm buttocks planted in his lap, and the plea- sure of handling the delightful mount of Venus, at the same time that he is fixed in, and enjoying it behind.[387]

And also offers some advice for potential threesomes:
> The performance would, doubtless, require an extent of parts; but whoever reflects on their proverbial extensive quality, will not doubt of their admitting with ease two guests, after a trial or two, and with sufficiency of natural or artificial lubrication, provided themselves could accommodate their entrance to the convenience of each other. . . .

> And in the way above alluded to, I am confident that might be effected. The woman must lie straight, on either side, and the man who attacks her in front must, after entering her, lift her uppermost leg on his buttock. The antagonist in the rear must then accommodate himself to her posture, and glide in likewise. . . .The men may knock her as hard as they will ; so as the woman is careful to keep her-

self exactly straight, and not to withdraw from one or the other, their violent shocks will only serve to make her more fixed and steady.[388]

Regardless of what in particular offended the Proclamation Society (probably all of the above), it is apparent that erotic texts, post-Cleland, tended to avoid the religious and social criticism of the previous centuries. In many ways, de Sade and his countryman Retif de la Bretonne were the writers who 'closed out' the old style of obscene. The style we recognize as 'pornography,' pioneered by Cleland and other European writers, is becoming more and more recognizable to our modern eyes.

By and large, however, it seems that the Proclamation Society did little more than proclaim—there are several surviving editorials, letters, and sermons arguing for the suppression of vice by members, but very little survives in the way of case records or lawsuits. This may be because the Proclamation Society was a largely upper-class society—it's members included, among others, "the Archbishops of Canterbury and York, seventeen bishops, six dukes, and eleven other peers," even though Wilberforce had hoped to recruit "persons of consequence in every line of life, the professions, members of both Houses [of Parliament], merchants in the city, aldermen, etc. In practice, the membership and especially the active (committee-serving) membership tended to contract towards the more exclusive circles of Westminster and the court."[389] Furthermore they were a very small society, never really exceeding more than 150 members from their foundation in 1787 to their absorption in 1802; a mere 15 years later. Either way, it seems that eventually middle-class rage and frustration at the inactivity bubbled over and resulted in the foundation of the Society for the Suppression of Vice.

The Society for the Suppression of Vice

IN 1802, The Society for the Suppression of Vice (hereafter, the Vice Society or the SSV) issued their first open letter to the public in the same year, titled *Society for the Suppression of Vice, Consisting of Members of the Established Church.* In it, they sounded the clarion call, insisting that "something must be done, and vigorously to check the impropriety of a luxurious and dissipated age."[390] Although they were full of praise for the Proclamation Society, "rejoyc[ing] in an opportunity of publicly acknowledging, with the upmost gratitude and respect, the great obligations of this country to the Proclamation Society," they also "lament[ed] that profaneness and immorality have encreased among us to such a degree, that to contend with them successfully requires more."[391] This is not to say that the SSV was hostile or antagonistic to the Proclamation Society—in fact, they hoped to work side by side with them: "[we are] hoping, by [our] joint efforts and influence to check the contagion of dissolute example and licentious practice."[392] Eventually the two societies combined forces, redoubling their efforts against the vice that seemed to seize England at every limb.

Although also consisting of several officials of the church, the Vice Society was initially much more secular and practical-minded, more in the model of the Society for the Reformation of Manners. Instead of tr   ying to win hearts and minds, and convince people to reform through sermons and editorials, the SSV elected to use the police and Courts as their primary weapons to "trace corruption to its source. . .disclose its covert recesses. . .drag offenders into light. . ..[and to] risque [their] personal safety against those whose trade is rapine, and whose profession is hatred and hostility," and most importantly, to "discharge the expenses necessary to support their prosecution."[393] Thus, the Vice Society was set up from

Brian M. Watson

the get-go as a legal society. In addition to giving their members advice on how to navigate and utilize the legal system, the group also published advice books for policemen in addition to placing charts in most of their public addresses which listed the crimes they could prosecute, the statute numbers, and the penalties.[394]

For example, under the "False Weights and Measures" category it listed 16 Statutes including "8 Hen c. c. 5, 11 Hen. 7.c.4. . .22&23 Ca.2.c.12. . .37 Geo.3. c.143." Under this, the Offence, Statutes, and Penalties subheadings listed "Persons using false Weights and Measures; 35 Geo. 3; Liable to a Penalty of 40s. for every Offence" respectively (see figure 9).

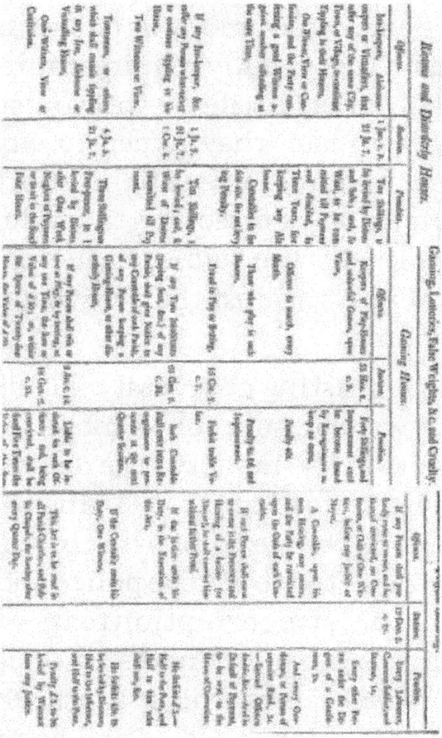

Figure 9: SSV Publication on the laws that could be used to prosecute sins.

However, when we turn to our topic, in comparison to the other offenses the Society for the Suppression of Vice prosecuted, the "Obscene Books and Prints" category was rather sparse, did not cite any statutes, and only said that "Persons selling obscene Books and Prints. . .May be indicted, imprisoned, and put in the pillory." By the middle of the century, however, in no small part due to their lobbying efforts, the SSV was able to add several more statutes and some increasingly exacting penalties to their charts.

Obscene Books and Prints.

Offence.	Statutes.	Penalties.
Persons selling obscene Books and Prints,	Com. Law.	May be indicted, imprisoned, and put in the Pillory.
N. B. Any Hawker, or Pedlar, found trading without a Licence, shall, on Confession or Proof, on the Oath of One Witness,	29 Geo. 3. c. 26.	Forfeit £40, by distress to be levied, or be committed to Gaol, or the House of Correction, till Penalty paid.

Figure 10: Detail of the above on the laws that could be used to prosecute obscene material.

Bursting so dramatically onto the scene, the Vice Society went quickly about its business, targeting all of the vices, profanities and immoralities that the *Proclamation* identified. In 1802 alone, the Vice Society prosecuted 220 shopkeepers and 218 pub owners for the Profanation of the Lord's Day, 20 individuals for the "frauds and abuses practiced in selling by FALSE WEIGHTS AND MEASURES," 26 for the "evil consequences resulting from LOTTERIES," and 5 houses and 11 persons for being brothels, gaming houses, or riotous and disorderly. They also successfully prosecuted 5 sellers of "BLASPHEMOUS, LICENTIOUS, AND OBSCENE BOOKS, AND PRINTS, as tending to inflame the minds and to corrupt the morals of the rising generation," more than the Proclamation Society had managed to prosecute in a decade in a half. Two were sentenced to six months imprisonment, one to twelve, one to six and then an additional two years when he was caught again in the same year.

Their description of obscene literature is interesting for several reasons. First is that the *argumentum ad liberos*, or the "think of the children" argument is utilized in relation to erotic works for just about the first time, which demonstrates how much the publication of *Onania* affected contemporary groups. It also shows that children's literacy was growing increasingly common, and that the burgeoning genre of children's literature was a concern of the SSV. Furthermore, they begged parents to pay attention to children's books they had been found to be:

> A most successful channel for the conveyance of infidel and licentious tenants. It is indeed no longer safe to trust the title of the books, the terms virtue and vice have no longer the same signification as formerly, and many a publication, which professed to instill virtuous principals into the mind, is calculated to destroy that respect for Religion, that regard for social and relative duties, and that abhorrence of vice.[395]

Hilariously enough, they might as well be talking about the book *Pamela*, which, as I noted, had by the 1800s become regarded as a slightly scandalous work. The language above is hardly unique though, it would be familiar to a parent who lived through the Comic Book Panic of the 1950s or 60s, or to contemporary parents who are warned about the public health crisis facing their children in the form of—perhaps unsurprisingly—pornography.

These 'protect the children' arguments by the Vice Society and others lends support to an idea presented at the very beginning of this book, that the concept of pornography as a category was tied to the increasing rates of literacy among the working class, women, and children. The English comedian and Anglican cleric Sydney Smith, noted that since the Society for the Suppression of Vice did not prosecute the wealthy it should be called "a society for suppressing the vices of persons whose income does not exceed £500 per annum."[396] In the same mode, a British politician refused to prosecute a book called *Political Justice* because it cost three guineas ($270 USD in 2010), reasoning that, "a three-guinea book could never do much harm among those who had not three shillings to spare."[397] Each of these quotations reveals the widespread goal—the protection and reform of the working classes.

This is a common trend that runs through all of the post-Curll prosecutions for obscene libel and pornography; the prosecuted individual is always a member of (or associated with) the middle or working class, and his dangerously sexy wares run the risk of corrupting the women, the children, and all who walk down the notorious Holywell Street, peering in the shop windows. This is the most interesting thing about the Vice Society's comments—that while the religious aspect of obscene libel is still present in 'blasphemous,' there is a much greater focus on the lewdness and sexiness of the books and prints. It was no longer religious or philosophical aspects that endangered the readers or incited them to revolt. Now, it was the mere hint or suggestion of sex or sexuality. This fear of sexuality was apparent in the earliest publications of the Vice Society, where they comment breathlessly that

> [T]he nature of the subject forbids such a description as would be necessary to convey a just notion of the extent of the evil which they have encountered. Suffice it to say, that the most corrupt device the morbid imagination of voluptuous sensuality ever yet conceived can scarcely be supposed to exceed in depravity the subjects of the publications discovered by the Society.[398]

And these publications were dangerous—one magistrate, proceeding over a Vice Society trial, said that "the mischief done to the community by such offences greatly exceeds that produced by murder," since murder has a definite boundary to the harm it causes, but the effects of corrupted morals can be endless.[399]

Even in the era of revolution; Napoleon on the Continent, and pro- and anti-Jacobin movements in England, the concern over erotic literature continued to grow. Part of the reason for the growing concern may have been the fact that there were so few laws and regulations against these types of works despite the 'obvious' need for them. Another reason, perhaps, was that constables (appointed by a local justice of the peace) were more likely to target obvious disorderly behavior such as drunkenness or brawling—remember that there was no real police force in London (or anywhere else in the world, really) until the 1829 Metropolitan Police Act, the SSV and other reformers like them were instrumental in establishing institution of state control over public behavior. Another major reason that the SSV became increasingly obsessed with porn was because, as the century progressed, obscene literature became—to their great dismay—much more accessible and forthrightly sexual.

To illustrate this point further, it is enough to point out that the Proclamation Society prosecuted books that were published over a half-century beforehand (such as *Fanny Hill*), and in some cases the books targeted were over a century old (such as *The School of Venus*). These were generally the types of works that we've covered for most of this book, works that combine philosophical ideas with slight eroticism. The members of the Proclamation Society seem to have been unaware of the more recent spate of titles coming out year by year, and instead seemed to be working with an old catalogue of works that they wished to prosecute. The first prosecutions of the Society for the Suppression of Vice were older works as well, many of them 'Italian,' suggesting texts by Pietro Aretino or Aretine imitators; first published in the 1500s. Unfortunately (or perhaps fortunately) for the SSV, there was a dramatic upswing in the number of new pornographic texts in the 1800s. As a result, as the century progressed, there was also a dramatic upswing in the number of Vice Society prosecutions. By 1857, Lord Campbell would note that the SSV had 159 prosecutions for obscenity under their belt, of which 154 were successful.[400]

The suggestion here is that, as the SSV's prosecutions and campaign intensified, so did the productivity and creativity of the pornographers. The Society for the Suppression of Vice and other associated moral reformers thought they were facing an organized campaign to destroy England; it was apparent to them, "beyond all reasonable doubt, that associations have been formed for the most nefarious purposes, which have threatened the very existence of civil society."[401] So they fought the pornographers in the streets with arrests, in the courts with lawyers, and in the government via lobbyists pushing for more vigorous laws. The pornographers of course, seemed to respond in kind, pushing the limits by writing and illustrating "most corrupt devices the morbid imagination of voluptuous sensuality," that they could. In many ways, *Fanny Hill* had been a precursor, with its separation of religious and social criticism from sensuality.[402] Despite its embrace of the latter, it began to pale in comparison to new works. In fact, *Fanny Hill* itself was found lacking and too drawn out; some entrepreneurs took it upon themselves to reissue the book with much less dialogue and many more creative sexual scenes.

It is necessary here to point out that I'm not trying to encourage the old stereotype of the hypocritical and prude Victorian. It would be far too easy to criticize the Vice Society's intentions and goals in the light of our supposedly modern and enlightened time. When the Society for the Suppression of Vice began their campaign they had widespread support amongst the British public, intellectuals, and politicians. The medical establishment underwrote the campaign with their theories of *spermatorrhea* (the fear that too many orgasms could devastate a man's mind and body) and onanism, and some like Joseph Alfred Conwell wrote that indulging in masturbation caused

> young men lose personal magnetism and attractiveness. . . .It is the duty of young men to become the fathers of an improved race – of children inheriting all the advantages of healthful vigor'. Here there is an onus placed on young men – a 'duty', no less – to cultivate and preserve a sound and robust constitution in order to beget healthy progeny. Clearly, the weak and sallow onanist is anathema to the perfection of 'health and strength' that characterises what Macfadden terms 'superb manhood.'[403]

Politicians strengthened medical diktats and the SSV's campaign with new laws and regulations, and it saw nearly universal sponsorship from the church. Advice writers like Sylvanus Stall in his 1897 *What a Young Boy Ought to Know* "counsels his (presumably worried) readers to 'Take plenty of exercise in the open air' and to 'Avoid all stories and trashy books and papers, but read plenty of good ones' in order that 'purity and strength may be measurably regained by those who have learned the vicious habit which is so prevalent among boys.'"[404]

Additionally, until the late 1820s, the SSV did extremely well financially, clearing more than £1000 per annum in subscriptions (about $94,000/£61,000 in 2015 money), and still maintained more than £500 per year thereafter.[405] Even one of their worst enemies, Richard Carlile, who engaged in a painful, multi-decade battle with the Vice Society for publishing the works of (philosopher) Thomas Paine, said that, "had you confined yourself to [suppressing vice], no honest or moral man would have complained of or objected to your conduct as a society."[406] These fears, concerns, and political organizing were not just a English phenomenon; chapters of the Society for the Suppression of Vice sprung up across the world —in Philadelphia, New York, Dublin, Paris, Amsterdam, and elsewhere. There is no doubt that their effect was felt among the writers and pornographers on Holywell Street, in London, as they heard of friends and business associates accosted and arrested. Despite this, or perhaps because of this, new books began to appear on the market in the 1820s and the 1830s. One of the most famous of these was *The Lustful Turk.*

Lusty Struggles

THE LUSTFUL TURK was first published between 1828 and 1830 by John Benjamin Brookes, and then republished by William Dugdale in 1857 (which will become important in a moment). Using the same form that *Pamela* does, the book purports to be a series of letters from Emily Barlow to her future sister-in-law, Silvia Carey. The plot begins on the premise that Emily is traveling to India in order to claim a fortune that a rich uncle has left in her name. She writes, "Oh, Sylvia! how cruel is the sacrifice exacted in our obedience to our parents; how happy had I been if this uncle of mine had never existed! My mother, my friend, my lover—all, all I hold dear—sacrificed to the prospect of possessing this uncle's wealth."[407] She promises to write to Sylvia very soon, but from Sylvia's perspective, Emily goes silent for a month.

Abruptly (for the reader), Sylvia receives a long letter from Emily, which begins with her heartbrokenness:

Dearest Sylvia—I think I see the expression of surprise you experience on perceiving my letter dated from this place [Algiers]. Oh, God, Sylvia, to what a wretched fate has the intended kindness of my

uncle devoted your miserable unfortunate friend.
Pity me, Sylvia; pity my wretchedness. . . . Oh God,
Sylvia, I have no longer any claim to chastity. Surely
never was poor maid so unfeelingly deprived of her
virtue. . . . In vain I resisted with all the strength
nature had bestowed on me. It was no use. In vain I
made the harem resound with my cries but no help
or assistance came to succour your poor friend[408]

The letter goes on to describe how her boat was captured
by Moorish pirates, how she was sold into slavery, and how
her first night in the Dey's harem goes. Playing up the 'innocent virgin captured by savage barbarian' card, when the 'Lustful Turk' kisses Emily, it arouses in her "nature, too powerful
nature. . .a sudden, new and wild sensations blended with my
shame and rage, which exerted themselves but faintly; in fact,
Sylvia, in a few short moments his kisses and his tongue threw
my senses into a complete tumult and an unknown fire rushed
through every part of me, hurried on by a strange pleasure,"
but when he tries to take it further, she fights back, to no avail.
Like Pamela, Fanny, and even Justine, Emily faints when the
letter reaches its physical and emotional height: "uttering a
piercing cry I sank insensible in the arms of my cruel ravisher.
How long I continued in this happy state of insensibility,
I know not."[409] Unlike Pamela, Fanny, and Justine however,
Emily leaves nothing to the imagination in describing her
rape beforehand:

[M]y petitions, supplications and tears were of no
use. I was on the altar, and, butcher-like, he was determined to complete the sacrifice; indeed, my cries
seemed only to excite him to the finishing of my
ruin, and sucking my lips and breasts with fury, he
unrelentingly rooted up all obstacles my virginity
offered, tearing and cutting me to pieces, until the
complete junction of our bodies announced that the

> whole of his terrible shaft was buried within me. . . .
> Dreadful, indeed, were my sufferings in being de-
> flowered. Never was poor maid so unceremoniously
> debauched, nor is it possible for anyone to suffer
> more cruel anguish than I did, in receiving my first
> lesson from this powerful Turk.[410]

After finishing with her, the Dey leaves to fight off an inva-
sion by an Arab tribe, and Emily recounts to Sylvie how she
met the other women in the harem, and they in turn told her
(in appropriately long-winded and detailed stories) how they
arrived at the harem and their first nights there. One of these
women asks her several questions, which reveal a great oncoming horror to Emily:

> She asked me whether I felt any pleasure when the
> Dey enjoyed me behind. I told her I did not under-
> stand what she meant by behind. She laughed most
> immoderately at my ignorance, and would scarcely
> credit what I had asserted, particularly as she knew
> the Dey was so fond of the other route. I requested
> her to explain herself. 'Are you not aware,' said she,
> 'that a woman has two maidenheads to take?' On my
> replying in the negative, she answered, 'You have,
> though. Under the altar of Venus is another grotto,
> a little more obscure, to be sure; but there the Dey
> will offer up his sacrifices with characteristic en-
> ergy.'[411]

Because she is English, she is even more horrified by this prop-
osition and she tells the Dey that she is upset and disturbed
by her oncoming fate: "I. . .told him in our country it was considered the most degrading crime that could be committed,
that it was punished with death." She further tries to convince
him by saying, "let the pleasures you confess I have afforded
you save me from what I consider would be the greatest dis-

grace I could possibly experience!" By this point, Emily seems to be suffering from Stockholm syndrome and is head over heels in love with him. He has become quite fond of her himself, but he is greatly upset by this request of hers and cries, "Can [you] think that any act of Ali would pollute [you]?. . . . I shall leave you to reflect, foolish slave, on your childishness in thus attempting to bind my pleasures by an oath made in a moment."[412] And with that, he storms out and leaves Emily alone, sinking to the couch in dismay.

In keeping with the epistolary format where all of the action takes place in letters written between the different characters, Emily tries to get back into the good graces of the Dey by writing to him, and announces, "Oh, Ali, I am with child; hasten to comfort your miserable slave. You cannot doubt my love. Since the day you overpowered my innocence (the day I consider the happiest of my existence, although truly it was a painful one)."[413] The Dey Ali writes back but refuses to flinch, and says that he "was aware of your being with child," but declares that "I am determined to tear myself from your tempting arms until I find your submission perfect." [414] There is no other option, Emily must submit wholly to the Lustful Turk.

And submit she does—because after all, this is a pornographic text, not a soap opera. As Lisa Sigel pointed out, "early nineteenth century pornography saw sexuality as happening through women (not only to women, as later works would do)," so Emily's submission allows the author to

> illustrate how religious teachings, standards of modesty and chastity, the relentless search for new pleasures, and the daily search to meet human needs had perverted humanity in the West. The Turkish harem offered a vision of sexuality without jealousies, class antagonisms, or false modesty. Stripping away these impediments allowed men and women to rediscover the strength of natural passions. . . Europe diminished men's sexuality, the

harem allowed it to grow rampant.[415]

Emily confesses via letter that she truly loves him, and will grant him anything he wants from her. Whether this is supposed to be Stockholm syndrome or just the regular ridiculousness of pornography is unclear, but either way, the Turk gets the object of his desire, and we have Emily here to give us a faithful account, albeit mixed in with some complicated emotions:

> [H]e divided my thighs to their utmost extension, leaving the route he intended to penetrate fairly open to his attack. He now got upon me, and. . .proceeded with great caution and fierceness; in short, he soon got the head entirely fixed. His efforts then became more and more energetic. But he was as happy as the satisfying of his beastly will could make him. He regarded me not, but profiting by his success, soon completed my second undoing; and then, indeed, with mingled emotions of disgust and pain, I sensibly felt the debasement of being the slave of a luxurious Turk. . .

> By my submission I was reinstated in his affections, and everything proceeds as usual. But the charm is broken. It is true he can, when he pleases, bewilder my senses in the softest confusion; but when the tumult is over, and my blood cooled from the fermentation he causes-when reason resumes its sway, I feel that the silken cords of affection which bound me so securely to him have been so much loosened that he will never again be able to draw them together so closely as they were before he subdued me to his abominable desires.[416]

The last sentence seems a little inconsistent with the rest of the tale, because Emily will be 'enjoying him to the utmost' a few short pages later—again, this is a transparently pornographic narrative, one that even modern audiences would read (mostly correctly) as pornographic. Aside from the hang-ups and fears around anal sex that Emily has that a modern viewer might not, there is not much different—but this hang-ups signal some of the ways that sexual culture was reorienting away from concerns over masturbation to concerns over homosexuality and perversion—something that the Lustful Turk leans much more into than Fanny Hill and her "criminal scene."

After these episodes, there is another long digression while another woman in the harem, 'The Grecian Slave' (who Emily conveniently "had been able to teach the English language") tells a long story of losing her beloved during a Turkish raid on her island and the slaughter of him and the priest who was about to marry them. She recounts how when she refused the Dey's sexual attentions he retaliated by poisoning her wine with a sleeping drug and then taking advantage of her. Suddenly, this letter ends abruptly and we hear from Sylvie, who was supposed to be Emily's sister-in-law before Emily's capture by pirates. Sylvie is profoundly and thoroughly disturbed and disgusted:

> Emily—It is impossible at once to shake off our earliest acquaintance; if it had been you ought not to have expected that I should have taken any notice of your disgusting letters. What offence have I ever given that you should insult me by writing in the language you have? Why annoy me with an account of the libidinous scenes acted between you and the beast whose infamous and lustful acts you so particularly describe?[417]

She goes on to describe what a horrible effect Emily's letters and conduct have had on her and Emily's mother, but notes in an offhand way that some missionaries are coming to Algeria to free slaves soon, and that if Emily has any sense of modesty left, that she should write and let her know that she wishes to "escape from the wretch who thus holds you in his thralldom."[418]

The book then takes a strange detour through the letters of those missionaries, Pedro and Angelo, the first of which writes several long letters describing his seduction and enjoyment of a local girl, the daughter of the Marquis de Mezzia. He describes this in a vaguely religious style (especially 'rod of Aaron'):

> *But never was conquest more difficult. Oh, how I* was obliged to tear her up in forcing her virgin defences! With what delicious tightness she clasped my rod of Aaron, as it entered the inmost recesses of her till then virgin sanctuary. How voluptuous was the heat of her young body! I was mad with enjoyment! ... Although Julia was much overcome with her suffering, still she reproachfully turned her lovely eyes swimming with pain and languor on me. At this instant, with a final energetic thrust, I buried myself up to the very hair in her. A shriek proclaimed the change in her state; the ecstasy seized me and I shot into the inmost recesses of the womb of this innocent and beautiful child as copious a flood of burning sperm as ever was fermented under the cloak of a monk; whereupon, oh, marvellous effects of nature, the lovely Mezzia, spite of her cruel sufferings, ceded to my vigorous impressments. The pleasure overcame the pain, and the stretching of her ivory limbs, the quivering of her body, the eager clasping of her delicate arms, clearly spoke that nature's first effusion was distilling within her.[419]

The letters go on to describe how the pair conspire to sell "young beauties over the sea to the great gratification of the Turks in Algiers and Tunis, but to the much greater gratification of ourselves, by well lining our own pockets with African gold."[420] The reason for this narrative detour is soon revealed: Emily's Dey has hired the pair of monks with his 'African gold' to kidnap and sell Sylvie to him because he is upset at the way she talked about him. He says he is "determined to pay the minx for calling me a beast if it lay in my power."[421]

In yet another letter, Emily walks in on the pair of them going at it and immediately faints from the shock. When she wakes up she is immediately reconciled with Sylvie, who begs "Forgive me, dearest. . .for the harsh letter I wrote you. Little did I then think that I too should fall a sacrifice to the dear wicked Dey."[422] Then, the 'dear wicked' Dey recounts to Emily in absurd detail what machinations he went through to kidnap and seduce her friend, and everything becomes 'sweet and charming,' almost like a fairytale ending:

> After this the Dey would often amuse himself with us alternately, compelling one of us to guide into the other his instrument and handle his pendant jewels; then he would throw his hand back and insert his finger into the gaping place that awaited its turn. In this way we were frequently (all three) dissolved at the same time in a flood of bliss.[423]

Both women become bodies, enslaved to the Lustful Turk, and the harem becomes a sort of 'pornotopia' of delight created for the reader. The lull does not hold, sadly, and "an awful catastrophe put an end to our enjoyments."[424] In an act of protest against anal sex, another girl in the harem cuts the Dey's penis off with his knife and then kills herself. The Dey, unfazed, has his physician cut off the remainder, preserves the 'members' (testicles) in glass jars for Sylvia and Emily, and sends them home to England.

On the level of language and appropriateness, *The Lustful Turk* is not that different from *Fanny Hill*. Although it is a bit more 'vulgar' with its language, it still avoids the common names and graphic description of genitalia such as 'cunt' or 'cock.' Additionally, it does not touch on many of the sexual acts or extremes that later works would. Like *Fanny Hill*, the work also places heterosexuality on a pedestal and avoids any reference to homosexuality, even lesbianism. Its main novelty and reason for its success might have been a forthright description of heterosexual anal sex. In Sigel's view, the anal sex "illustrates the pleasure of the harem and then undercuts it as a utopia because complete control can lead to degeneracy in sexuality as in politics," which seems like an accurate reflection of attitudes towards anal sex in the era, but it also seems that just the novelty of the scene would have made the book a better seller as nineteenth century erotic writers sought new niches and tried to check as many boxes as possible. The bondage scene in the book (the Dey ties Sylvie up and flogs her) also seems to be a gesture towards completion, even though bondage scenes had quite a long history in England and Europe as a whole, dating all the way back to the 1500s.

On a philosophical level, however, *The Lustful Turk* was terribly upsetting to Victorian moralists—not only does it involve rape, it involves the willing participation of English women in fornication and adultery with an infidel and a foreigner. Nor are Emily and Sylvia punished as they should be —at the end of the novel Emily is working on marrying an "Irish earl, who I have a presentiment will be found worthy of acceptance," and might be able to "erase the Dey's impression from my heart."[425] Furthermore, it presents female sexuality in a manner that must have deeply disturbed the Society for the Suppression of Vice, who declared that "women are elevated in the scale of society and the suavity of manners . . . they have a mild, conciliating, forbearing, and civilizing spirit."[426] It was no wonder then, that when the Society for the Suppression of Vice caught wind of this publication they brought a legal case against a certain William Dugdale for publishing and selling it; a legal case that would rock the world of English literature to its very foundations, and be used by the American and British governments to discipline and punish for over a century.

Campbell's Law

THE LUSTFUL TURK was first published between 1828 and 1830 by John Benjamin Brookes, and then piratically republished by William Dugdale in 1857, without permission or reservation. Dugdale, born in 1800 had by this been a publisher for about three decades (since 1822). Early on in his life he had joined radical (for his time) free speech groups called 'Painites' after Thomas Paine, famous for his arguments in *Rights Of Man* that resulted in his trial *in absentia.* According to Lisa Sigel, the groups that Dugdale belonged to "alternately espoused democratic revolution, violent overthrow of Parliament, full freedom of the press, of association, and over movement, free love, abolition of slaver, utopian landholding schemes, rational religion and deism."[427]

By 1828 Dugdae had become known as a printer that was eager to mix liberal political philosophy with bawdy writing and aggressive slanders of the elite, and, along with 53 other shops, ran a side specialty in pornographic literature as it was profitable.[428] He had become infamous as "the principal source of such publications in the country."[429] By 1857, he had been prosecuted by the Society for the Suppression of Vice at least nine times, and his constant mocking of them frustrated them to no end. So when he republished *The Lustful Turk* in 1857, they were determined to use him as an example, exhibit A in their case to the government on why a law specific to obscene publications was needed.

To nobody's surprise, Dugdale was (once again) convicted of publishing obscene libel, the same crime Edmund Curll had been prosecuted for over 130 years before. Like Curll though, he was sentenced not only for his erotic texts, but for the fact that he also specialized in political material that was seen as dangerous and seditious. Despite over 50 years of lobbying, from 1802 to 1857, the Society for the Suppression of Vice had not been successful in getting major vice legislation passed. In 1817, the SSV's Secretary, George Pritchard, testified before the House of Commons about their crusade. When asked how many prosecutions the Vice Society had launched, Pritchard testified, "between thirty and forty, in all of which they have succeeded...[but] in consequence of renewed intercourse with the continent [after the Napoleonic War], incidental to the restoration of peace, there has been a great influx...of the most obscene articles of every description."[430]

The House of Commons continued questioning him on the nature of the prosecutions, eventually asking his opinion on the adequacy of the current laws against obscene literature. Pritchard responded that the current libel law was "by no means adequate to the suppression of such offenses," and explained that the process of obtaining a warrant through a bill of indictment was too difficult. He declared, "I do not see how this evil can be effectively put a stop to, unless constables and other persons are enabled to seize such offenders without a warrant." He further testified that many dealers were able to escape with impunity, and that many shops on Holywell Street were able to openly display obscene books and prints for sale.[431]

Although the House of Commons did not immediately act on his testimony, by 1824, the Society had succeeded in getting an addition to the 1824 Vagrancy Act that declared,

> every Person wilfully [sic] exposing to view, in any Street, Road, Highway, or public Place, any obscene Print, Picture, or other indecent Exhibition ... shall

be deemed a Rogue and Vagabond, within the true Intent and Meaning of this Act; and it shall be lawful for any Justice of the Peace to commit such Offender ... to the House of Correction, there to be kept to Hard Labour for any Time not exceeding Three Calendar Months.[432]

In lobbying for this law, the SSV was specifically targeting Holywell Street in London, which was notorious for its 'obscene prints, pictures and other indecent exhibitions,' that were visible from the street. Unfortunately for the SSV, the 1824 Act did not define what a 'public place' was, and so they found themselves lobbying for revisions for another 14 years. The 1838 Vagrancy Act extended the earlier Act to include the display of such material inside a shop or house. Though this law was more stringent, it still required 'public display,' and it still did not grant the SSV power to seize and destroy material. Furthermore, they were frustrated by individuals like Dugdale, who had associates or relatives run his business while he was in jail. Finally, the Vagrancy Act was found wanting because it did not stipulate increased punishment for repeat offenders, such as Dugdale. A greater, more powerful Act was needed, and the 1857 trial of William Dugdale and his associate William Strange, launched by the Society, would provide this impetus.

During the course of the trial, the Society managed to impress upon the mind of the judge, Lord John Campbell, First Baron Campbell, the great danger presented by obscene literature. Curious, Campbell examined *The Lustful Turk* and the other books that Strange and Dugdale were accused of publishing. Disgustedly, he declared his "astonishment and horror," particularly at the low price at which it was sold, and declared it to be a "disgrace to the country." He proclaimed that it was "high time that an example should be made," and sent Dugdale to prison for a year, the maximum allowed under the law.[433] Not to belabor the point, but Campbell's revulsion at the low cost and ease of access is a further example of how the definition of indecency hinged upon whether groups such as children or the poor were able to gain access to it.

A couple of days later, on May 11th, Campbell announced to the House of Lords that he had "learned with horror and alarm that a sale of poison more deadly than prussic acid, strichnine, or arsenic—the sale of obscene publications and indecent books—was openly going on."[434] Confirming the double standard for members of the lower and upper classes, Campbell noted that the poison available was not alone "indecent books of a high price, which was a sort of check," but that "the most licentious and disgusting [material] w[as] coming out week by week, and sold to any person who asked for them, and in any numbers."[435] Six weeks later, he introduced the Obscene Publications Act into the House of Lords.

There is little purpose in documenting here all the twists and turns of the Act through the House of Lords and Commons, as it has been chronicled many times. The surprising aspect of the process (for people who believe the stereotype of Victorian prudishness) is how much resistance the Act initially encountered in the Houses. Opposition was led by Lord Chancellor Cranworth, and supported by Lords Lyndhurst, Brougham and Wensleydale, all of whom opposed the bill on the grounds that there was no way of defining what the bill sought to suppress. Lord Lyndhurst commented in a wonderfully snarky British way that, "what is the interpretation which is to be put on the word 'obscene?' I can easily conceive that two men will come to entirely different conclusions as to its meaning."[436]

Furthermore, the consensus was that the bill granted constables too much power without enough oversight. In its original form, based on the strength of one person's testimony, the authorities were allowed to enter and search any building and then seize and destroy any material they thought might be obscene. The Lords noted that these authorities were not well-known for their aesthetic or cultural judgment. The resistance was so strong and bitter that Campbell began to lose hope and signaled that he might drop the bill. This could not stand! The Society for the Suppression of Vice leaped into action, organizing a letter-writing lobbying campaign from its members and from the public as a whole. Shortly thereafter, Campbell, sounding greatly relieved, proclaimed to the House of Lords that he had received strong support for the bill from, "various Members of that House, from clergymen of all denominations, from many medical men, from fathers of families, and from young men who themselves had been inveigled into those receptacles of abomination against which his Bill was directed."[437] The debate over the law was publicized in newspapers and pamphlets across London, and by the time the bill reached the House of Commons, it saw near-universal support from "nearly all shades of the press. . . . Campbell and the Society got their act with only minor amendments."[438]

Campbell was only finally able to sell the Act to the Lords by promising that it would apply "exclusively to the works written for the single purpose of corrupting the morals of youth and of a nature calculated to shock the common feelings of decency in any well-regulated mind," and that any book that made any pretensions of being literature or art, classic or modern, had nothing to fear from the law.[439] The real enemy, to Campbell and the press, were the Holywell Street pornographers. The irony in this argument is that less than three decades later "the law would be used against the classical works the Lords had wanted to guard, and especially against current literature."[440] Indeed, this same act would be used to target and threaten the works now-famous authors such as James Joyce and D.H. Lawrence until the 1960s, over a century later. The impact of this law on England and its colonies in North America, Asia, and Australia—and on other Western cultures generally—can hardly be understated.

By far the best example of the worldwide influence and impact of the vice suppression movement is the one that was taking place across the Atlantic, first in New York City and then in the United States as a whole. Anthony Comstock first began his rise to fame and notoriety in the post-Civil Way New York City, by embarking on a mission as personal as Campbell's—the total and outright extermination of licentious literature in America. Because of his young age (mid-twenties), Comstock was among "among the first to understand that new and burgeoning business" of obscene literature.[441] Instead of being attracted, Comstock wrote that he was made aware of "'the appalling fact that there was an organized business, systemically carried on where 169 [obscene] books were openly advertised in circulars.'"[442] Offended, he worked alone "rigorously and unapologetically... enforcing the laws against trafficking in obscenity" by using the police to arrest of the offenders he found.[443]

Working as a vigilante however, would only get Comstock so far, and many of the cases were thrown out of court or simply dropped. What would truly empower Comstock, and allow him to ascend was that his crusade struck a chord in a group of people with access to time, money, and power: the Young Men's Christian Association. One of the board members, Morris Jesup, a wealthy banker and devout Christian, was a major advocate for the 1865 anti-obscenity law that the 1873 Comstock Act would ride on. And in 1872, Morris happened to notice a letter on the desk of the YMCA's secretary from Anthony Comstock.

The letter was a plea from Comstock for money, describing his campaign against a publisher of erotic books named William Haynes. Although the publisher had died shortly after he learned Comstock was after him, his wife, Mary Haynes, still had in her possession many of the books and plates.[444] She had offered to sell them to Comstock, but he, not having any money, turned to the YMCA.[445] Morris Jesup intervened, writing a check for $650—$500 for the plates and the books, and $150 for Comstock himself—"Comstock and his audience [had] found each other."[446] After he spoke to them in 1872, they assembled a Committee on Obscene Literature and for Suppression of Vice and appointed Comstock as its head: "from the perspective of the members of the committee, they had begun a battle. They then hired Comstock to help them fight it."[447]

And fight it, Comstock did. His earliest cases were rather straightforward, and carried the support of many YMCA members. It was only his later cases that would arouse so much controversy and solidify the historical image of him as excessive and intolerant. The William Haynes case described above was Comstock's first YMCA-supported victory. His next one was against George Ackerman, whose stock was raided and destroyed. Comstock found and destroyed, by his own words "5500-6000 Obs[cene] cards, ½ ton Letter Press, 4000 Pictures, 52 Steel & 50 copper plates, 142 woodcuts" as well as from two brothers named Barkley "2000 old letters, 2000 circulars, 100 photographs, and 100 obscene books...[and a] Lot of Rubber Goods."[448]

Perhaps because of his youth and his ability to understand the mind and culture of the New York clerks, but Comstock, as he made his arrests, especially the arrests of the Barkley brothers, he began to see that the distribution system "operating through the mails was more important than the sales over the counter" and that in order to truly succeed he would have to gain control over the mail system.[449] By 1872 he had successfully pushed for a copycat Obscene Publications Act, referred to as the Act for the "Suppression of Trade in, and Circulation of, Obscene Literature and Articles of Immoral Use" or the Comstock Laws, and went about using his newly granted powers immediately. Indeed, both the Societies for the Suppression of Vice in England and the United States put their newly-granted powers to use immediately, and by December of the same year, Lord Campbell was able to declare 'Mission Accomplished' over London pornographers:

> He was told that informations [sic] had been laid against dealers of the publications in question in Holywell Street; that warrants had been granted and searches made; and that large quantities of these abominable commodities had been found, and the parties owning them summoned before the magistrates. . .at last he was told, it was now in the quiet possession of the law, for the shops where these abominations were found had been shut up, and the rest of the houses were now conducted in a manner free from exception.[450]

If true, this did not remain the case for very long. No doubt the Holywell Street authors lay low for a few years, but less than a decade later the Saturday Review reported that "the situation was as bad as ever, and that 'the dunghill is in full heat, seething and steaming with all its old pestilence.'"[451]

The Romance of Lust

THE FINAL DECADES of the 1800s saw a veritable renaissance of pornography in England and other places, with new books being issued by the week. To provide a small selection, visitors to London's Holywell Street in the years following the Obscene Publications Act would see such titles as; *Intrigues in a Boarding School* (1860), *Confessions of a Lady's Maid* (1860), *How to Raise Love or The Art of making Love, in more ways than one* (1863), *Lucretia or the Delights of Cunnyland* (1864)—which is a more obscene version of the Merryland books we discussed—or even *The Inutility of Virtue*, which was cheekily printed for the 'Society of Vice' (1865).

Selective purchasers were rewarded when specialized

Brian M. Watson

genres and keywords began to develop, similar to modern-day pornographic subgenres: the boarding school, virgin confessions, nunneries, sex guides, flagellation—each with their own standard plots and tropes, much like a modern-day romance novel. It makes little difference which title one might buy, as nearly all of them saw a dramatic increase in the amount of sex and sexual positions at the expense of plot, narrative, and characterization, sometimes to the point of absurdity. Plot and style became a tattered scrap of plausibility to throw over scenes of debauchery, much like modern pornography videos using "pizza delivery," or the "plumber's visit" as a substitute to plot. One of the most obscene and absurd was the multi-volume *The Romance of Lust* which began appearing as early as 1859.

Some of this renaissance was attributable to William Dugdale's release from prison, but other publishers, such as John Hotten and William Lazenby, soon realized the profits to be made. All of the above titles and hundreds more are noted, described, and excerpted in a series of erotic indexes: *Index Librorum Prohibitorum* (Index of Prohibited Books, 1877), *Centuria Librorum Absconditorum* (A Hundred Hidden Books, 1879) and *Catena Librorum Tacendorum* (A Series of Silenced Books, 1885). Originally privately published, this trilogy was originally attributed to fake author 'Pisanus Fraxi,' and they are essentially whirlwind bibliographies of pornographic books—an early IMDB of pornography.[452]

The man behind the curtain, so to speak, was Henry Spencer Ashbee, who, on the surface, was a quite reputable and successful Victorian gentleman. Born in 1834 to moderately successful Kentish parents, Robert and Frances Ashbee, Henry Spencer would go on to become an extremely successful businessman himself when he married his wife, Elizabeth Lavy (their son Charles became a famous artist). His new father-in-law made him the head of a small branch of the textile company Charles Lavy & Co, and under Ashbee's management the

258

firm grew to be tremendously successful in England, France, Spain, Belgium and the United States. Much of Ashbee's success is attributed to his amazing grasp of languages and literature—as a child he had been educated in Greek, Latin, modern languages, and literature. He never attended university or college, but his grasp of French and Spanish were so good that he had an entry in the French version of *Who's Who* and was elected to a prestigious post as a Spanish literary critic.

His fluency also aided him in his obsessive and secret hobby; a hobby that ended up becoming the great passion of his life. Behind the scenes, "he was engaged in the ambitious project of becoming the century's leading collector and bibliographer or erotic books. Ashbee emerges as the archetypical Victorian gentleman with a secret."[453] He began this hobby probably under the influence of a close friend of his, but eventually—probably due to a lot of money and a lot of time to read—he began to be obsessive about his collection, buying copies of every erotic text he came across. His trips across Europe on business helped in this goal, and he even made friends with a British ambassador who would smuggle erotic books into England in government bags (which could not be searched).

Ashbee's group of friends met as a club called the Cannibal Club, beginning in the middle of 1863. Founded by Sir Richard Francis Burton, the famous adventurer and linguist, the group began having private dinner parties with members of elite British society that judged themselves as connoisseurs of fine pornography. Ashbee, along with the rest of the Club was profoundly disturbed by what he saw as the backwards sexual morality and 'hyper-prudishness' of English and American society at the time. The reason for the odd name of the club was because Burton had always maintained an interest in cannibalism, and was bitterly disappointed that he never managed to see and perhaps participate in it. The interest in cannibalism was not limited to Burton: one Cannibal begged

Burton to acquire the skin of an African girl so he might bind his volumes of the Marquis de Sade in it.[454]

In reality, the meetings of the Cannibal Club, jokingly called 'orgies' by Burton, were excuses for the members to get rip-roaringly drunk with group of likeminded men—no topic of conversation was out of bounds. The members were diverse, but some of the major figures included Richard Monckton Milnes, 1st Baron Houghton, the conservative politician and poet whose erotic literature collection was only surpassed by another member of the club; Edward Sellon, a translator and author of several erotic works; James Campbell Reddie, an openly homosexual translator of French and Italian erotic novels, and a pioneering erotic bibliographer whose work Ashbee would depend on; Frederick Hankey, a major Conservative politician; George Augustus Sala, the famous reporter and erotic novelist; Algernon Charles Swinburne, the taboo poet and playwright; and of course Henry Spencer Ashbee, the erotic bibliographer and encyclopedist, the man who helped to tie all of these disparate counterculture threads together.

The Cannibal dinners also provided a fertile breeding ground for collaboration and cooperation. Nearly every single member, at one time or another would turn his hand towards the creation pornographic material. They made themselves an audience for erotic material. Some works even became collaborations between two or more members, such as the *Mysteries of Verbena House* (1882), a heavily pornographic novel that focuses on the flagellation and birching of schoolgirl after schoolgirl by the headmistress. The work was started by Sala, but ended up being completed by Reddie when Sala either lost interest or failed to finish. Reddie also took up the completion of *The Sins of the Cities of the Plain* (1881), the work of another Cannibal, Simeon Solomon, the homosexual Pre-Raphaelite painter, when Solomon was convicted of public indecency and disgraced in 1873. The work was supposedly the 'true' biography of a Victorian rentboy named Jack Saul, likely based on the real-life John Saul in Ireland, but recounts a number of homosexual encounters in graphic detail.

The members also took the opportunity of the meetings to buy, sell, and recommend erotic literature to each other, much of which was available from a friend of the club, the aforementioned William Dugdale, or Swinburne's publisher John Camden Hotten. In the days after Club meetings it is possible to see Ashbee, Swinburne, and others writing to their booksellers for copies of a new or rumored work, such as such as *The Romance of Chastisement, Exhibition of Female Flagellants*, or the satirical opera *Lady Bumtickler's Revels*, all published by Hotten. Additionally, the members would read erotic works they had discovered or written to the club. For example, at one meeting in 1865, Swineburne waxed poetically about the new edition of Whitman's *Leaves of Grass* that included several poems celebrating sensual and romantic love between men.

In his early forties, Henry Spencer Ashbee decided he needed to set himself to a new project, as a way of giving back to all of his friends who had helped him collect these erotic and pornographic books—he decided to write a trilogy of *Indexes* of erotic literature. In his first Index, *Index Librorum Prohibitorum*, published in 1877, he described his reasons for doing this:

> That English erotic literature should never have had its bibliographer is not difficult to understand. First and foremost the English nation possesses an ultra-squeamishness and hyper-prudery peculiar to itself, sufficient alone to deter any author of position and talent from taking in hand so tabooed a subject; and secondly English books of that class have generally been written with so little talent delicacy or art that in addition to the objectionableness of the subject itself they would undoubtedly be considered

Brian M. Watson

by most bibliographers as totally unworthy of any
consideration whatever.[455]

In writing the *Indexes,* Ashbee partially hoped to preserve
the transient pornographic texts that were the most likely to
be destroyed. As a result, many of his excerpts are the only surviving record of these books that we have today. Preempting
the charge that his commentaries are obscene, Pisanus Fraxi
insists that, "in treating of obscene books it is self-evident
that obscenities cannot be avoided," adding immediately that
in his own text, he will never be caught using an "impure
word when one less distasteful but equally expressive can be
found."[456] And, anyways, nobody was going to be aroused by
his commentaries:

> The passions are not excited. Although the citations
> I produce are frequently licentious, being as a mat-
> ter of course those which I have considered the
> most remarkable or most pungent in the books from
> which they are extracted; yet I give only so much as
> is necessary to form a correct estimate of the style
> of the writer, of the nature of the book, or the course
> of the tale, not sufficient to inflame the passions.
> This could only be accomplished by the perusal of
> the books in their entirety, by the reader giving him-
> self up in fact to the author. My extracts on the con-
> trary will, I trust and believe, have a totally oppos-
> ite effect and as a rule will inspire so hearty a disgust
> for the books they are taken from, that the reader
> will have learned enough about them from my pages
> and will be more than satisfied to have nothing fur-
> ther to do with them.[457]

As any of the other upper-class men of the Cannibal Club
would have, Ashbee knew that his indexes and his life's work
faced the greatest danger after he died. Rather than let it pass

into the hands of his family, where it surely would have been destroyed—Ashbee was on as good terms with his son as de Sade was, which is to say, not good terms at all—he willed the entire collection to the British Library and Museum.

If it had just been these books however, it would have only taken a couple of moments for the British Museum to either refuse the bequest or to choose to destroy it. However, along with his pornography collection, Ashbee also had the world's largest collection of *Don Quixote* and Cervantes manuscripts and prints. Some of the manuscripts and artworks are original and priceless, and he spent as much acquiring them (if not more) as he did erotic material. Therefore, in order to obtain the Cervantes material, the British Museum had to take the erotica (excepting duplicates) as well.

Gibson records the dilemma of the Museum on finding out the terms of the bequest: on the subject of the obscene books, the Museum stated that, "[we] have gone through the whole of them and have packed six boxes the duplicate copies. He asked the permission of the Trustees to destroy them."[458] Peter Mendes has speculated that, along with the duplicates, the Museum "destroyed the greater part of Ashbee's collection of 'poorly produced, illustrated pornographic fiction (particularly in English) of the nineteenth century,' perhaps some hundred items."[459] Since no other copies of many of these books seem to have survived, they have now been lost to research forever—except in Ashbee's *Indexes*. However, what remains in the so called 'Private Case,' is an invaluable asset to any researcher of sexuality or literature—it is the first time these books escaped the flames. Furthermore, after the Private Case was established, it allowed other erotic collectors, many of them Ashbee's friends, to will their rare material to that collection—entire books have been written from research there, including this one.

There is a chance that among the books destroyed by the British Library, there were copies of a certain text called *My*

Secret Life by 'Walter,' which is an 11-volume erotic master-piece that totals in at around 4,000 pages and over a million words, which puts it in among one of the longest works of literature ever composed, and by far the longest erotic work ever composed. It is quite likely that Henry Spencer Ashbee was the author of this work, and most scholars (including myself) support Ashbee's biographer Ian Gibson in this argument.[460] The books that *were* preserved were stored in a part of the British Library called the Private Case, which was completely off limits to the public. Only recently have the public and academics been allowed to peruse the books, but there are still a number of strict rules surrounding it. When I visited, there were all kinds of safeguards in place—for example, you had to read these books under the supervision of librarians, and you were not allowed to leave them on your desk if you went to the bathroom or got up to stretch your legs. Furthermore, if you were leaving for lunch, you had to return them to the circulation desk, where they would be placed in a chest and securely padlocked. The fact that these restrictions still surround and control much of the Ashbee collection shows the legacy of the Obscene Publications Act echoing down to today.

Knowing what we do about Henry Spencer Ashbee, it would be surprising to think that there were books that could shock even him. For example, in one of his Indexes he comments that a certain book, *The Romance of Lust*, contains scenes "not surpassed by the most libidinous chapters of [de Sade's] Justine. The episodes, however, are frequently most improbable, sometimes impossible, and are as a rule too filthy and crapulous. No attempt is made to moderate the language, but the grossest words are invariably employed."[461] A brief survey of the work, which maunders through 300-plus dense pages of description, would give this impression as well—*The Romance* is a blow-by-blow account of the amorous career of a boy (and then a man) named Charles, told from his point of view. He begins his tale in his 15th year, and states that along with his two younger sisters, "Mamma treated us all as children, and was blind to the fact that I was no longer what I had been. . .my passions were awakening."[462]

In a revealing detail about how differently children were raised, and how beds were shared in an earlier time, Charles notes that:

> My sisters and I all slept in the same room. They together in one bed, I alone in another. When no one was present, we had often mutually examined the different formations of our sexes. We had discovered that mutual handlings gave a certain amount of pleasing sensation; and, latterly, my eldest sister had discovered that the hooding and un-hooding of my doodle, as she called it, instantly caused it to swell up and stiffen as hard as a piece of wood. My feeling of her little pinky slit gave rise in her to nice sensations, but on the slightest attempt to insert even my finger, the pain was too great. We had made so little progress in the attouchements that not the slightest inkling of what could be done in that way dawned upon us.[463]

The death of his father and the increasing illness of his mother causes her to hire a governess named Evelyn to educate and discipline Charles and his two sisters, Mary and Eliza. The mother describes the children to Evelyn as "somewhat spoiled, and unruly; but there is a horse, and Susan will make you excellent birch rods whenever you require them. If you spare their bottoms when they deserve whipping, you will seriously offend me." This, as they say, is pretty blatant foreshadowing, and it is not too long afterwards that we have our first blatantly sexual scene, one of flagellation. Charles' sister Mary refuses to do something that Evelyn commanded, and as a result she is placed on 'the horse,' which was a device used

Brian M. Watson

to administer corporal punishment. Charles' description of it reads like a sex device from a BDSM catalog:

> [Evelyn] placed [Mary] on it, held her firmly with one hand while she put the noose round her with the other, which, when drawn, secured her body; other nooses secured each ankle to rings in the floor, keeping her legs apart by the projection of the horse, and also forcing the knees to bend a little, by which the most complete exposure of the bottom, and, in fact, of all her private parts too, was obtained.... The rod whistled through the air and fell with a cruel cut on poor Mary's plump little bottom. The flesh quivered again, and Mary, who had resolved not to cry, flushed in her face, and bit the damask with which the horse was covered. . . . Cut succeeded cut, yell succeeded yell —until the rod was worn to a stump, and poor Mary's bottom was one mass of weals and red as raw beef. It was fearful to see, and yet such is our nature that to see it was, at the same time, exciting.[464]

Inadvertently, for a teenage boy, Charles quickly becomes infatuated with Evelyn and watches her undress every night in the bedroom he shares with her and his sisters. Being so naive he, of course, never thinks of "applying [his] fingers for relief," and remains innocent. Innocent, at least for a few more pages (and two months later), until his mother is visited by a friend, Mr. B (who seems to have the most reoccurring name in English erotica) and his wife. One night, when trying to get something from a closet, he hears them coming and hides, peeking through a crack in the door:

> [Mr. B] got up, and lifted her on the edge of the bed, threw her back, and taking her legs under his arms, exposed everything to my view. She had not so much hair on her mount of Venus as Miss Evelyn,

but her slit showed more pouting lips, and appeared more open. Judge of my excitement when I saw Mr. Benson unbutton his trousers and pull out an immense cock. Oh, dear, how large it looked; it almost frightened me. With his fingers he placed the head between the lips of Mrs. Benson's sheath, and then letting go his hold, and placing both arms so as to support her legs, he pushed it all right into her to the hilt at once. I was thunderstruck that Mrs. Benson did not shriek with agony, it did seem such a large thing to thrust right into her belly. However, far from screaming with pain, she appeared to enjoy it.[465]

A few days later, Mr. B is forced to leave on business, and his wife, Mrs. Benson, who apparently cannot last more than a day or so without getting off, ropes Charles into visiting her room. Then, in one long-winded and glorious night, she "initiat[es Charles] into all the rites of Venus. . .the *ne plus ultra* [highest peak] of erotic pleasure." The next 50 pages describe, in endless details, all of the rites Mrs. Benson initiates him in:

It was a long bout indeed, prolonged by Mrs. Benson's instructions, and she enjoyed it thoroughly, encouraged me by every endearing epithet, and by the most voluptuous manoeuvres. I was quite beside myself. The consciousness that I was thrusting my most private part into that part of a lady's person which is regarded with such sacred delicacy caused me to experience the most enraptured pleasure. Maddened by the intensity of my feeling I at length quickened my pace. My charming companion did the same, and we together yielded down a most copious and delicious discharge.[466]

As was quite common in earlier pornographic novels, such

as *Luisa Sigea* or *The School of Venus*, Mrs. Benson also educates (initiates) Charles in anatomy and biology: "My dear Charles, do you see that little projection at the upper part of my quim, that is my clitoris, and is the site of the most exquisite sensations. . .you will find as you titillate it with your tongue or suck it, that it will become harder and more projecting," and cautions him to be careful about how many times in a day he has sex: "I must consider your health. You have already done more than your age warrants, and you must rise and go to your bed to recover, by a sound sleep, your strength."

She also educates him on how to manage his affairs, which is perhaps the only code of morals that is followed throughout the book. She lectures that he must "show great discretion and ready wit. . .[for] discretion is the trump card of success," and most importantly, he must let all his lovers "for some time imagine that each possesses you for the first time. . .you must enact the part of an ignoramus seeking for instruction."[467] This shows that educational texts still remained as relevant and important for nineteenth century readers as much as they were for sixteenth century readers.

Shortly thereafter, Charles "felt my opportunity was at hand to initiate my darling sister into the delightful mysteries that I had just been myself instructed in," and proceeds to instruct his older sister Mary in "all [the ways] of kissing and toying with your charming little Fanny," then turned to his younger sister Eliza, commenting that, "A reflection struck me that it would be necessary to initiate my sister Eliza in our secrets, and although she might be too young for the complete insertion of my increasingly large cock, I might gamahuche [perform oral sex on] her while fucking Mary, and give her intense pleasure. In this way we could retire without difficulty to spots where we should be quite in safety, and even when such was not the case, we could employ Eliza as a watch, to give us early notice of any one approaching. It will be seen that this idea was afterwards most successfully carried out to the immense increase of my pleasure."[468] The rest of the book is, quite simply, an exercise in increasing bawdiness, endless sex, and trampling of all societal boundaries. The second volume includes his orgies with his sisters and an older gentleman named James MacCallum, and the siblings' seduction of their new governess, Miss Frankland. The end of the second volume and the beginning of the third concerns Charles' 'seduction' by his aunt and uncle, and then the seduction of an extremely young village boy named Dale by him and his uncle. The fourth book reaches the height of indulgence and hedonism when all of the parties come together in a tumult:

> [M]yself in my aunt's cunt, which incest stimulated uncle to a stand, and he took to his wife's arse while her nephew incestuously fucked her cunt. The Count took to the delicious and most exciting tight cunt of the Dale, while her son shoved his prick into his mother's arse, to her unspeakable satisfaction. Ellen and the Frankland amused themselves with tribadic extravagances.[469]

And so on. The fourth volume comes to a close with a description of the children of the assorted couples, and how they too were, "initiated in all love's delicious mysteries by their respective parents." With a final commentary by Charles, the book ends: "we are thus a happy family, bound by the strong ties of a double incestuous lust. It is necessary to have these loved objects to fall back upon, for alas! All the earlier partakers of my prick are dead and gone."[470]

All considered, *The Romance of Lust* manages to cover voyeurism, sexual education, masturbation, heterosexual sex, lesbianism, male homosexuality, flagellation, anal sex, double penetration, incest, pedophilia, and coprophilia, on the short list. Unlike the stories that this book began with, there is almost no dialogue, and very little plot that is not related to sex—or serving as a vehicle, segue, or bridge to another sexual encounter. Nor is there really an effort at philosophizing or any sort of moral struggle. And this was considered one of the better-written and planned pornographic works of the 19th century by 'foremost' experts.

The reality is that by the mid-1800s, these erotic works had matured into something resembling modern pornography in all but name—and as the word 'pornography' became more and more popular, all erotic literature came to fall under that umbrella. *The Romance of Lust* as well as *My Secret Life* and all similar works of that genre have followed the 'Cleland' strategy to the logical extreme, becoming purely sexual. The word 'pornography' gave authors and artists something to aspire to, something to categorize their work by, but it was also used encompassingly by authorities in an attempt to exert control over any number of works, including ones that 'made pretensions of being literature' and should not have had anything to fear from Campbell's law.

This is what we will discuss in the closing chapters of this book, before turning to visual pornography in the form of photography and film. If the period between 1750 and 1857 was the period where the cultural battles reached their greatest frenzy and created the genre of pornography, then the following century, from 1857-1960 marks the high water point of the use of the Obscene Publications Act as a bludgeon against any work that was found morally questionable. It is also the period of time that lead to the eventual turning of the tides and the defeat of the law. Let us go, ever onwards, to the end of our story.

PART IV: LA PETITE MORT / *FUTUUMESHI* (1900-1961) [471]

8

1900 — 1960: Sexology, Psychology, Filmography

Hick's Test[472]

A S DEMONSTRATED by *The Romance of Lust*, the 1857 Obscene Publications Act did little to nothing to control the rising tide of obscenity and pornography. If you will recall, Lord Baron Campbell only managed to get the 1857 Act passed by promising that it would apply exclusively to "works written for the single purpose of corrupting the morals of youth and of a nature calculated to shock the common feelings of decency in any well-regulated mind," and that any book that made any pretensions of being literature or art, classic or modern, had nothing to fear from the law.

The tremendous irony of Campbell's theater was that less than three decades later "the law would be used against the classical works the Lords had wanted to guard, and especially against current literature."[473] The shift occurred in 1868, with the *Regina v. Hicklin* decision. The case concerned a man named Henry Scott, a bookseller from Wolverhampton, who reprinted an old anti-Catholic pamphlet called *The Confessional Unmasked: shewing the depravity of the Romish priest-*

hood, the iniquity of the Confessional, and the questions put to females in confession. The text itself is nearly-ridiculously dry and boring theological pamphlet whose arguments and comments go as far back as the Reformation, and many passages bear a remarkable similarity to *Venus in the Cloister* and other works we've touched on. The 'sauciest' it really gets is when it talks about how priests question women about sex with their husbands, and about how priests seduce women (by overcoming their modesty)—the same story that goes back to Boccaccio or Aretino. The pamphlet itself was even somewhat aware of the stir that it was causing, assuring the potential reader that "some of the more sordid details. . . were being kept in the relative obscurity of the Latin tongue, 'but the time may come when it will become out bounden through painful duty to rouse the indignation of Englishmen at the expense of their modesty' lest Roman Catholic priests 'convert an Eden into a Sodom.'"[474] In the hands of the anti-Catholic William Murphy however, the pamphlet became weaponized, and after a series of firebrand lectures in Birmingham an Irish Catholic mob of 50-100,000 people gathered to storm his lecture hall, forcing the Mayor to supplement his police force with some 400 soldiers (including 100 cavalry) and a force of some 600 special constables.[475]

But to newly-empowered government officials, there was a chance, however small, that a child might be corrupted through reading the text, so they seized the work and ordered it destroyed. Scott was also brought to trial under the 1857 Obscene Publications Act. During the first trial, however, he proclaimed that his *intentions* had just been to insult Catholics, not to corrupt children. The court accepted this argument, but the prosecutors appealed the decision to the Queen's Bench, the supreme court in England. Justice Cockburn held that any work that could

> deprave and corrupt those whose minds are open
> to such immoral influences, and into whose hands

a publication of this sort may fall... [anything that] suggest to the minds of the young of either sex, or even to persons of more advanced years, thoughts of a most impure and libidinous character

was prosecutable obscenity.[476] The Hicklin Test, as it came to be called, widened the definition of obscenity from works written 'for the sole purpose of corrupting the morals of youth' to works that 'deprave and corrupt,' and those that 'may fall' into the hands of anyone with an ability to read them. In other words, it was no longer just the youth that needed to be protected, but the minds of the entire British public. The intention of the author was irrelevant, all that mattered was protecting the innocence of the public.

Following the Hicklin decision, groups such as the National Vigilance Association (another reformation group, established in 1885) seized on it as a new weapon in their battle "for the enforcement and improvement of the laws for the repression of criminal vice and public immorality."[477] Utilizing a strategy developed by Anthony Comstock and the American Society for the Suppression of Vice, these groups would purchase copies of books they found obscene and then prosecute the publishers for allowing the book to fall into their hands. Additionally, government authorities, particularly the Home Office (which controlled products which could be imported into England), used the same strategy to target books that were printed on the Continent and then brought into England. The Hicklin Test enabled the prosecution of any book found suspect, whether it was a work of literature such as Emile Zola's *La Terre* (prosecuted in 1888), or a medical text that explained sex and contraception such as *The Fruits of Philosophy* (prosecuted in 1877). With such descriptions as:

[T]he exterior orifice commences immediately below [the Mons Veneris]. On each side of this orifice is a prominence continued from the mons veneris,

> which is largest above and gradually diminishes as
> it descends. These two prominences are called the
> Labia Externa, or external lips. Near the latter end
> of pregnancy they become somewhat enlarged and
> relaxed, so that they sustain little or no injury dur-
> ing parturition[478]

The latter book was not meant to be particularly pornographic. Nor does it seem that the author's single purpose was
to corrupt the morals of youths—in fact, the stated purpose
was, "not to gratify the idle curiosity of the light-minded. . .
[but] for utility in the broad and truly philosophical sense of
the term." This was even recognized at the trial, where the
jury noted that they "entirely exonerate the defendant from
any corrupt motives in publishing it."[479] However, the jury
held, at the same time, that "we are unanimously of opinion that the book in question is calculated to deprave public
morals." For Justice Cockburn, that was a verdict of guilty.

The jury's split statement shows the discrepancy between
the intentions of the Obscene Publications Act and its expan-
sion under Hicklin Test. The 'problem' with *The Fruits of Philosophy* was not its 'obscenity,' but the fact that it explained
and advocated for birth control—its advocacy for 'onanism'
was the reason it, along with Zola's *La Terre*, was found to deprave public morals. This is also illustrated by the prosecution of Havelock Ellis' second volume of *The Psychology of Sex*,
also known as *Sexual Inversion*. If obscenity was contingent
upon authorial intention, then Ellis was especially innocent:
"I had not at first proposed to devote a whole volume to sexual
inversion. It may even be that I was inclined to slur it over as
an unpleasant subject, and one that it was not wise to enlarge
on."[480] Knowing it was not wise; Ellis went to lengths to make
his text scientific, even to the point of publishing it (1896) in
German, the contemporary *lingua franca* of science. Nonetheless, when translated into English the following year, the work

quickly came under fire. The 'problem' with Ellis' work for the Home Office was that he refused to criminalize or pathologize homosexual relationships:

> I realized that in England, more than in any other country, the law and public opinion combine to place a heavy penal burden and a severe social stigma on the manifestations of an instinct which to those persons who possess it frequently appears natural and normal. It was clear, therefore, that the matter was in special need of elucidation and discussion.[481]

Ellis was not only cautious in his language—he also prepared "an elaborate defense and assembled a team of medical experts to prove the book's scientific merit."[482] However, his name did not appear on the indictment—the name of his bookseller did. The bookseller pleaded guilty after an intimidating lecture by the magistrate, and Ellis' elaborately planned defense never saw the light of day. Unable to have his day in court, he was left powerless and had to publish his books in Paris or the United States. Even then, American authorities were only slightly more lenient, allowing Ellis' works to be purchased by only by doctors and medical students.[483]

Ellis' trial was instructional for both government prosecutors and modern authors. The former found a new strategy in targeting publishers and booksellers, and the latter realized that representations of sexuality in any form, especially queer sexuality, was to invite prosecution. The advantage to targeting publishers instead of authors was manifold; first, it allowed prosecutors to sidestep the issue of literary merit or artistic value; second, a publisher was much less likely to 'put it all on the line' and engage in a full defense of one novel or author; finally, this strategy allowed exploit of the Hicklin Test, which defined obscenity as something that fell into the wrong hands as opposed to the 1857 Obscene Publications Act, which defined it as authorial intent. The result of this was that publishers began to require that authors revise their work before publication. Additionally, many authors engaged in self-censorship or complete silencing, to avoid calling attention to themselves through subtlety, or to avoid the risk altogether.

The Grey Elderly Ones

ONE EXAMPLE of this latter strategy is *Maurice* (1971), by E.M. Forster. *Maurice* is a *bildungsroman* and biography of a gay man, Maurice Hall. The work is far too subtle to be 'written exclusively for the purpose of corrupting the morals of youth.' For example, Maurice himself is not aware of his own 'inversion' until the second part of the novel, nearly a hundred pages in, and Forster himself noted that Maurice's puzzlement was deliberate. Regardless, the novel's focus on his relationships with Clive and then Alec was *verboten* for the time. The erasure of homosexuals from public discourse is even demonstrated when Maurice visits his family doctor and says that there is something wrong with him: the doctor cannot figure out the issue at all, saying he is clean of any STDs. Maurice himself has to say that he is "an unspeakable of the Oscar Wilde sort," to which the doctor replies "rubbish, rubbish... Listen to me Maurice, never let that evil hallucination that temptation from the devil occur to you again."[484] The fact that Forster was already a popular author by the time he wrote *Maurice* (1913-4), meant that the chance of his work falling into the 'wrong' hands was too high. Forester of course, realized this, and did not publish the book during his lifetime. Compounding the problem was that *Maurice* had a deliberately happy ending—the *Terminal Note* to *Maurice* says that:

> A happy ending was imperative. I shouldn't have bothered to write otherwise! I was determined that

in fiction anyway two men should fall in love and remain in it for the ever and ever that fiction allows. . .Happiness is its keynote—which by the way has had an unexpected result: it has made the book more difficult to publish. . .If it ended unhappily, with a lad dangling from a noose or with a suicide pact, all would be well, for there is no pornography or seduction of minors. But the lovers get away unpunished and consequently recommend crime. [485]

His deliberacy in its revision and diligence in building a personal archive to contextualize it is evidence that he intended *Maurice* to eventually be published, in "a Happier Year."[486]

Forster was not the only author to engage in self-censorship —most of his contemporaries engaged in it or were forced to by their publishers—but the total suppression of *The Psychology of Sex* and *Maurice* remains an extreme example. On the other end of the spectrum was a writer that declared outright contempt for and war upon the Obscene Publications Act: D.H. Lawrence. The near-hounding of Lawrence by the Home Office, newspaper critics, and moral societies from the 1915 burning of *The Rainbow* to the posthumous trial (1960) of *Lady Chatterley's Lover* (1929) was tantamount to decades-long governmental crusade against him. Lawrence responded with a campaign of his own by continuing to write and by targeting English censors with vitriol in poetry such as *Nettles* (1930) and in pamphlets such as *Pornography and Obscenity* (1929), which will be examined below.

The government became 'aware' of Lawrence in 1915, the middle of World War I, where his publication of *The Rainbow* was immediately met with newspaper criticism of its frank discussion of sex. *The Rainbow* is a family history of three generations of the Brangwen family, beginning with Tom Brangwen falling in love with Lydia, a Polish refugee. The next section of the book concerns the tumultuous relationship between Lydia's daughter Anna and her husband Will. However, the vast majority of the book—over three-quarters of it—is focused on Anna and Will's daughter, Ursula. *The Rainbow* focuses intently on the subtle politics of relationships, at the expense of all else. This is apparent from the first chapter, "How Tom Brangwen Married a Polish Lady," to the last pages of the novel, where Ursula dwells on a lost lover. Lawrence's novel is a study of love, a word that is repeated over a hundred times in it, and seems to crop up every ten pages.

Specifically, *The Rainbow* focuses on the tensions between love, lust, and power. Both Lydia and Anna 'give in' to men and masculine lust, which is described as uncontrollable: when Anna rejects Will's advances he "became a mad creature, black and electric with fury. The dark storms rose in him, his eyes glowed black and evil," and he "force[s] his will upon her."[487] Lydia is nearly subsumed and erased by Tom, but Anna, who represents a transition from absolute patriarchy, is not completely powerless: when Will had finished "getting his satisfaction of her" she "strikes back," dashing, goading, harassing him (in her words), until he "recognized her as the enemy."[488] The tempestuous war between the two of them continues, alternating between intense hostility and overwhelming love, until they are complete strangers to each other. Only then, when they treat each other as equals are they transformed:

> He was the sensual male seeing his pleasure, she was the female ready to take hers: but in her own way. . . She was another woman under the instance of a strange man. He was a stranger to her, seeing his own ends. Very good. . .They abandoned in one motion the moral position, each was seeing gratification pure and simple. . .he lived in a passion of sensual discovery with her.[489]

The battle between the pair is essentially a conflict over

love and power, over the need for control and dominance in the relationship. Whereas Lydia was essentially controlled and dominated by her husband, Anna and Will, alienated from each other over the course of years, manage to have a rapprochement by finally seeing each other as equals and taking what they want from each other.

If the visceral descriptions were not disturbing to censors, the account of Ursula's life, which takes up most of the book was undoubtedly so. Representing (to Lawrence) the most important and modern generation in the Brangwen family, Ursula is the first woman who has the freedom to choose between love and power, to control or refuse the masculine lust that is foisted upon her, or even pursue alternate routes. For example, when she begins a relationship with Anton Skrebensky, a British soldier, she does not 'give in' to his entreaties or physical goading:

> He appropriated her. There was a fierce, white cold passion in her heart. . .like a soft weight upon her, bearing her down. . . but still her body was the subdued, cold, indomitable passion. . . She received all the force of his power. . . She was cold and unmoved as a pillar of salt.[490]

Despite the fact that his "will was set and straining with all its tension," he is "annihilated" and her pillar of salt "burn[s] and corrod[es]" him.[491] Under the moral standards for books at the time, the two fates for women were supposed to be marriage and reward or whoredom and punishment— Lawrence's Ursula subverts both of these. When Anton returns from fighting the Boer War years later, the pair end up getting engaged and having sex. However, Ursula abruptly decides that "'I don't think I want to marry you [Anton]... I don't want to be with other people' she said. 'I want to be like this. I'll tell you if ever I want to marry you.'"[492] Anton breaks off their engagement, marries another woman, and sails for India, and Ursula finds that she is pregnant. Disaster for the whore seems to loom—but it never manifests, as Ursula miscarries, and then carries on with her life, stronger than before—she becomes the protagonist of Lawrence's next novel, *Women In Love* (1920).

On top of Ursula's subversions and Lawrence's descriptions, two final nails would drive the coffin shut for a censorship case: Ursula's lesbian relationship with her teacher, Ms. Iver, and the questioning of Christianity by various characters. Ursula's relationship with Ms. Iver was not subtle—Lawrence describes it even more openly than some of his heterosexual relationships, and they indeed "become intimate."[493] Furthermore, both Ms. Inger and Anna question Christianity; Ms. Inger saying that *"religions* were local [but] Religion was universal. Christianity was a local branch," and Anna saying "It is impudence to say that Woman was made out of Man's body, when every man is born of a woman."[494] Regardless of which particular alerted or disturbed them, the police were quick to obtain a warrant under the 1857 Obscene Publications Act and seize all copies of *The Rainbow* for destruction. Like Ellis, they targeted the publisher of the novel, Methuen, and forced them to renounce the book and burn all copies. The publisher was not happy as they had attempted to get Lawrence to "moderate the manuscript and he had twice refused."[495] The case led to a blacklisting of Lawrence in England, its colonies, and America—the Home Office and others would go after his *Women in Love*, *Lady Chatterley's Lover*, and his other novels, poetry and plays—he was even forced to use a pseudonym (Lawrence H. Davidson) on textbooks he wrote, to avoid scrutiny.

Admirably or foolishly, Lawrence never changed his focus or declined an opportunity to attack his censorial adversaries. For example, when he published a book of poetry, *Pansies* (1928), Scotland Yard demanded that he remove 12 controversial poems or face prosecution, which he did, saying they were "not terribly important bits."[496] However, using the publicity he secretly printed 500 copies of the original book, with the offending poems added back in, but for 'private' publication only. When they had all sold, he announced this through his publisher, who said that "in the event of any action taken, which I do not consider likely, it would have to be proved that the book was likely to fall into the hands of people who were liable to be morally influenced by it."[497] Lawrence was well-aware of the distinction between the original 1857 Act and the Hicklin Test, and knew he had a good case if it were to go to trial. Indeed, it seems that he deliberately instigated the authorities in hope of this. Unfortunately for Lawrence, the Director of Public Prosecutions was also well-aware of the distinction, and refused to proceed in the issue, even if the Home Office wanted to pursue editions sent overseas.[498]

Lawrence's name alone seemed to be enough to bring down the police—an exhibition of his paintings in 1929 caused the police to dig up an even earlier act, the 1842 Vagrancy Act, in order to charge the gallery owner, Mr. St. John Hutchinson, with exhibiting indecent prints. When he appeared before the magistrates, Hutchinson argued that "the raid amounted to a new form of censorship. 'I have not been able to find any case in which serious paintings have been brought into a police court and a magistrate has been asked to decide whether they were obscene.'"[499] Whether or not the magistrate was in agreement, he said he would dismiss the case if Hutchinson would agree to pay a fine of five pounds, which he agreed to, not willing to risk further prosecution as Lawrence may have been. The whole episode particularly enraged Lawrence, and he quickly responded to the trial with his landmark essay, *Pornography and Obscenity* (1929), where he noted that "when the police raided my picture show, they did not in the least know what to take. So they took every picture where the smallest bit of the sex organ of either man or woman showed."[500]

Pornography and Obscenity serves as a very useful insight into Lawrence's understandings of sex and sexuality, and his use of them in his novels. It is also a useful tool for understanding the impacts of Obscene Publication Acts on artists and authors alike, and how they worked though the ideas of pornography and obscenity and made their own distinctions. Lawrence begins the essay by stating "what they [pornography and obscenity] are depends, as usual, entirely on the individual."[501] Noting that pornography means "the graph [*drawing*] of the harlot [*porno*]" and obscene meant "that which might not be represented on stage" he points out the same issue that Lord Lyndhurst did a half-century earlier: "what is obscene to Tom is not obscene to Lucy or Joe."[502] In Lawrence's view, it is mob-rule and mob-understanding that decide the obscene "*Vox Populi, Vox Dei*, don't you know. If you don't we'll let you know it."[503] But Lawrence suggests a shift for the popular understanding of pornography, because

> even I would censor genuine pornography, rigorously. . .what is pornography, after all this? It isn't sex appeal or sex stimulus in art. It isn't even a deliberate intention on the part of the artist to arouse or excite sexual feelings. There's nothing wrong with sexual feelings in themselves, so long as they are straightforward and not sneaking or sly. . .Pornography is the attempt to insult sex, to do dirt on it. This is unpardonable.[504]

The 'grey elderly ones' that Lawrence targeted were, in his eyes, responsible for putting dirt on sex and love.

In a funny way, as he continues to describe the differences he sees between pornography and obscenity, Lawrence brings us full circle in our narrative to this point:

> We take it, I assume, that pornography is something base, something unpleasant. In short, we don't like

it. And why don't we like it? Because it arouses sexual feelings? I think not. No matter how hard we may pretend otherwise, most of us rather like a moderate rousing of our sex. It warms us, stimulates us like sunshine on a grey day. . . Half the great poems, pictures, music, stories of the whole world are great by virtue of the beauty of their sex appeal. Titian or Renoir, the Song of Solomon or Jane Eyre, Mozart or Annie Laurie, the loveliness is all interwoven with sex appeal, sex stimulus, call it what you will. . . Perhaps it may be argued that a mild degree of sex appeal is not pornographical, whereas a high degree is. But this is a fallacy.

Boccaccio at his hottest seems to me less pornographical than Pamela or Clarissa Harlowe or even Jane Eyre or a host of modern books or films which pass uncensored. At the same time Wagner's Tristan and Isolde seems to me very near to pornography, and so, even, do some quite popular Christian hymns.[505]

As he would say in *Apropos of Lady Chatterley's Lover*: "I want men and women to be able to think sex, fully, completely, honestly, and cleanly. Even if we can't act sexually to out complete satisfaction, let us at least think sexually, complete and clear."[506] The police and the censors that called them out were "the grey elderly ones" that "belong[ed] to the last century, the eunuch century... the century that has tried to destroy humanity, the nineteenth century...of purity and the dirty little secret."[507] Sexuality and its artistic representation, the last barrier in polite conversation and public discourse, was the battleground on which Lawrence fought for the right to express himself. However, he was repeatedly stymied by a prosecutorial strategy that targeted publishers or gallery owners who were not willing to risk a full trial. As a result, Lawrence was left with an unwarranted reputation as a pornographer and nearly chased out of Britain by the end of WWI. A long period of self-imposed exile compounded by ill health and his death in 1930 left him unable to challenge the reputation in court, and he did not live to see the turning point in his struggle.

The Battle of the Lonely Well

AT THE SAME TIME Lawrence was castigating 'grey elderly ones,' in his pamphlet, another trial over obscene literature was taking place, one that holds augurs for the mid-century shift that produced the 1959 obscenity law—the 1928 trial over Radclyffe Hall's *The Well of Loneliness*. Like *Maurice* and *The Rainbow*, Hall's novel is a *bildungsroman* that documents a characters childhood and coming of age. Unlike Lawrence, Hall was not interested in frank depiction and description of sexuality. In fact, the most 'obscene' or suggestive line in the novel occurs when the main character kisses another woman "full on the lips, as a lover."[508] While Forester was much more cautions and hesitant about publishing a novel that discussed or featured homosexuality, Hill was not reticent at all. In a very real sense, Hill combined Lawrence's aggressive agenda with Forster's topic of choice. Although it would be easy to propose that it was Hall's mention of homosexuality brought down official censure, the fact that Virginia Woolf published a book (*Orlando*) in the same year and on the same topic discounts that suggestion. The difference is that Hall treated *The Well of Loneliness* as a polemic against the British establishment, especially the homophobic attitudes of the time.

The *Well of Loneliness* tells the story of Stephen Gordon, the daughter—despite the name—of two upper-class English parents, Anna and Sir Philip Gordon. To explain the name: when Anna conceives, Sir Philip is struck by "how much he longed for a son" and they take to calling the fetus Stephen.[509] As the narrator puts it, "'Man proposes—God disposes,'" and Stephen is born a girl. Sir Philip however, "insisted on calling the infant Stephen...[and] was stubborn, as he could be at times over whims."[510] From a very young age however, Stephen manifests signs of 'sexual inversion' as Ellis called it, and "became aware of an urgent necessity to love. She adored her father, but that was quite different... it was other with Collins, the housemaid."[511] When Stephen becomes infatuated with Collins her father notices and begins to "study his daughter gravely," reading late at night a book by a certain German, Karl Heinrich Ulrichs—the first sexologist to propose a theory of homosexuality.[512] He is unable to tell his wife of his suspicions about their daughter and:

> committed the first cowardly action of his life... In his infinite pity for Stephen's mother, he sinned very deeply and gravely against Stephen, by withholding from that mother his own conviction that her child was not as other children... 'There's nothing for you to understand,' he said firmly, but I like you to trust me in all things.[513]

The narrator injects a value judgment against Sir Philip in saying that he 'sinned very deeply and gravely.' Furthermore, when he is unable to tell Stephen herself about his discoveries, he is described as setting "the lips of his spirit to the cup and his spirit must drink the gall of deception. There are some things that even God should not ask... 'My dear, don't be foolish, there's nothing strange about you."[514]

Stephen's first inkling that something might be different about her comes when a friend named Martin confesses his love for her and she is disturbed: she "stare[ed] at him in a kind of dumb horror, staring at his eyes that were clouded by desire, while gradually over her colourless face there was spreading an expression of the deepest revulsion—terror and revulsion."[515] It is only when she falls in love with an older woman, Angela Crossby, and declares it, does the book reach its rhetorical (and obscene) height

> Stephen answered 'I know that I love you, and that nothing else matters in the world'...all that [Angela] was, and all that she had been and would be again, perhaps even to-morrow, was fused at that moment into one mighty impulse, one imperative need, and that need was Stephen. Stephen's need was now hers, by sheer force of its blind and uncompromising will to appeasement. Then Stephen took Angela into her arms, and she kissed her full on the lips, as a lover.[516]

The discovery of the affair by the narrator's mother casues her to say that her daughter was "unnatural... this thing you are is a sin against creation."[517] It is in this moment that Stephen "found her manhood," and when she discovers her father's books on sexology, Hall paints a pathetic (in the *pathos* sense) picture: holding her fathers "old well-worn Bible. [Stephen] demand[ed] a sign from heaven—nothing less than a sign from heaven she demanded. The Bible fell open near the beginning. She read: 'And the Lord set a mark upon Cain...' Then Stephen hurled the Bible away."[518]

The rest of the novel continues more or less in this sense, with Hall creating scenes to show that Stephen is congenitally 'inverted' and blameless for her identity. She becomes a novelist, and then serves as an ambulance driver in the War, where she falls in love with another woman named Mary. By the end of the novel, she determines that in order to 'protect' Mary, she must 'martyr' herself and send Mary away.[519] Her novel ends with a famous appeal that describes the ghosts of all the people she knew

> calling her by name, saying... 'Stephen, Stephen, speak with your God and ask Him why He has left us

Brian M. Watson

forsaken!'. . . And now there was only one voice, one
demand; her own voice into which those millions
had entered. . .'God,' she gasped, we believe; we have
told You we believe. . .We have not denied You, then
rise up and defend us. Acknowledge us, oh God, before the whole world. Give us also the right to our
existence!'[520]

Hall's brazenness and forthrightness was something that
the Home Office could not tolerate, especially as her publisher began importing books that had been secretly printed
in Paris.[521] Relying on their usual strategy of targeting a publisher and thereby bypassing the danger of a trial about literary merit, the authorities organized an elaborate sting operation to seize all copies of the book in England.

Hall and her publisher had prepared for this—before the
book was even finished she wrote to her publisher to say that
she would not allow even one word to be altered "I have put
my pen at the service of some of the most persecuted and
misunderstood people in the world... So far as I know nothing of the kind has ever been attempted before in fiction."[522]
When the publisher was named in the indictment, he used a
loophole in the law to say that "Miss Radclyffe Hall wished
to be heard under section 32 of the Customs Act as 'another
person,'" allowing her to go on trial.[523] She would be able
to speak her 'one voice, one demand.' Within two weeks she
managed to line up the 'cream' of the British literary establishment to testify in her favor: Arnold Bennett, T.S. Eliot,
E.M. Forster, Julian Huxley, Rose Macaulay, George Bernard
Shaw, Lytton Strachey, and Leonard and Virginia Woolf.[524]

Not all of these figures were there enthusiastically—many
of them thought that Hall was too daring, too polemical, and
risked exposure and scandal to the entire literary or Blooms-
bury group of London. Woolf commented on this in her letters: "most of our friends are trying to evade the witness box;

for reasons you may guess. But they generally put it down to the weak heart of a father, or a cousin who is about to have twins."[525] Woolf also expressed reservations over Hall and her book: "no one has read her book; or can read it... so our ardour in the case of freedom of speech gradually cools... we are already beginning to wish it unwritten."[526] Luckily for Woolf, she would not end up testifying. The defense lawyer opened his case by saying that it was his intention "to call his distinguished witnesses to testify that the book was not obscene, and those who had passed the 1857 Obscene Publications Act never intended it to be used against such a book."[527] The purpose of the trial became immediately clear—the defeat of the Hicklin definition of obscene literature. Unfortunately, the prosecution had chosen its judge wisely, and the judge had pre-determined that *The Well of Loneliness* was obscenity, according to the files of the Director for Public Prosecution examined by Alan Travis.[528] Using the powers of the 1857 Act that was under question, Justice Biron declared that he had the right to define obscenity:

> The evidence that is being offered me is expert evidence as to whether or not the book is a piece of literature. That is not the point. The book may be a very fine piece of literature and yet be obscene. Art and obscenity are not disassociated. . .I agree it has considerable merits, but that does not prevent it from being obscene, and therefore I shall not admit this expert evidence.[529]

As Woolf put it, "in what cases is evidence allowable? This last, to my relied, was decided against us: we could not be called as experts in obscenity, only in art."[530]

With the very purpose of the trial invalidated, Hall's defense collapsed. They were unable to prove that the book had merit or that the 1857 Obscene Publications Act was being used in the wrong way—the Act itself was being used to suppress the questioning of the Act. When the judge announced his decision a week later, he was "clear that it was lesbianism itself rather than any particular passage of the book that was being condemned... the better an obscene book is written, the greater is the public to whom it is likely to appeal. The more palatable the poison, the more insidious it is."[531] After an hour of his speech, Hall seemed to try to cry out with the voice at the end of her novel

> **Miss Radclyffe Hall**: 'I protest, I emphatically pro-test.'
> **Sir Chartres Biron**: 'I must ask you to be quiet.'
> **Hall**: 'I am the author of this book—'
> **Biron**: 'If you cannot behave yourself in Court I shall have to have you removed.'
> **Hall**: 'Shame!'[532]

And she was silenced. Furthermore, Hall's appeal was denied and, much to her dejection, all copies of her book were destroyed in England and the Commonwealth countries of Australia, New Zealand, India, South Africa, and Canada.

The 1928 trial of *The Well of Loneliness* was a formative and important one for England's literati. Over 40 of them had been present at the trial, and the other 115 that had been invited no doubt followed the trial closely. In many ways, this would mark the low point for the writers and the high point for the application of the 1857 Obscene Publications Act and its Hicklin Test. The first sign that the tide was shifting was the already-mentioned 1929 symposium on "The 'Censorship' of Books" in which several of Hall's key experts would argue for the need for reform. Ellis, for example noted that "it is said, indeed, that we have no censorship. If that is so, we have what is worse...call it the Inquisition."[533] Forster commented that "I consider that the Act, as at present interpreted, is both unfair to writers and against the public interest, but all I can do is indicate [it]... Non-pornographic books, like *The Well of Loneliness*, ought not to be suppressed."[534] Woolf herself even contributed, arguing that the law was harmful to England and "even more serious is the effect upon the writer... [he] is uncertain what may or may not be judged as obscene... he will be asked to weaken, to soften, to omit."[535] The symposium and its arguments represented the first organized effort by writers to argue in public about the law.

Furthermore, Hall's trial was instructional to American publishers and lawyers, who would learn the lessons of Hall's trial well. In February of the following year, the American publishers Covici-Friede bought the rights to the book from Knopf, who refused to publish after the British trial.[536] They then hired Morris Ernst as their lawyer, the co-founder of the ACLU and the author of a book on the legal history of obscenity, *To The Pure.* Ernst and Covici-Friede seem to have learned three things from the first trial: 1) the defense would have to exercise control over how and by whom the book would be seized, 2) the Obscene Publications Act and the Hicklin Test would have to be the central target of the trial, not societal acceptance of lesbianism, and 3) the literary merit of the work would have to be proved and linked to the original intentions of Campbell when writing the 1857 Act.[537] They sent a copy of the first American edition of *The Well of Loneliness* to the New York Society for the Suppression of Vice, who fell for the bait. Charges of obscenity were brought against the publishers in New York by the NYSSV and attorney general of New York. But, by April of 1929, after reading the book, the judges of the New York Court of Special Sessions cleared the book of any obscenity charges, stating that: "the book in question deals with a special social problem, which, in itself, cannot be said to be in violation of the law unless it is written in such a manner as to make it obscene... and tends to deprave and corrupt minds open to immoral influence."[538]

This, to me, marks a clear shift in the tide against the 1857 Obscene Publications Act. Granted, the decision was in another country, and the defense used a remarkably smart strat-

Brian M. Watson

egy to ensure a case favorable to them, but the United States had been using the British Hicklin Test as a way to determine prosecutable obscenity., and furthermore, the ruling created a precedent that English lawyers could then exploit in their arguments. Ernst succeeded in identifying the weak spot in the armor of the Test, the same spot that its supporters considered strength: its broadening of the 1857 Obscene Publications Act and the attendant results was not the intention of the original law. Four years later, in 1933, Ernst would go on to defend Joyce's *Ulysses* before the Supreme Court and succeed there as well, opening the way for its publication in England a few years later, in 1936. The *Well of Loneliness* was freely published in England in 1946. The same strategy would also be successfully copied in 1959 by publisher Barney Rosset and Charles Rembar in their defense of D.H. Lawrence's *Lady Chatterley's Lover* and John Cleland's *Fanny Hill* in front of the United States Court of Appeals.

The 1857 Obscene Publications Act would be revised in 1959 to include the author's right to argue for literary merit along with the requirement that the entire work be considered, not just individual sections. Even the long-dead 'pornographer,' D.H. Lawrence finally got his day in court in a showdown between the Queen's Bench and Penguin books and *Lady Chatterley's Lover* was deemed 'not obscene' in 1961. The age of the obscene moderns was over.

Photography and Filmography

PERHAPS AS YOU'VE GOTTEN CLOSER to the end of this book you have begun to wonder more and more about why I have limited the discussion to books, engravings and erotic artwork. That might be surprising for a work that claims to be about the history of pornography and obscenity, especially because when people think 'porn' they're most likely to think about dirty pictures or hardcore movies, or one of the thousands of pornographic websites on the Internet. The first things to come to your mind aren't usually the works of the Italian father of pornography, Pietro Aretino, or the poetry of libertine Earls, or the dark philosophies of the Marquis de Sade. No, the first things that come to your mind are more likely to be *Playboy Magazine*, websites such as pornhub.com or kink.com, or even a more personal experience with pornographic material.

Part of the reason we have spent so much time in focusing on history of the book, or on erotic artwork and engravings, is, as I said at the beginning of this book, pornography has a longer history than we usually assume it does. Roughly, this narrative has run from the years 1350-1950, from the Renaissance to the Cold War. It is a long period of time, which covers everything from the Reformation to the English, American and French Revolutions, and, in all honesty, the rise of photography and videography comes at the tail end of that period —the first (surviving) erotic image is from 1839, and the first (vaguely) erotic video by 1894, and the first forthrightly pornographic one not until 1908. This is one reason why I have not yet covered photography or film.

The other reason, the major one, is that context matters. As I have repeatedly commented throughout this book, there is no pornography without obscenity, no obscenity without erotica. In the beginning, the first recognizably pornographic works combined social, religious, and political critique and sometimes educational information along with erotic and obscene titillation in order to create a product that our modern eyes wouldn't always see as pornography (such as *Merryland*). It took several important court cases and a pair of reformation societies along with a major Obscene Publications Act to actually create the legal and cultural concept of pornography in the English world, as well as similar developments elsewhere. Even the word, 'pornography,' dates as late as 1857. So the purpose of this final section is to address the history of visual (photographic and film) pornography and how it fits into the history of pornography as a whole.

The first major breakthrough in photographic technology originated from the experiments of Louis Daguerre, who invented the process known as daguerreotype, and whose technology was given to the world by the French nation in 1839. Daguerreotypes were a major breakthrough because they allowed a photographic exposure to be taken in a matter of minutes, versus the hours of exposure that used to be required. To make a daguerreotype, early photographers took a cleaned and polished copper plate and covered it with a thin layer of silver iodide—by candlelight, in order to avoid any exposure to light. The image is revealed by exposing it to mercury vapors (very dangerous and nauseating), and then washing it in salty water. This labor-intensive process, combined with the high cost of the materials, made daguerreotypes only available for the financially well-off. It was not until 1853 when the Englishman Fredrick Scott Archer's negative on glass process allowed printing on paper in unlimited amounts.

As proof of my statement that literature provided the model and context for pornography, erotic photography followed the same process as erotic literature. In the beginning, photographs were expensive (as much as a week's salary for the average person), and their high cost limited the purchasers to the upper-classes. The first publishers and connoisseurs saw this as a good thing, as the prices kept the number of customers to a manageable level, and confined to "social classes respected for their moral integrity and ethical stability."[539] The improved technology which allowed mass printing and lowered costs was what caused things to become, "'problematic' in the pleasure-dampening and prudish Victorian sense." But when the process became easier, and photography became more widespread and more of an industrial process, then the moral outcry and demands for regulation began. By the 1860s, paper photographs were being sold by hawkers or booksellers in London's Holywell Street or in the Grands Boulevards district of Paris. As Alexander Dupoy explains in his *Erotic Photography*:

> The moral question of circulation to the general public was not a problem when it only concerned the daguerreotypes, as the excessive cost ensured a limited distribution to the elite. It now became a problem, as it was possible for every soldier, school-boy, young man or even young woman to acquire or have access to a licentious image, even if the image was academic. The mid-nineteenth century was a time of great confusion between moral order and artistic aestheticism.[540]

The subjects of the first images were of landscapes or objects —it was difficult to photograph nudes or people because it took several minutes to take the picture, and people had a tendency of moving, especially if said people were having sex. Regardless, where there is a will, there is a way. According to Dupouy, a certain optician named Noël-Marie Paimal Lebours claimed to have taken the first nude photograph by 1841, but Michael Koetzle notes in *1000 Nudes*, a history of erotic photography, that "Rudolf Brettschneider ("Die Erotik in der Photographie" - Eroticism in Photography -, 1931) mentions the year 1849, while Joseph Maria Eder ("Die Geschichte der Photographie" - The History of Photography –1932) would have a nude photograph appear in 1844," but either way the first images would have required heavy preparation: "powder or white makeup was applied to faces. Bodies were forced into tortuous stances and left exposed to the blazing sun for minutes at a time."[541] When the first commercial photographs went on sale in France, they were available from the offices of opticians, and in the salons of high-end art dealers —not in shady backstreet alleyways (that would come later).

Brian M. Watson

The original nudes were shot almost like an artistic painting:

They mimicked artists and painters by making pastiches of their compositions and the use of accessories, including draping, columns and fabric. In fact, most of the precursors of photography came directly from painting. The interconnection between the two processes seemed obvious: photographers were inspired by painters, and painters made use of photography. With photography, artists no longer had to put up with models who either did not turn up or were late.[542]

But this does not mean that all erotic photographs were sweet and innocent photographs; it only look seven years from the announcement of the technology to the first commercially available daguerreotype of people having sex!

Figure 11. An example of an 'artists study' [The Uwe Schied Collection]

Figure 12. An early image from 1890 [The Uwe Schied Collection].

As the French were the first to pioneer and master daguerreotypes and photography, Paris became the center of the trade in erotic and obscene images, just as it had once served as the center for erotic and obscene books. In 1848, only 13 studios existed in all of Paris, but by 1860, there were over 400! All of them claimed to be reputable joints that only took pictures of individuals and families, but in fact, most of them traded and profited from the sale of nude images to any customer that had the money. The lewd pictures were also sold near train stations by hawkers, and in the streets of London, Paris, Amsterdam, Philadelphia, New York, other European and American cities, and were also sent via mail to customers. All of these activities caused the Societies for the Suppression of Vice in England and America to begin targeting and prosecuting the sellers, along with their decades-long fight against obscene literature.

A police report from Paris illustrates how much the trade had boomed: in 1850, exactly 60 photographs had been seized, but by 1860, ten years later, the police were confiscating thousands of examples. By 1875 the number had ballooned to 130,000 photographs with "lewd" subjects. The prosecutions began. It seems the first lucky individual prosecuted for erotic photography was one Félix Moulin, about whom not much is known. He was prosecuted in 1851 and sentenced to one month in prison and a fine of 100 francs. The court decision in his case "'maintained that a great number of the pictures confiscated' at his studio and his deal Malacrida's place were so obscene. . . that even the enunciation of their titles (...) would represent an offense under the law against the dissemination of lewd literature."[543] The fines faced by female models was worse—in 1857, four women were sentenced to *six* months in prison on top of the hundred franc fine. By the 1850s erotic photography had finally taken the leap into pornography and a half-century later film would progress at the same rapid clip.

By the 1900s, film technology began to take off. As with photography, the technology was pioneered first by a Frenchman, named Louis Le Prince, and then improved by the American inventor Thomas Edison. The technology was rather basic in the beginning, just a strip of pictures printed on film and then rotated in a loop with a high-speed shutter to create the illusion of movement. In 1894 Edison's studio recorded a vaguely erotic short, titled *Carmencita*, which featured a Spanish dancer who twirled and posed on film for the first time. The short was considered scandalous in some places because Carmencita's underwear and legs could be seen in the film, but Edison's studio followed it up two years later with the even more controversial *Fatima's Coochie Dance*, which "starred an Egyptian belly dancer whose appearance at the 1893 Columbus Exposition in Chicago was still the subject of condemnation and complaint, three years on."[544] The far most explosive video released that year however was *The May Irwin Kiss*, an 18 second film of a Victorian couple kissing, or rather pecking in a somewhat awkward and forced manner. Chicago journalist Herbert Stone called it "beastly... manifested to gargantuan proportions and repeated three time over, it is absolutely disgusting. Such things call for police interference."[545] There were several uproars in newspaper editorials across the country, and cries for censorship from the Roman Catholic Church, and calls for prosecution—although these calls do not seem like they were followed up on, perhaps because Edison was so highly respected by the American public, but also perhaps because there was no law in place to deal with erotic films yet.

For the decade or so following Edison, there were several innovators in different countries that recorded short clips or scenes such as *Apres le Bal – Le Tub*, which features a naked woman being bathed by her maid, but the first surviving 'hardcore' pornographic film dates from 1908 France: *A Les Culs d'Or (At the Golden Bottom)*. As Dave Thompson explains, the title board

> Dissolves to a view of a country inn, its white plaster walls weather-beaten and stained. A portly, middle-aged and waxed-mustachioed musketeer, clad in all the finery one would expect rom that noble profession, stands outside, knocking on the door and hammering on an outdoor table. He has traveled far and is in need of sustenance.
>
> The innkeeper, however, has no food. But, unwilling to disappoint so distinguished a customer, he instead

ushers the visitor to a seat, then hastens to where one of his staff, a pretty, plump young girl, is cleaning glasses. They exchange some words, then she approaches their guest, leads him to another table, far more secluded than the first, pours him a drink and informs him what is really on the menu—herself.

With every scene ushered in by one more in a dizziying panopoly of excruciating puns, each allaying some form of physical intimatcy with a food stuff, the cavalier samples each 'dish' in turn: the seafood *la crevette*, as he extracts one finger from between her legs and tastes it; *asperges en branches* (an asparagus dish) as he removes his own pants; *saucisse* (sausage), *moule* (mussel), the chicken and mushroom hors d'oeuvre *bouchees a le reine*; and so on, until the cavalier's climax marks the end of the first course, and the innkeeper serves up the dessert, a second naked girl, cross-legged on a serving platter. The trio fall upon one another with gusto, *sandwich a la gousse*, and there the reel—and the film—concludes.[546]

The film is available for viewing on Wikimedia Commons.[547] Another early film from the same year also survives—*A L'Ecu d'Or ou la Bonne Auberge (At the Golden Crown or The Right Inn*. The word 'l'ecu' literally means 'crown' but is also a euphemism for a vagina). The film begins with a hotel maid cleaning up a room with a (newly-invented) vacuum cleaner when the screen announces, in silent movie format, that she has "une riche idee" [a good idea]. She begins to use the sucking end of the (presumably off) vacuum as a dildo, until she is walked in on by the newlywed husband and wife whose room she is supposed to be cleaning. The pair drag her off to the bed and the trio all begin to take their clothes off. The group all fall into the bed, there is a scene of oral sex, a scene of 69-ing, face-sitting, intercourse, and then the four minute long movie ends.

These movies were never distributed to the public, of course, and it seems like they were recorded by private groups for a small audience, which would have limited it and kept it out of the public (and police) eye.

As with photography before it, and books before that, film eventually became cheaper and more widespread, began appearing in the alleyways and under the counter at stores, and eventually lead to arrests, prosecution and jail time. The Czech movie *Ecstasy* (1933), for example, featured scenes of nudity, and perhaps the first female orgasm shown in a major theatrical release. The scandal of these scenes lead to cries for the seizing and banning of the offensive material, and lead to the Hayes Code in the United States, which more or less successfully banned erotic material from Hollywood movies for the next 30 years. It was challenged in 1964 by the motion picture *The Lovers,* which tells the story of a woman named Jeanne Tournier who 'rediscovers' love through adultery with a much younger man named Bernard, and eventually leaves her husband to start a new life. If the film were released today, it would probably barely garner an R-rating, and would be unlikely to stir up any significant drama.

However, at the time, the state of Ohio found that it was disturbing enough to label the movie as obscene and to prosecute and fine a certain Nico Jacobellis to the tune of $2,500 ($18,500 in 2013 dollars). The Ohio Supreme Court supported the state in both its obscenity charge and in its fine, but the US Supreme Court reversed the decision, arguing that the film was not obscene and was therefore protected as free speech. As to *why* the film was protected free speech? Well, the Justices quickly ran into problems explaining their rationales–even though the Court ruled 6-3 in favor of Jacobellis, the individual Justices gave four very different opinions as to *why* the film was not obscene, none of them agreeing with the others. The most famous opinion however, came from Judge Potter Stewart, when he wrote that "I shall not today attempt

Brian M. Watson

further to define the kinds of material I understand to be embraced within [hardcore pornography], and perhaps I could never succeed in intelligibly doing so. But I know it when I see it, and the motion picture involved in this case is not that."[548] Stewart's comment that he "knew it when he saw it" is proverbially famous because it seems to sum up so much of the argument over pornography and obscenity—to some extent, we all know it when we see it. Full freedom of pornographic expression was not available in the United States until 1988's *California v. Freeman,* which effectively legalized hardcore pornography. By the 1990's in the United Kingdom, most forms of pornographic expression were allowed, but different formats and genres still remain problematic and there have been in recent years increasing attempts at regulation. And so we come to the modern day, where the internet has created a pornotopia of easily-accessible and free pornography—we are living in the worst nightmare of the Society for the Suppression of Vice.

9

Conclusion

I N HIS FINAL (and most modern) *Index*, Henry Spencer Ashbee, perhaps the scholar emeritus of the pornography field, comments that:

> We cannot fail to perceive that while in the former books [like Fanny Hill] the characters, scenes, and the incidents are natural, and the language not unnecessarily gross, those in the latter are false, while the words and expression employed are of the most filthy description. CLELAND's characters--Fanny Hill, the coxcomb, the bawds, and the debauchees with whom they mix, are taken from human nature and do only what they could and would have done under the very natural circumstances in which they are placed; whereas the persons in the latter works are the creations of a disordered brain, quite unreal, and what they enact is either improbable or impossible. Thus, the nature of English erotic fiction is changed.[549]

Ashbee argues that "immoral and amatory fiction. . .must unfortunately be acknowledged to contain, *cum granum salis* [with a grain of salt], a reflection of the manners and vices of the times—of vices to be avoided, guarded against, reformed. . . . English Erotic Novels, I repeat, are sorry productions."[550] That language of his—'vices to be avoided, guarded against, reformed,'—sounds suspiciously similar to the mission statement of the Society for the Suppression of Vice. In truth, it is likely the best one-sentence summary of their entire project. "Better were it," Ashbee continues, "that such literature did not exist. I consider it pernicious and hurtful to the immature, but at the same time I hold that, in certain circumstances, its study is necessary, if not beneficial."[551]

As is no doubt obvious by this point, I agree with Ashbee's contention that the study of pornography is necessary. I would not go so far as to argue that I think it would be better if pornography (and everything that word implies) did not exist, because, as shown here, these sorts of representations have been used in Western culture since 'the beginning.' Renaissance writers, building off Greek and Roman formats, were empowered by the printing press and enthusiastically embraced the erotic as a method of communication and critique. So popular were these writings that the 1593 Council of Trent was the first to outlaw them, and the first to see that ban backfire when Italian bawdy writing spread across Italy, and then Europe. After all, as Pietro Aretino in the 1500s, or Earl Rochester in the 1600s would gleefully point out, everyone looks the same naked or having sex. All bodies, common, holy, or royal are reducible to the same basic parts—the body is the ultimate leveler of class.

All along the way, erotic discourse, obscene libel, and pornography have been negotiated, defined, argued over, and enabled by the printing press, the book, and the market. As Lisa Siegel puts it, rather than "merely engaging in the libidinal, [pornography] emerged from the very movements that defined the modern world: humanism, the scientific revolution, and the Enlightenment."[552] I have shown in this history how erotic, obscene, and pornographic material played a role in the Reformation and Counter-Reformation, two of the great shapers of European history. I have also detailed how it interacted and revealed the history of some of our most powerful cultural institutions, such as privacy, marriage, or sexuality. Obscene materials played a major role in emergent capitalism, with Edmund Curll and his commodification of erotic literature, and reactions against said obscene material helped create manners and propriety in Samuel Richardson's *Pamela*. Obscenity and pornography played major roles in the intellectual and creative life of the French Revolution and in shaping how the new technologies of photography and film would be interpreted and regulated.

The impacts of the genre hardly end there, as it has contributed to Western culture in many significant ways. For example, it was a powerful informer of the Modern art—one can easily argue that James Joyce or D.H. Lawrence would not have been as significant without the controversies over sex (and sexuality) that surrounded and informed their work. The work of the Society for the Suppression of Vice also continued to have an impact well into the twentieth-century; for example, 13 'obscene' paintings by D.H. Lawrence were seized by the British government in 1929 from the Warren Gallery in London. The paintings were then prosecuted under the 1838 Vagrancy Act that the Vice Society had lobbied for, only "spared from being burned on condition that they were never exhibited in Britain again."[553]

In the introduction, I asked what changed between Rochester and Rossetti—why Rossetti's *Jenny* inspired such a diatribe against the poet, whereas Rochester only seemed to briefly miff King Charles II. The short answer is that the contexts and the audience changed and with them, the interpretations. Rochester's *Satyre*, which combined the erotic with political criticism, could comfortably exist in the same world as *Venus in the Cloister*, which combined philosophic ideas with erotic titillation, and was written for, to, and by the upper classes. *Jenny*, however, existed in the same world as *The Romance of Lust*, separated by only four years. *Jenny* and *The Romance* existed in a post-Obscene Publications Act world. The Society for the Suppression of Vice had finally been triumphant in convincing the government of the danger that obscene publications presented, because they could be purchased and consumed by any member of the increasingly literate public. Rochester lived in a world where mistresses, affairs, and eroticism were—for the upper classes—acceptable. Rossetti lived in a world where middle- and upper-class reformers had largely succeeded in creating and enforcing public morality and prostitues were regarded as a threat to the moral, social, and health system. As a result, the *Satyre* was, in its context, a poem that, although critical of the King, did not upset the balance of things. *Jenny*, however, with its idealization of a 'common' prostitute, outraged decency, sacrificed purity, and falsified history—not just because the prostitute was a danger to the morals of the working-classes, but because of the terrible fears that surrounded masturbation and sexuality.

The intervening story of the movement from erotic discourse to pornography is thus a mirror-history to the rise of privacy, sexuality, capitalism, morality, and the middle class. Starting with Edmund Curll's commodification of any work even vaguely licentious or scandalous, and the government's response of making obscene libel prosecutable by the temporal courts, the push and pull between profit and enforcement would ultimately divorce eroticism from the earlier social, political religious criticism that usually accompanied it. *Fanny Hill* was retrospectively momentous in that it separated the erotic and critical voices, and disposed of the critical. *Justine* was retrospectively momentous because it signaled the high-water mark, and ultimate culmination, of the libertine critique of society that would only be revived in a more reserved format under James Joyce, D.H. Lawrence, and others. The failure of *Fanny*'s prosecution demonstrated a gap in the church and state alliance that had worked in tandem for centuries, and it was this gap that middle-class religious and moral reform groups organized against, empowered by a shift in attitude by the larger culture. As the government would not prosecute the producers, sellers, or consumers of erotic works, the Societies used the courts as a weapon while simultaneously lobbying for more weaponry.

The landmark 1857 Obscene Publications Act, drafted by the Society for the Suppression of Vice, represented the culmination of this effort and they were able to declare victory over obscene literature. In retrospect however, the declaration was a premature one, and Holywell Street (and its wares) went on existing. Like the Edmund Curll who had once set up shop near it, Holywell stubbornly went on existing, past the death of Lord Campbell in 1861, and past the dissolution of the Society for the Suppression of Vice in the 1880s, until it was destroyed in the early 20th century to make room for Kingsway and Aldwych. By then, however, it had made the jump from books to daguerreotypes, photography, and film.

With the rise of modernity and the Internet, the Society for the Suppression of Vice's worst nightmare has been realized; unfettered access to unlimited pornography throughout all levels of society. On top of this, there has been no serious and sustained effort by either the government or by moral societies to challenge this new norm. Though battle-scarred and dusty, and perhaps only temporarily, it seems that pornographers of Europe and America can declare a sort of victory. In an age of unlimited access to pornography, however, it is perhaps even more important to realize that the nature and forms of pornography are historically constructed, have changed before, and can change again. And indeed, as a new wave of pornographic restrictions sweep across the United Kingdom and as American state after state declares pornography a public health crisis, and that pornography today is far worse than it has ever been, perhaps we are beginning to see another shift of that pendulum.

10

Thank-yous & Sources Cited

As with any book, there are always a million people to say thank you to. To begin, I would like to say thank you to Ashleigh and Sara, as without their love, support and encouragement the first draft of this book would not have been possible. Thank you for endless encouragement, critique, and gentle smacks when I got down on myself or discouraged. An updated thanks go out to Jacquelyn who saw me through a rewrite of this whole damn thing, and even though she didn't really understand why I was killing myself encouraged me anyways. Thank you to Heather for love, friendship, and telling me what to do with my life after my book, and for Sarah for staying the most unlikely but still best friend post KSC. A big something goes out to Kenzie, who—though NRE was fast, overpowering, explosive, and sweet—taught me to be more myself—in every way—by simply being themselves. It is a gift I haven't really learned to appreciate yet, but am still discovering. Finally, a thank you to Zoe, for continuing to support and look after me in small and thoughtful ways that I didn't even know I needed (and for loving me in big ones, that I always need).

Secondly, I also need to thank my parents and family, who without their teaching, humor and a good deal of head-shaking over my graduate work, I never would have been in the position of achieving the things I have in life so far. The third part of my major thanks goes to Reddit's AskHistorians community, for pushing me to write for a general audience, for giving me an outlet in which my research did not seem weird, and to my fellow moderators, who have been my best of friends and confidantes.

In the field of academics, I would like to thank Dr. Jonathan Rose, my M.A. advisor at Drew University, both for his founding and development of book history and SHARP— The Society for the History of Authorship, Reading, and Publishing—and for his encouragement, critique and excellent classes that gave me the breadth of knowledge to delve into this topic so deeply. Furthermore, I would like to thank Bradford Mudge at University of Colorado Denver ceaselessly for both reading an early version of my Master's Thesis and offering pages of critiques and edits and for giving me advice and constructive criticism in writing this book. Unending praise to him for allowing me to use excerpts from his translations in *When Flesh Becomes Word* in this writing of this book. In the same vein, many thanks to Lisa Siegel of DePaul University for her (very pointed) critique of my M.A. thesis. Furthermore, I need to thank Nicolas Germana and Anne-Marie Mallon of Keene State College for encouraging by love of history and literature, the two things that really took me to Drew University and into my field as a whole.

Additional thanks go to Southern New Hampshire University for (unknowingly) hosting me while writing the vast majority of this manuscript. Thanks especially to Chelsey Lemley of SNHU who dealt patiently and kindly with every single one of my weird technical issues. Thanks to the staff of the British Library for helping me and dealing patiently with my million and a half requests for hard-to-find and rather-weird pornographic manuscripts. Additional thanks to the Kinsey Insitute and Library for the same thing – I started writing this book there, and now I am a graduate student again, working everyday there. That is something to be thankful for.

Additional thanks to the Bernicke Rare Book & Manuscript Library in New Haven, the National Library of Scotland, the University of Manchester Library, the Bibliotheque nationale de France, especially for dealing with my terrible French requests. And finally, Indiana University Bloomington, where I am again a graduate student, in Library Science and Archives —turns out it's just about where I belonged in the first place.

Final thanks in no particular order go to Thomas Froh for libertinism, Kelly Nilsson for being my role model in all things life, Courtney Small for tea and inspiration, Denise and Mat for sex talk and hosting me like a traveling bum, Mike, Chris, Margaret, Danielle & Kerstyn for being major bros of the AHA team *and* Cait, Hunter, Davey, and Will for killing at the NCPH panel, Cait for her helpfulness in telling me about sex, books and children of ye olde times, Jimmy Buttram (no, that's not a typo) & Andrew T for being the best roommates and driving across the country with me, everyone in my Drew University and Indiana University Bloomington cohorts, Billy Procida for who knows, but he knows, Ivy and last but not least everyone in my Psi Upsilon family for their love, support, and endless willingness to be my drinking buddies and friends.

Bibliography

1. "An Act for the Punishment of idle and disorderly Persons, and Rogues and Vagabonds, in that Part of Great Britain called England.." legislation.gov.uk. www.legislation.gov.uk/ukpga/1824/83/pdfs/ukpga_18240083_en.pdf (accessed October 3, 2013), p. 669 no. IV. [PDF]
2. "Regina v. Hicklin."Wikisource. https://en.wikisource.org/wiki/Regina_v._Hicklin (accessed November 12, 2013).
3. "A Thirteenth-Century Castilian Sumptuary Law." The

Business History Review, vol. 37, no. 1/2, 1963, pp. 98–100. JSTOR, JSTOR, www.jstor.org/stable/3112097.

4. "begin, v.". OED Online. October 2016. Oxford University Press.

5. "Letter from Mr Pritchard to Lrd Campbell," Jauary 1858, Social Evil Extracts Album, part 1, NVA Papers, Fawcett Library.

6. "Letter Writing and the Rise of the Novel: The Epistolary Literacy of Jane Johnson and Samuel Richardson." The Pen and the People: English Letter Writers 1660-1800, by Susan E. Whyman, Oxford University Press, 2011, chapter 5.

7. "Novel Pleasure." The Cambridge Companion to Erotic Literature, by Bradford Keyes. Mudge, Cambridge University Press, 2017, p. 130.

8. "pornography, n.". OED Online. October 2016. Oxford University Press.

9. Andrew Gordon Craig, "The Movement for the Reformation of Manners, 1688–1715," unpubl. Ph.D. diss., University of Edinburgh, 1980.

10. Anon. A Congratulatory Epistle from a Reformed Rake, to John F------g, Esq ; upon the New Scheme of Reclaiming Prostitutes. Printed for G. Burnet, 1758.

11. Anon. Supplement To The Historical Portion Of The 'Records Of The Most Ancient And Puissant Order Of The Beggar's Benison And Merryland, Anstruther', Being An Account Of The Proceedings At The Meeting Of The Society, Together With Excerpts, Stories, Bon-Mots, Speeches, And Songs Delivered Thereat. 'Anstruther,' Printed for Private Distribution, 1892, p.

12. Anonymous [Edward Sellon]. Ophiolatreia: an Account of the Rites and Mysteries Connected with the Origin, Rise and Development of Serpent Worship ... the Whole Forming an Exposition of One of the Phases of Phallic ... Worship. Privately Printed, 1889.

13. Anonymous. The Lustful Turk. New York: Masquerade Book, 1990.

14. Anonymous. The Romance of Lust. New York: Grove Press, 1968. Some Grove Press editions of this work falsely attribute it to Edward Sellon, who write several erotic books for William Dugdale, including The

New Epicurean noted above.

15. Archives, The National. "Currency Converter." The National Archives, The National Archives, Kew, Surrey TW9 4DU, 1 Mar. 2006, www.nationalarchives.gov.uk/currency/default0.asp.

16. Aretino, Pietro, and Nargaret Rosenthal. Aretino's Dialogues. University of Toronto Press, 2005.

17. Aretino, Pietro, and Samuel Putnam. The Works of Aretino: Translated into English from the Original Italian. Covici-Friede, 1933.

18. Arnold, Amanda. "The War on Porn Is Back." Jezebel, Jezebel.com, 20 Sept. 2017, jezebel.com/the-war-on-porn-is-back-1810469452.

19. Arnstein, Walter L. "The Murphy Riots: A Victorian Dilemma." Victorian Studies, 1 Sept. 1975, www.jstor.org/stable/3826732?seq=1#page_scan_tab_contents.

20. Ashbee, Catena Librorum Tacendorum, pg. 185. Published as Volume III of Ashbee, Henry Spencer. The Encyclopedia of Erotic Literature, Being Notes Bio-Biblio-Icono-Graphical and Critical, on Curious and Uncommon Books. New York: Documentary Books, Inc., 1962.

21. Ashbee, Henry Spencer. Catena Librorum Tacendorum: Being Notes Bio- Icono- Graphical and Critical, on Curious and Uncommon Books. London, Privately Printed, 1885.

22. Ashbee, Henry Spencer. Index Librorum Prohibitorum; Bio-Biblio-Icono-Graphical and Critical Notes on Curious, Uncommon and Erotic Books. London, Privately Printed, 1877.

23. Augustine, Saint. The Works of Saint Augustine Part Two -- Letters. Vol. 4, New City Press, 2005.

24. Bailey, Beth. "The Vexed History of Children And Sex." The Routledge History of Childhood in the Western World, edited by Paula S. Fass, Routledge, 2015.

25. Baines, Paul, and Pat Rogers. Edmund Curll, Bookseller. Clarendon Press, 2007.

26. Barclay, Katie, and Merridee L. Bailey, editors. Emotion, Ritual and Power in Europe, 1200-1920: Family,

State and Church. Palgrave Macmillan, 2017, especially chapter 3,

27. Baron, Hans. Crisis of the Early Italian Renaissance. Princeton University Press, 1955.
28. Black, Jeremy. The British and the Grand Tour. Routledge, 2011.
29. Boccaccio, Giovanni. The Decameron. Translated by G. H. McWilliam, Franklin Library, 1981.
30. British Broadcasting Corporation. "William Wilberforce." BBC - Religions. http://www.bbc.co.uk/religion/religions/christianity/people/williamwilberforce_1.shtml (accessed September 14, 2013).
31. Brundage, James A. Law, Sex, and Christian Society in Medieval Europe". University of Chicago Press, 1987.
32. Buchanan, Robert Williams. The fleshly school of Poetry, and other phenomena of the day. London: Strahan& Co., 1872.
33. 'Charles II, 1662: An Act for preventing the frequent Abuses in printing seditious treasonable and unlicensed Bookes and Pamphlets and for regulating of Printing and Printing Presses.', Statutes of the Realm: volume 5: 1628-80 (1819), pp. 428-35. URL: http://www.british-history.ac.uk/report.asp?compid=47336.
34. Chorier, Nicolas. The Dialogues of Luisa Sigea. Locus Elm Press, 2015. Electronic Kindle version.
35. Clark, Peter. British Clubs and Societies 1580-1800: The Origins of an Associational World . Clarendon Press, 2000.
36. Cleland, John. Memoirs Of A Woman Of Pleasure. Printed for G. Fenton, 1749, p. 5.
37. Cleugh, James. The Divine Aretino. Stein and Day, 1966, p. 23; Chubb, Thomas Caldecot. Aretino, Scourge of Princes. Reynal & Hitchcock, 1940.
38. Commonwealth Legal Information Institute. "English Reports: DOMINUS REX v. CURL." English Reports 1795. www.commonlii.org/uk/cases/EngR/1795/1184.pdf (accessed May 1, 2013).
39. Contributors, Multiple. Onania: or, the Heinous Sin of Self-Pollution, and All Its Frightful Consequences. H. Cooke, 1756.

40. Dabhoiwala, Faramerz. The Origins of Sex: A History of the First Sexual Revolution. Penguin Books, 2013.

41. De Sade, Marquis. Justine, Philosophy in the Bedroom and Other Writings. Translated by Richard Seaver and Austryn Wainhouse, Grove Press, 1965.

42. Defoe, Daniel. Reformation of Manners: a Satyr. Publisher Not Identified, 1702.

43. DeJean, Joan. The Reinvention of Obscenity: Sex, Lies, and Tabloids in Early Modern France. The University of Chicago Press, 2002.

44. Doror Wahrman, The Making of the Modern Self. Yale University Press, 2004

45. DuPont, Ellen. "Henry Havelock Ellis." The Embryo Project Encyclopedia. http://embryo.asu.edu/pages/henry-havelock-ellis (accessed November 27, 2013).

46. Dupouy, Alexandre. Erotic Art Photography. Parkstone Press, 2004.

47. Ellis, Havelock, Lord Charles Darling, Stephen Foote, E.M. Forster, Virginia Woolf, and Carrol Romer." The 'Censorship' of Books." The Nineteenth Century and After DCXXVI (1929): 433-450.

48. Emck, Katy. "Female Transvestism and Male Self-Fashioning in As You Like It and La Vida Es Sueno." Reading the Renaissance: Culture, Poetics, and Drama, edited by Jonathan Hart, Garland Pub, 1996.

49. Ernst, Morris L. To The Pure: A Study of Obscenity and the Censor. New York: The Viking Press, 1929.

50. Fissell, Mary. "When the Birds and the Bees Were Not Enough: Aristotle's Masterpiece." The Public Domain Review, 19 Aug. 2015, publicdomainreview.org/2015/08/19/when-the-birds-and-the-bees-were-not-enough-aristotles-masterpiece/.

51. For more on scribal culture. Clanchy, M.T. "Parchment and Paper: Manuscript Culture 1100–1500." A Companion to the History of the Book, edited by Simon Eliot and Jonathan Rose, Blackwell, 2007.

52. Forster, E. M. Maurice; A Novel. New York: Norton, 1971.

53. From the Preface to the First Edition, a copy which is available online: Ellis, Hav-

elock. "Studies in the Psychology of Sex, Volume 2."Project Gutenberg. http://www.gutenberg.org/files/13611/13611-h/13611-h.htm (accessed November 20, 2013).

54. Fubini, Riccardo. "Humanism and Scholasticism." Interpretations of Renaissance Humanism, edited by Angelo Mazzocco, Brill, 2006.

55. Fuller, Wayne Edison. Morality and the Mail in Nineteenth-Century America. Urbana, Ill.: University of Illinois Press, 2003.

56. Fysh, Stephanie. The Work(s) of Samuel Richardson. Newark: University of Delaware Press, 1997, p. 57-58.

57. Gallup, Inc. "Older Americans' Moral Attitudes Changing." Gallup.com. N.p., 03 June 2013. Web. 19 Oct. 2016.

58. Gayle, Damien. "UK to Censor Online Videos of 'Non-Conventional' Sex Acts." The Guardian, Guardian News and Media, 23 Nov. 2016, www.theguardian.com/technology/2016/nov/23/censor-non-conventional-sex-acts-online-internet-pornography.

Knibbs, Kate. "Selling Erotic Ebooks Is Illegal in Germany Before 10pm ." Gizmodo, Gizmodo.com, 22 June 2015, gizmodo.com/selling-erotic-ebooks-is-illegal-in-germany-before-10pm-1713112318. "[As of this writing SC9 in Utah, HR549 in Virginia,] HJR 166 in Alabama, HR 364 and HR 447 in Georgia, HR 113 in Hawaii, HF 1788 and SF 1605 in Minnesota, HCR 38 in Missouri, HCR 1002 in Oklahoma, H 3887 in South Carolina, HR 112 in Texas, and SCR 29 in West Virginia. Other resolutions, like Arkansas's HR 1042, Kansas's HR 6016 (SR 1723 died in the Senate), Oklahoma's HCR 1006, and Virginia's HJ 549, have had success in one chamber. Other states have adopted or signed their versions of the resolution. South Dakota unanimously passed SCR 4 in January. Tennessee's governor signed SJR 35 on April 24th. The most recent passed resolution is Louisiana's HCR 100, which has slightly different language from the others: pornography is deemed a "hazard" instead of a crisis, and the victims are specified as "Louisiana children."

59. George III, King. "By the King: A Proclamation for the Encouragement of Piety and Virtue, and for preventing and punishing of Vice, Profaneness and Immorality." In Part the First: Address to the Public from the Society for the Suppression of Vice, Setting Forth, With a List of the Members, the Utility and Necessity of such an Institution and its Claim to Public Support. London: Printed for the Society, 1803.

60. Gibson, Edmund. A Sermon Preached to the Societies for Reformation of Manners At St. Mary-Le-Bow, on Monday January the 6th, 1723. John Wyat at the Rose in St. Paul's Church-Yard, 1723.

61. Gibson, Ian. The Erotomaniac: the Secret Life of Henry Spencer Ashbee. Faber, 2001.

62. Gooding, Richard. "Pamela, Shamela, and the Politics of the Pamela Vogue." Eighteenth-Century Fiction, vol. 7, no. 2, 1995, pp. 109–130., doi:10.1353/ecf.1995.0021.

63. Hall, Radclyffe. The Well of Loneliness. New York: Anchor Books, 1990.

64. Hansard's Parliamentary Debates, HL Deb 03 July 1857 vol 146 cc864-7, http://hansard.millbanksystems.com/lords/1857/jul/03/committee. (Accessed October 5th, 2013). Discussion of SSV lobbying in M. Hardcastle (ed.), Life of John, Lord Campbell, London, 1881, vol II, p. 353.

65. Hansard's Parliamentary Debates, HL Deb 07 December 1857 vol 148 cc226-7. http://hansard.millbanksystems.com/lords/1857/dec/07/return-moved-for (Accessed October 5th, 2013).

66. Hansard's Parliamentary Debates, HL Deb 11 May 1857 vol 145 cc102-4. http://hansard.millbanksystems.com/lords/1857/may/11/sale-of-poisons-and-poisonous (Accessed October 3rd, 2013).

67. Hansard's Parliamentary Debates, HL Deb 25 June 1857 vol 146 cc327-38 http://hansard.millbanksystems.com/lords/1857/jun/25/second-reading (Accessed October 5th, 2013)

68. Harper, Kyle. From Shame to Sin: The Christian Transformation of Sexual Morality in Late An-

tiquity. Harvard University Press, 2016.

69. Hartley, L. P. The Go-Between. New York Review of Books, 2011.

70. Horowitz, Helen Lefkowitz. Rereading Sex. New York: Knopf, 2002.

71. Ingram, Martin. "Courtship and Marriage, C. 1500–1750." The Routledge History of Sex and the Body: 1500 to the Present, edited by Sarah Toulalan and Kate Fisher, Routledge, 2016.

72. Ingram, Martin. Church Courts, Sex and Marriage in England, 1570-1640. Cambridge University Press, 1994 and Addy, John. Sin & Society: in the Seventeenth Century. Routledge, 2014.

73. Johns, Adrian. Piracy: the Intellectual Property Wars from Gutenberg to Gates. The University of Chicago Press, 2011, chapters 2 and 3.

74. Johnson, James William. A Profane Wit: The Life of John Wilmot, Earl of Rochester. University of Rochester Press, 2009 discusses this on p. 181-82 and Greene, Graham. Lord Rochester's Monkey: Being the Life of John Wilmot, Second Earl of Rochester. Pengiun Books, 1988 on p. 106-8. Both refer to Haley, K. H. D. The First Earl of Shaftesbury. Clarendon Press, 1968: A letter dated January 20, 1674, reported that "my Lord Rochester fled from

75. Johnson, James William. A Profane Wit: The Life of John Wilmot, Earl of Rochester. Rochester, NY: U of Rochester, 2004. Print. And The Libertine. Dir. Lauence Dunmore. Perf. Johnny Depp, Samantha Morton, John Malkovich. The Weinstein Company, 2004. DVD.

76. Kassel, Lauren. "MEDICAL UNDERSTANDINGS OF THE BODY, C.1500–1750" The Routledge History of Sex and the Body, 1500 to the Present, edited by Kate Fisher and Sarah Toulalan, pp. 57-74.

77. Kennedy, Maev. "Lawrence 'Obscenities' Finally Get a Showing." The Guardian, Guardian News and Media, 22 Nov. 2003, www.theguardian.com/uk/2003/nov/22/books.arts.

78. Kidnie, Margaret Jane, and Philip Stubbes. "A Critical Edition of Philip Stubbes's Anatomie of Abuses."

ETheses -- Birmingham University, University of Birmingham, 4 Apr. 1996, etheses.bham.ac.uk/4435/1/Kidnie96PhD_redacted.pdf.

79. Knowlton, Charles. "Fruits of Philosophy: A Treatise on the Population Question." Gutenberg.org. http://www.gutenberg.org/files/38185/38185-h/38185-h.htm (accessed November 20, 2013).

80. Koetzle, Michael. 1000 Nudes: Uwe Scheid Collection. Taschen, 2001, p. 11.

81. La Petite Morte (French): 'The sensation of orgasm as likened to death, literally, the little death.'

82. Langford, Paul. "Chapter, 8 Personal Nobility." Public Life and the Propertied Englishman: 1689-1798, Clarendon Press, 1998, pp. 540–575.

83. Lawner, Lynne, and Pietro Aretino. I Modi: The Sixteen Pleasures: an Erotic Album of the Italian Renaissance. Northwestern University, 1988.

84. Lawrence, D. H. Sex Literature and Censorship: Essays. New York: Twayne Publishers, 1953

85. Lawrence, D. H. The Rainbow. New York, NY: Signet Classic, 2009

86. Ley, David J. The Myth of Sex Addiction. Rowman & Littlefield, 2014.

87. Luther , Martin. Weimarer Ausgabe. VIII, Deutscher Taschenbuch Verlag, 1987

88. Luther, Martin. Against the Roman Papacy: An Institution of the Devil. Translated by Jaroslav Pelikan, vol. 40 of Luther's Works, Concordia and Fortress Press, 1957.

89. Mackie, Erin Skye. Rakes, Highwaymen, and Pirates: the Making of the Modern Gentleman in the Eighteenth Century. Johns Hopkins University Press, 2014.

90. Manchester, Colin. "Lord Campbell's Act: England's First Obscenity Statue." The Journal of Legal History 9, no. 2 (1988): 223-241

91. Mann, Nicholas. "The origins of humanism." The Cambridge Companion to Renaissance Humanism. Ed. Jill Kraye. Cambridge: Cambridge U Press, 1966. 1-20

92. Marcus, Steven. The Other Victorians: a Study of

Sexuality and Pornography in Mid-Nineteenth-Century England. Basic Books, 1964 for discussion on pornotopia, which is widely viewed with skepticism by current researchers.

93. Mason, Diane. The Secret Vice Masturbation in Victorian Fiction and Medical Culture. Manchester University Press, 2014

94. McKeon, Michael. The Secret History of Domesticity: Public, Private, and the Division of Knowledge. Johns Hopkins University Press.

95. Meibom, Johann Heinrich. A Treatise of the Use of Flogging in Venereal Affairs Also of the Office of the Loins and Reins. ... By John Henry Meibomius, M.D. Made English from the Latin Original by a Physician. To Which Is Added, a Treatise of Hermaphrodites. Printed for E. Curll, 1718, Preface.

96. Mia Korpiola, Between Betrothal and Bedding: Marriage Formation in Sweden 1200–1600 (Leiden: Brill, 2009).

97. Millot and L'Ange in Mudge, Bradford K. When Flesh Becomes Word: An Anthology of Early Eighteenth-Century Libertine Literature. Oxford University Press, 2004

98. Monger, George P. Marriage Customs of the World: From Henna to Honeymoons. ABC-CLIO, 2005, pgs 23-25,

99. Moulton, Ian Frederick. Before Pornography. Oxford [England: Oxford University Press, 2000

100. Moulton, Ian Frederick. Before Pornography: Erotic Writing in Early Modern England. Oxford University Press, 2000, p. 14.

101. Moulton, Ian. "Erotic Representation, 1500–1750." The Routledge History of Sex and the Body: 1500 to the Present, edited by Sarah Toulalan and Kate Fisher, Routledge, 2016, pp. 207–222.

102. Mudge, Bradford Keyes. The Whore's Story: Women, Pornography, and the British Novel, 1684-1830. Oxford University Press, 2000.

103. Muir, Edward. The Culture Wars of the Late Renaissance: Skeptics, Libertines, and Opera. Harvard University Press, 2007, p. 63.

104. Muzzarelli, M. G. "Reconciling the Privilege of a Few with the Common Good: Sumptuary Laws in Medieval and Early Modern Europe." Journal of Medieval and Early Modern Studies, vol. 39, no. 3, 2009, pp. 597–617, doi:10.1215/10829636-2009-006.

105. News, Bay City. "Kink.com Buys SF Armory." SFGate, 9 Jan. 2007, www.sfgate.com/news/article/Kink-com-buys-SF-Armory-3326129.php.

106. NoFap Community. "About NoFap® and FAQs." NoFap, Reddit, 21 Nov. 2017, www.reddit.com/r/NoFap/wiki/index.

107. O'Malley, John W. Trent: What Happened at the Council. Boston, MA: Harvard University Press, 2013.

108. Pallavicino, Ferrante. The Whores Rhetorick: Calculated to the Meridian of London, and Conformed to the Rules of Art. Printed for George Shall in Stone-Cutter-Street, 1683.

109. Palliser, D. M., et al. The Cambridge Urban History of Britain. Cambridge University Press, 2000

110. Paul, Charles K. William Godwin: His Friends and Contemporaries. Roberts Brothers, 1877.

111. Peakman, Julie. The Pleasure's All Mine: A History of Perverse Sex. Reaktion Books, 2016.

112. Pepys, Samuel. "Saturday 8 February 1667/68." The Diary of Samuel Pepys, www.pepysdiary.com/diary/1668/02/08/.

113. Pepys, Samuel. "Sunday 28 May 1665." The Diary of Samuel Pepys, www.pepysdiary.com/diary/1665/05/28/.

114. Pepys, Samuel. "Sunday 9 February 1667/68." The Diary of Samuel Pepys, www.pepysdiary.com/diary/1668/02/09/. Hilariously enough, this supposedly comprehensive Pepys source chooses to suppress the mastuabatory language about his prick. The full text is in a comment right below the source text.

115. Pepys, Samuel. "Wednesday 1 January 1667/68." The Diary of Samuel Pepys, www.pepysdiary.com/diary/1668/01/.

116. Pepys, Samuel. A Pepysian Garland. Edited by Hyder E Rollins, Harvard University Press, 1971, p. 72–77.

117. Phillips, John. Sade: the Libertine Novels. Pluto Press, 2001, p. 4.

118. Political State, xxviii (August 1724), 207. Available at https://books.google.com/books?id=NXZYAAAAcAAJ&lpg=PA207&ots=R25ayFDQdW&dq=Why%20is%20poor%20Curll%20hunted%20down%20by%20the%20Society%20for%20Reformation%20of%20Manners%20for%20his%20unprofitable%20starving%20Bawdry%3F&pg=PP7#v=onepage&q=Why%20is%20poor%20Curll%20hunted%20down%20by%20the%20Society%20for%20Reformation%20of%20Manners%20for%20his%20unprofitable%20starving%20Bawdry?&f=false

119. Qtd in Ashbee, Henry Spencer. Index Librorum Prohibitorum; Bio-Biblio-Icono-Graphical and Critical Notes on Curious, Uncommon and Erotic Books. London, Privately Printed, 1877, p 117-126.

120. Quinlan, Maurice J. Victorian Prelude, a History of English Manners. Hamden, Conn.: Archon Books, 1965

121. Reformation Society. An Account of the Societies for Reformation of Manners in England and Ireland: with a Persuasive to Persons of All Ranks to Be Zealous and Diligent in Promoting the Execution of the Laws against Prophaneness and Debauchery for the Effecting a National Reformation. 3rd ed., Printed for B. Aylmer and A. Bell, 1700.

122. Richardson, Samuel, et al. The Novels of Samuel Richardson: Complete and Unabridged; Heinemann, 1902, History of Pamela.

123. Richardson, Samuel. Pamela. London: J.M. Dent, 1914, title page.

124. Robert Issac Wilberforce, The Life of William Wilberforce (London 1838)

125. Roberts, M. J. D.. Making English Morals: Voluntary Association and Moral Reform in Nineteenth-

Century England. Cambridge, UK: Cambridge University Press, 2004, p. 75. Roberts was able to examine the bank records of the SSV, held at Hoare's Bank in London.

126. Roberts, MJD. "Making Victorian Morals? The Society for the Suppression of Vice and its Critics 1802-1888." Historical Studies 21, no. 83 (1981): 157-73

127. Rochester, John Wilmot, 2nd Earl of. "A Satyre on Charles II."Goucher College.faculty.goucher.edu/eng211/a_satyre_on_charles_ii.htm (accessed May 5, 2013), lines 1-9.

128. Rochester, John Wilmot. "The Farce of Sodom, or The Quintessence of Debauchery."Wikisource, the Free Online Library, 1689, en.wikisource.org/wiki/The_Farce_of_Sodom,_or_The_Quintessence_of_Debauchery.

129. Rochester, John Wilmot. John Wilmot, Earl of Rochester: The Poems and Lucina's Rape. Edited by Keith Walker and Nicholas Fisher, Wiley-Blackwell, 2010, p. 104-5.

130. Rogers, Pat, and Paul Baines. "The Prosecutions of Edmund Curll, 1725-28." The Library, vol. 5, no. 2, Jan. 2004, pp. 176–194., doi:10.1093/library/5.2.176.

131. Rossetti, Dante Gabriel. "Jenny ."Poetry Foundation. http://www.poetryfoundation.org/poem/184527 (accessed May 5, 2013), lines 1-4.

132. Roy Porter and Lesley Hall, Facts of Life. The Creation of Sexual Knowledge in Britain, 1650–1950 (New Haven, Conn., and London, Yale University Press, 1995), pp. 6–7

133. Sasha Roberts, 'Let Me the Curtains Draw: The Dramatic and Symbolic Properties of the Bed in Shakespearean Tragedy', in Staged Properties in Early Modern English Drama, ed. Jonathan Gil Harris and Natasha Kord (Cambridge: Cambridge University Press, 2002)

134. Schroeder, H. J., translator. The Canons and Decrees of the Council of Trent. Tan Books, 2011, pgs. 278-283.

135. Scott, John. An Account of Societies for the Reformation of Manners, and the Suppression of Vice with Answers to Objections Against Them Second Edition, Enlarged. W Rawson, 1807.

136. See Hopkins, Amanda, and Cory Rushton. The Erotic in the Literature of Medieval Britain. D.S. Brewer, 2007.

137. Sherlock, Thomas. "A Letter on the Earthquakes in MDCCL." In Discourses Preached at the Temple Church. Oxford: Clarendon Press, 1812. 325-338, pgs. 325-27.

138. Shoemaker, R. B. "The Decline Of Public Insult In London 1660-1800." Past & Present, vol. 169, no. 1, Jan. 2000, pp. 97–131., doi:10.1093/past/169.1.97.

139. Sigel, Lisa Z. Governing Pleasures: Pornography and Social Change in England, 1815-1914. Rutgers University Press, 2002

140. Sigel, Lisa Z. International Exposure: Perspectives on Modern European Pornography, 1800-2000. Rutgers University Press, 2005

141. Skjelver, Danielle Mead. "German Hercules: The Impace of Scatology on the Definition of Martin Luther as a Man 1483-1546." Pittsburgh Undergraduate Review, vol. 14, no. 1, 2009, pp. 30–78., Available at: www.academia.edu/1016951/German_Hercules_The_Impact_of_Scatology_on-_the_Image_of_Martin_Luther_as_a_ Man_1483-1546.

142. Smith, Preserved. The Life and Letters of Martin Luther. Routledge, 2016

143. Society, for the Suppression of Vice Part the First: Address to the Public from the Society for the Suppression of Vice, Setting Forth, With a List of the Members, the Utility and Necessity of such an Institution and its Claim to Public Support . London: Printed for the Society, 1803, pgs 34-35.

144. Society, for the Suppression of Vice Part the Second: Address to the Public from the Society for the Suppression of Vice, Containing an Account of the Proceedings of the Society from its Original In-

stitution. London: Printed for the Society, 1804, pg. 26.

145. Society, For the Suppression of Vice, The Constable's Assistant: Being a Compendium of The Duties and Powers of Constables and other Peace Officers, chiefly as they relate to the Apprehending of Offenders, and the laying of Information before Magistrates. Villiers Street, London: Printed for the Society, 1808.

146. Society, For the Suppression of Vice. Society for the Suppression of Vice, Consisting of Members of the Established Church. WIth a Brief Abstract of Proceedings in 1802. Bridge-Street, Blackfriars, London: Printed for the Society, 1803, p. 5.

147. Souhami, Diana. The Trials of Radclyffe Hall. New York: Doubleday, 1999

148. Stewart, Potter. "Jacobellis v. Ohio." Findlaw, 22 June 1964, caselaw.findlaw.com/us-supreme-court/378/184.html.

149. Stolberg, Michael. "EXAMINING THE BODY, C. 1500–1750." The Routledge History of Sex and the Body, 1500 to the Present, edited by Kate Fisher and Sarah Toulalan, pp. 91–105.

150. Stone touches on this, but see also Fass, Paula S. The Routledge History of Childhood in the Western World. Routledge, 2015, chapters 3-5, and Lascarides, V. Celia., and Blythe Simone Farb. Hinitz. History of Early Childhood Education. Taylor and Francis, 2013.

151. Stone, Lawrence. The Family, Sex and Marriage in England, 1500-1800. Harper & Row, 1977.

152. Strange, John. Reports of Adjudged Cases in the Courts of Chancery, King's Bench, Common Pleas, and Exchequer: from Trinity Term in the Second Year of King George I. to Trinity Term in the Twenty-First Year of King George II. II, Printed by A. Strahan and W. Woodfall, Law-Printers to the King for G.G. and J. Robinson, W. Otridge, 1795.

153. Straus, Ralph. The Unspeakable Curll. Chapman & Hall, 1927

154. Swinburne, Algernon Charles. The Swineburne

Letters. Vol. 2 : 1869-1872. Edited by Cecil Y Lang, vol. 2, Yale Univ. Press , 1974

155. Taylor, Leslie. ""I Made up My Mind to Get It": The American Trial of "The Well of Loneliness" New York City, 1928-1929." Journal of the History of Sexuality 10, no. 2 (2001): 250-286. http://www.jstor.org/stable/3704816 (accessed December 10, 2013)

156. The Decameron of Giovanni Boccaccio. Translated by John Payne. Blue Ribbon Books, 1931

157. The National Archives (UK)."Records of the National Vigilance Association."The National Archives. https://www.nationalarchives.gov.uk/a2a/records.aspx?cat=106-4nva&cid=0#0 (accessed November 15, 2013).

158. The Times. "Novel Condemned as Obscene." The Times (London), November 17, 1928,

159. The Times."Alleged Obscene Novel. Proceedings at Bow-Street." The Times (London), November 10, 1928,

160. Thomas, Donald. A Long Time Burning; The History of Literary Censorship in England. New York: Praeger, 1969

161. Thompson, Dave. Black and White and Blue: Adult Cinema from the Victorian Age to the VCR. ECW Press, 2007

162. Timbs, John. Doctors and patients, or, Anecdotes of the Medical World and Curiosities of Medicine. London: Richard Bentley and Son (1876), p. 151.

163. Tosh, John. Manliness and Masculinities in Nineteenth-Century Britain. Pearson Longman, 2005, p. 61-82.

164. Toulalan, Sarah and Fisher, Cate. "INTRODUCTION" The Routledge History of Sex and the Body, 1500 to the Present, edited by Kate Fisher and Sarah Toulalan, pp. 1-20.

165. Toulalan, Sarah. Imagining Sex: Pornography and Bodies in Seventeenth-Century England. Oxford University Press, 2011.

166. Travis, Alan. Bound and Gagged: A Secret His-

tory of Obscenity in Britain. London: Profile Books, 2000, p. 9.

167. Trumbull proposes that he killed himself, but other sources are more divided. Trumbull, C.G. Anthony Comstock, Fighter. New York: Fleming H. Revell Company, 1913

168. Turner, James. Schooling Sex: Libertine Literature and Erotic Education in Italy, France, and England 1534-1685. Oxford University Press, 2003

169. Vickery, Amanda. The Gentleman's Daughter: Women's Lives in Georgian England. Yale University Press, 1999, p. 52.

170. Wagner, Peter. Eros Revived: Erotica of the Enlightenment in England and America. Paladin, 1990

171. Watson, Brian. "'A Poison More Deadly': Defining Obscenity in the West." NOTCHES BLOG, 25 Aug. 2016, notchesblog.com/2016/05/10/a-poison-more-deadly-defining-obscenity-in-the-west/.

172. Watson, Brian. "The Victorian with a Secret." NOTCHES, 12 Dec. 2017, notchesblog.com/2017/12/12/the-archetypical-victorian-with-a-secret-henry-spencer-ashbee/. Another large bit of it is indebted to indebted to my article for The Edinburgh History of Reading 'Hellfire and Cannibals: 18th and 19th Century Erotic Reading Groups and Their Manuscripts' (forthcoming).

173. White, Matthew. "Selected Death Tolls for Wars, Massacres and Atrocities Before the 20th Century." Twentieth Century Atlas - Historical Body Count, 1 Jan. 2012, necrometrics.com/pre1700a.htm#30YrW.

174. Wohl, Anthony S. "The Murphy Riots." The Victorian Web, 4 Apr. 2002, www.victorianweb.org/religion/Murphy_Riots.html.

175. Woolf, Virginia. The Diary of Virginia Woolf, Vol. 3 1925-1930.Ed. Anne Oliver Bell with Andrew McNeillie. New York: Harcourt, 1980

176. Woolf, Virginia. The Letters of Virginia Woolf, Vol. 3: 1923-1928. Ed. Nigel Nicolson and Joanne Trautmann. New York: Harcourt, 1978

177. Wyngaard, Amy S. "Sade, Réage and Transcend-

ing the Obscene." The Cambridge Companion to Erotic Literature, edited by Bradford Keyes. Mudge, Cambridge University Press, 2017

178. Youssef, H. "The History of the Condom." Journal of the Royal Society of Medicine, vol. 86, Apr. 1993, pp. 226–228., www.ncbi.nlm.nih.gov/pmc/articles/PMC1293956/pdf/jrsocmed00099-0056.pdf.

179. Ziegler, Philip. The Black Death. New York, NY: John Day Co., 1969.

ABOUT THE AUTHOR

I am a historian of the book and sexuality, an archivist, and a researcher. I have especial interest in the history of privacy, sexual categories, obscene/pornographic literature, intersectionality and queer theory.

I started undergrad at Keene State College, a small liberal arts college in New Hampshire, where I grew up. I originally wanted to be a teacher but quickly moved to focusing on academia. I received M.A. in History & Culture from Drew University, where I focused on the history of the book and obscenity censorship. I am currently pursuing a MLIS in Archives and Digital Humanities at Indiana University Bloomington.

My first book, *Annals of Pornographie: How Porn Became Bad*, resulted in an appearance on Conan O'Brien and elsewhere. Currently, I work as a pre-professional assistant at Scholarly Communications at IUB, focusing on Open Access, and I am a pre-professional archivist at the Kinsey Institute. I am researching my next book, which is on the historiography of porn studies between the end of WWII and the start of the Reagan and Thatcher 'rebellions.' I have a number of forthcoming book chapters in the *Edinburgh History of Reading, Literature's Kinkiest Corners* and elsewhere.

I am also a volunteer moderator for the world's largest academic history forum, AskHistorians, and I am the co-host and editor of The AskHistorians Podcast. You can contact me at www.brimwats.com or via email at:

b m watson 1989 AT gmail .com

Thank you.

[1] "begin, v.". OED Online. October 2016. Oxford University Press.

Brian M. Watson

[2] "pornography, n.". OED Online. October 2016. Oxford University Press.

[3] Moulton, Ian Frederick. Before Pornography. Oxford [England: Oxford University Press, 2000, p. 8. The treatise on prostitutes was *Le Pornographe ou La Prostitution réformée* by Restif de la Bretonne. First used in modern sense in Charles Anthon, "Dictionary of Greek and Roman Antiquities," New York, 1843: "Pornography, or obscene painting, which in the time of the Romans was practiced with the grossest license, prevailed especially at no particular period in Greece, but was apparently tolerated to a considerable extent at all times. Parrhasius, Aristides, Pausanias, Nicophanes, Chaerephanes, Arellius, and a few other [pornographoi] are mentioned as having made themselves notorious for this species of license."

[4] Johnson, James William. *A Profane Wit: The Life of John Wilmot, Earl of Rochester*. University of Rochester Press, 2009 discusses this on p. 181-82 and Greene, Graham. *Lord Rochester's Monkey: Being the Life of John Wilmot, Second Earl of Rochester*. Pengiun Books, 1988 on p. 106-8. Both refer to Haley, K. H. D. *The First Earl of Shaftesbury*. Clarendon Press, 1968: A letter dated January 20, 1674, reported that "my Lord Rochester fled from Court some time since for delivering (by mistake) into the King's hands a terrible lampoon of his own making against the King, instead of another the King asked him for."

[5] Buchanan, Robert Williams. The fleshly school of Poetry, and other phenomena of the day. London: Strahan& Co., 1872, pgs. 66-69. Ruskin, in reviewing the poems before publication, was also discouraging, saying that he would "be sorry if you [Rossetti] laid the [poem] before the public... [it has] too great boldness for common readers." See the Rossetti Archive's webpage on Jenny: http://www.rossettiarchive.org/docs/3-1848.raw.html

[6] Rochester, John Wilmot, 2nd Earl of. "A Satyre on Charles II."Goucher College.faculty.goucher.edu/eng211/a_satyre_on_charles_ii.htm (accessed May 5, 2013), lines 1-9.

[7] Rossetti, Dante Gabriel. "Jenny ."Poetry Foundation. http://www.poetryfoundation.org/poem/184527 (accessed May 5, 2013), lines 1-4.

[8] ibid, lines 139, and 372.

[9] Johnson, James William. *A Profane Wit: The Life of John Wilmot, Earl of Rochester*. Rochester, NY: U of Rochester, 2004. Print. And *The Libertine*. Dir. Laurence Dunmore. Perf. Johnny Depp, Samantha Morton, John Malkovich. The Weinstein Company, 2004. DVD.

[10]Gayle, Damien. "UK to Censor Online Videos of 'Non-Conventional' Sex Acts." *The Guardian*, Guardian News and Media, 23 Nov. 2016, www.theguardian.com/technology/2016/nov/23/censor-non-conventional-sex-acts-online-internet-pornography. Knibbs, Kate. "Selling Erotic Ebooks Is Illegal in Germany Before 10pm ." *Gizmodo*, Gizmodo.com, 22 June 2015, gizmodo.com/selling-erotic-ebooks-is-illegal-in-germany-before-10pm-1713112318. "[As of this writing SC9 in Utah, HR549 in Vir-

ginia,] HJR 166 in Alabama, HR 364 and HR 447 in Georgia, HR 113 in Hawaii, HF 1788 and SF 1605 in Minnesota, HCR 38 in Missouri, HCR 1002 in Oklahoma, H 3887 in South Carolina, HR 112 in Texas, and SCR 29 in West Virginia. Other resolutions, like Arkansas's HR 1042, Kansas's HR 6016 (SR 1723 died in the Senate), Oklahoma's HCR 1006, and Virginia's HJ 549, have had success in one chamber. Other states have adopted or signed their versions of the resolution. South Dakota unanimously passed SCR 4 in January. Tennessee's governor signed SJR 35 on April 24th. The most recent passed resolution is Louisiana's HCR 100, which has slightly different language from the others: pornography is deemed a "hazard" instead of a crisis, and the victims are specified as "Louisiana children." Arnold, Amanda. "The War on Porn Is Back." *Jezebel*, Jezebel.com, 20 Sept. 2017, jezebel.com/the-war-on-porn-is-back-1810469452.

[11] NoFap Community. "About NoFap® and FAQs." *NoFap*, Reddit, 21 Nov. 2017, www.reddit.com/r/NoFap/wiki/index.

[12] Ley, David J. *The Myth of Sex Addiction*. Rowman & Littlefield, 2014.

[13] News, Bay City. "Kink.com Buys SF Armory." *SFGate*, 9 Jan. 2007, www.sfgate.com/news/article/Kink-com-buys-SF-Armory-3326129.php. As of 2017 Kink.com had ceased filming at the Armory.

[14] Gallup, Inc. "Older Americans' Moral Attitudes Changing." Gallup.com. N.p., 03 June 2013. Web. 19 Oct. 2016.

[15] Moulton, Ian. "Erotic Representation, 1500–1750." *The Routledge History of Sex and the Body: 1500 to the Present*, edited by Sarah Toulalan and Kate Fisher, Routledge, 2016, pp. 207–222. See Marcus, Steven. *The Other Victorians: a Study of Sexuality and Pornography in Mid-Nineteenth-Century England*. Basic Books, 1964 for discussion on pornotopia, which is widely viewed with skepticism by current researchers.

[16] For example, the Wife of Bath, some versions of the Gawain, branches of the *Mabinogi*, and other sources. See Hopkins, Amanda, and Cory Rushton. *The Erotic in the Literature of Medieval Britain*. D.S. Brewer, 2007, among others.

[17] See for example, Baron, Hans. *Crisis of the Early Italian Renaissance*. Princeton University Press, 1955. Although Baron's work has been criticized by Eugenio Garin and Paul Oskar Kristeller for being too prescriptive, he remains important in shaping my understanding. Also see Mazzocco, Angelo. *Interpretations of Renaissance Humanism*. Brill, 2006. Mazzocco and Blacks essays provide an excellent grounding.

[18] Mann, Nicholas. "The origins of humanism." *The Cambridge Companion to Renaissance Humanism*. Ed. Jill Kraye. Cambridge: Cambridge U Press, 1966. 1-20, p. 2.

[19] This is somewhat an oversimplification, as there was overlap and back-and-forth and a great deal of cooperation, as Mann and others point out,

but the greater point still stands. See also Fubini, Riccardo. "Humanism and Scholasticism." *Interpretations of Renaissance Humanism*, edited by Angelo Mazzocco, Brill, 2006.

[20] O'Malley, John W. Trent: What Happened at the Council. Boston, MA: Harvard University Press, 2013., p. 38.

[21] Boccaccio, Giovanni. *The Decameron*. Translated by G. H. McWilliam, Franklin Library, 1981. p. 27-28.

[22] - Ibid, p. 40.

[23] Ibid, p. 45.

[24] Ibid, p. 46.

[25] Ibid, p. 46.

[26] Ibid, p. 47.

[27] Ibid, p. 47.

[28] Ibid, p. 183-4.

[29] Ibid, p. 185.

[30] Ibid, p. 186

[31] Ibid, p. 253

[32] Ibid, p. 254.

[33] Ibid, p. 255.

[34] Ibid, p. 256.

[35] Dabhoiwala, Faramerz. *The Origins of Sex: A History of the First Sexual Revolution*. Penguin Books, 2013, p. 144.

[36] *The Decameron of Giovanni Boccaccio*. Translated by John Payne. Blue Ribbon Books, 1931, p. 184. This footnote even makes a bizarre appearance in a 2015 edition of the book in Amazon Kindle format.

[37] Ziegler, Philip. The Black Death. New York, NY: John Day Co., 1969.

[38] McWilliams, *The Decameron*, p. 15-6. Boccaccio's entire description of the plague years through the introduction is straightforwardly terrifying.

[39] For more on scribal culture. Clanchy, M.T. "Parchment and Paper: Manuscript Culture 1100–1500." *A Companion to the History of the Book*, edited by Simon Eliot and Jonathan Rose, Blackwell, 2007, pp. 194–206.

[40] Ibid, p. 205.

[41] Quoted in ibid, p. 198.

[42] Cleugh, James. *The Divine Aretino*. Stein and Day, 1966, p. 23; Chubb, Thomas Caldecot. *Aretino, Scourge of Princes*. Reynal & Hitchcock, 1940, p. 8.

[43] Chubb, p. 19.

[44] Cleugh, p. 24.

[45] Ibid, p. 25.

[46] Ibid, p. 33.

[47] Ibid, p. 35.

[48] Qtd in Whitcomb, Merrick. *Literary Source-Book of the German Renaissance.* University of Pennsylvania, 1899, p. 79.

[49] Qtd in Chubb, p. 51.

[50] Chubb, p. 57.

[51] From both Cleugh p. 47 and Chubb, p. 67.

[52] Cleugh, p. 48.

[53] Chubb, p. 79

[54] Aretino, Pietro, and Samuel Putnam. The Works of Aretino: Translated into English from the Original Italian. Covici-Friede, 1933, p. 252.

[55] Lawner, Lynne, and Pietro Aretino. *I Modi: The Sixteen Pleasures: an Erotic Album of the Italian Renaissance.* Northwestern University, 1988, Sonnet 1.

[56] Cleugh, James. *The Divine Aretino, Pietro of Arezzo, 1492-1556.* London: A. Blond, 1965.

[57] Aretino, Pietro, and Margaret Rosenthal. *Aretino's Dialogues.* University of Toronto Press, 2005, p. 15.

[58] Ibid, p. 16-17.

[59] Ibid, p. 19-20.

[60] Ibid, p. 22.

[61] Ibid, p. 24.

[62] Ibid, p. 27.

[63] Muzzarelli, M. G. "Reconciling the Privilege of a Few with the Common Good: Sumptuary Laws in Medieval and Early Modern Europe." *Journal of Medieval and Early Modern Studies*, vol. 39, no. 3, 2009, pp. 597–617, doi:10.1215/10829636-2009-006.

[64] Ibid, p. 599.

[65] "A Thirteenth-Century Castilian Sumptuary Law." *The Business History Review*, vol. 37, no. 1/2, 1963, pp. 98–100. *JSTOR*, JSTOR, www.jstor.org/stable/3112097.

[66] Emck, Katy. "Female Transvestism and Male Self-Fashioning in As You Like It and La Vida Es Sueno." *Reading the Renaissance: Culture, Poetics, and Drama*, edited by Jonathan Hart, Garland Pub, 1996, pp. 76.

[67] Ibid.

[68] Aretino, *Dialogues*, p. 29.

[69] Ibid, p. 59.

[70] Ibid, p. 60.

[71] Ibid, p. 61.

[72] See *Barclay, Katie, and Merridee L. Bailey, editors. Emotion, Ritual and Power in Europe, 1200-1920: Family, State and Church. Palgrave Macmillan, 2017,* especially chapter 3, Monger, George P. *Marriage Customs of the World: From Henna to Honeymoons.* ABC-CLIO, 2005, pgs 23-25, Sasha Roberts, 'Let

Brian M. Watson

Me the Curtains Draw: The Dramatic and Symbolic Properties of the Bed in Shakespearean Tragedy', in *Staged Properties in Early Modern English Drama*, ed. Jonathan Gil Harris and Natasha Kord (Cambridge: Cambridge University Press, 2002), also of interest may be Mia Korpiola, *Between Betrothal and Bedding: Marriage Formation in Sweden 1200–1600* (Leiden: Brill, 2009).

[73] Aretino, p. 61.

[74] Ibid, p. 62.

[75] Ibid, p. 65.

[76] Ibid, p. 65.

[77] Ibid, p. 68.

[78] Ibid, p. 102.

[79] Ibid, p. 86.

[80] Ibid, p. 103.

[81] Ibid, p. 106.

[82] Ibid, p. 108.

[83] Ibid, p. 117

[84] Ibid, p. 157.

[85] Ibid, p. 158.

[86] Cleugh, final chapter.

[87] Chubb, p. 451.

[88] Luther , Martin. *Weimarer Ausgabe*. VIII, Deutscher Taschenbuch Verlag, 1987, p. 203.

[89] Dabhoiwala, p. 12.

[90] Brundage, James A. *Law, Sex, and Christian Society in Medieval Europe"*. University of Chicago Press, 1987, p. 3.

[91] Augustine, Saint. *The Works of Saint Augustine Part Two -- Letters*. Vol. 4, New City Press, 2005., p 253.

[92] Harper, Kyle. *From Shame to Sin: The Christian Transformation of Sexual Morality in Late Antiquity*. Harvard University Press, 2016, p. 7.

[93] See Ingram, Martin. *Church Courts, Sex and Marriage in England: 1570-1640*. Cambridge University Press, 1987, Karras, Ruth Mazo. *Unmarriages: Women, Men, and Sexual Unions in the Middle Ages*. University Of Pennsylvania, 2014, and Addy, John. *Sin & Society in the Seventeenth Century*. Routledge, 2014.

[94] Dabhoiwala, p. 7.

[95] Ibid.

[96] Smith, Preserved. *The Life and Letters of Martin Luther*. Routledge, 2016, p. 44.

[97] Qtd in Oettinger, Rebecca Wagner. *Music as Propaganda in the German Re-*

formation. Routledge, 2016, chapter 6.

[98] Much of this section draws from Skjelver, Danielle Mead. "German Hercules: The Impace of Scatology on the Definition of Martin Luther as a Man 1483-1546." *Pittsburgh Undergraduate Review*, vol. 14, no. 1, 2009, pp. 30–78., Available at: www.academia.edu/1016951/ German_Hercules_The_Impact_of_Scatology_on_the_Image_of_Martin_ Luther_as_a_Man_1483-1546.

[99] Luther, Martin. *Against the Roman Papacy: An Institution of the Devil.* Translated by Jaroslav Pelikan, vol. 40 of *Luther's Works*, Concordia and Fortress Press, 1957.

[100] O'Malley, John W. *Trent: What Happened at the Council.* Harvard University Press, 2013, p. 12

[101] Ibid, p. 18.

[102] Ibid.

[103] Ibid, p. 186.

[104] Ibid, p. 226.

[105] Ibid.

[106] See Ingram, Martin. *Church Courts, Sex and Marriage in England: 1570-1640.* Cambridge University Press, 1987, Karras, Ruth Mazo. *Unmarriages: Women, Men, and Sexual Unions in the Middle Ages.* University Of Pennsylvania, 2014, and Addy, John. *Sin & Society in the Seventeenth Century.* Routledge, 2014.

[107] Stone, Lawrence. *The Family, Sex and Marriage in England, 1500-1800.* Harper & Row, 1977, p. 6. Although there is much to critique in Stone (more on that later) he remains essentially right, in my opinion, that the family as an institution was much more open and widespread (dispersed amongst non-biological members) in the 16th and 17th centuries than it would be later.

[108] Moulton, Ian Frederick. *Before Pornography: Erotic Writing in Early Modern England.* Oxford University Press, 2000, p. 14.

[109] Schroeder, H. J., translator. *The Canons and Decrees of the Council of Trent.* Tan Books, 2011, pgs. 278-283.

[110] Ibid.

[111] White, Matthew. "Selected Death Tolls for Wars, Massacres and Atrocities Before the 20th Century." *Twentieth Century Atlas - Historical Body Count*, 1 Jan. 2012, necrometrics.com/pre1700a.htm#30YrW.

[112] Muir, Edward. *The Culture Wars of the Late Renaissance: Skeptics, Libertines, and Opera.* Harvard University Press, 2007, p. 63.

[113] Ibid, p. 93.

[114] As is likely obvious, I am using the seventeenth century English edition, because the author's Italian is unfortunately not. Pallavicino, Ferrante. *The Whores Rhetorick: Calculated to the Meridian of London, and Conformed to the*

Brian M. Watson

Rules of Art. Printed for George Shall in Stone-Cutter-Street, 1683, p. 2.

[115] Ibid, p. 7

[116] Ibid, p. 11.

[117] Ibid, p. 40.

[118] Ibid, p. 61.

[119] Muir, p. 94.

[120] Pallavicino, p. 67.

[121] Ibid, p. 86.

[122] Kidnie, Margaret Jane, and Philip Stubbes. "A Critical Edition of Philip Stubbes's Anatomie of Abuses." *ETheses -- Birmingham University, University of Birmingham*, 4 Apr. 1996, etheses.bham.ac.uk/4435/1/Kidnie96PhD_redacted.pdf, p. 269.

[123] Turner, James. *Schooling Sex: Libertine Literature and Erotic Education in Italy, France, and England 1534-1685*. Oxford University Press, 2003, p. viii.

[124] Qtd. in MOULTON, IAN FREDERICK. "Crafty Whores: The Moralizing of Aretino's Dialogues." *Critical Survey*, vol. 12, no. 2, 2000, pp. 88–105. *JSTOR*, JSTOR, www.jstor.org/stable/41557045, p. 100.

[125] Pepys, Samuel. "Wednesday 1 January 1667/68." *The Diary of Samuel Pepys*, www.pepysdiary.com/diary/1668/01/.

[126] Pepys, Samuel. "Saturday 8 February 1667/68." *The Diary of Samuel Pepys*, www.pepysdiary.com/diary/1668/02/08/.

[127] Pepys, Samuel. "Sunday 9 February 1667/68." *The Diary of Samuel Pepys*, www.pepysdiary.com/diary/1668/02/09/. Hilariously enough, this supposedly comprehensive Pepys source chooses to suppress the mastuabatory language about his prick. The full text is in a comment right below the source text.

[128] Sarah Toulalan has a detailed account, which this section is indebted to, in Toulalan, Sarah. *Imagining Sex: Pornography and Bodies in Seventeenth-Century England*. Oxford University Press, 2011.

[129] DeJean, Joan. *The Reinvention of Obscenity: Sex, Lies, and Tabloids in Early Modern France*. The University of Chicago Press, 2002, p.

[130] Millot and L'Ange in Mudge, Bradford K. *When Flesh Becomes Word: An Anthology of Early Eighteenth-Century Libertine Literature*. Oxford University Press, 2004, p. xvi

[131] Qtd in ibid, p. 25.

[132] Ibid, p. 6.

[133] Ibid.

[134] Ibid, p. 8.

[135] Ibid, p. 9.

[136] Aretino, p. 43-44.

[137] Ibid.

[138] Mudge, p. 10.

[139] Ibid, p. 11.

[140] Ibid.

[141] Toulalan, p. 55.

[142] Millot and L'Ange in Mudge, *When Flesh Becomes Word*, p. 9.

[143] Mudge, *When Flesh Becomes Word*, p. 306, ft. 6.

[144] Ibid, p. 15.

[145] Ibid.

[146] Mudge, p. 306-7, fn. 7.

[147] Kassel, Lauren. "MEDICAL UNDERSTANDINGS OF THE BODY, C.1500–1750" *The Routledge History of Sex and the Body, 1500 to the Present*, edited by Kate Fisher and Sarah Toulalan, pp. 57-74

[148] Stolberg, Michael. "EXAMINING THE BODY, C. 1500–1750." *The Routledge History of Sex and the Body, 1500 to the Present*, edited by Kate Fisher and Sarah Toulalan, pp. 91–105.

[149] Toulalan, Sarah and Fisher, Cate. "INTRODUCTION" *The Routledge History of Sex and the Body, 1500 to the Present*, edited by Kate Fisher and Sarah Toulalan, pp. 1-20.

[150] Millot and L'Ange in Mudge, p. 19.

[151] Ibid, p. 41.

[152] Ibid, p. 25.

[153] Ibid, p. 30.

[154] Ibid, p. 34.

[155] Ibid, p. 45.

[156] Chorier, Nicolas. *The Dialogues of Luisa Sigea*. Locus Elm Press, 2015. Electronic Kindle version. Location 139.

[157] Ibid.

[158] See fn 35 above.

[159] Chorier, location 241.

[160] Ibid, location 411-422.

[161] Peakman, Julie. *The Pleasure's All Mine: A History of Perverse Sex*. Reaktion Books, 2016, p. 109-143.

[162] Ibid, p. 109.

[163] Chorier, location 429-443.

[164] Ibid, locations 610-649.

[165] Fissell, Mary. "When the Birds and the Bees Were Not Enough: Aristotle's Masterpiece." *The Public Domain Review*, 19 Aug. 2015, publicdomainreview.org/2015/08/19/when-the-birds-and-the-bees-were-not-enough-aristotles-masterpiece/.

Brian M. Watson

[166] Roy Porter and Lesley Hall, *Facts of Life. The Creation of Sexual Knowledge in Britain, 1650–1950* (New Haven, Conn., and London, Yale University Press, 1995), pp. 6–7

[167] Qtd in Fissell. John Cannon, Memoirs of the Birth, Education, Life and Death of: Mr. John Cannon. Sometime Excise Officer & Writing Master at Mere Glastenbury & West Lydford in the County of Somerset. (1743). Somerset Record Office, Ms. DD/SAS C/1193/4, p. 41. For a modern edition, see *The Chronicles of John Cannon, Excise Officer and Writing Master*, ed. John Money, (Oxford: Published for the British Academy by Oxford University Press, 2010). (Fissell's footnote)

[168] Chorier, locations 953-957.

[169] Ibid, locations 1056-1065.

[170] Ibid.

[171] Ibid, locations 1073-78.

[172] Ibid, location 1086.

[173] Hartley, L. P. *The Go-Between*. New York Review of Books, 2011, p. 1.

[174] Rochester, John Wilmot. *John Wilmot, Earl of Rochester: The Poems and Lucina's Rape*. Edited by Keith Walker and Nicholas Fisher, Wiley-Blackwell, 2010, p. 104-5.

[175] Johnson, James William, p. 19.

[176] Stone, p. 501-17

[177] Johnson, p. 19.

[178] Ibid, p. 20.

[179] Ibid, p. 31-2.

[180] Black, Jeremy. *The British and the Grand Tour*. Routledge, 2011, p. 76-77, but the entire chapter as a whole.

[181] Johnson, p. 46.

[182] Greene, 35.

[183] Vickery, Amanda. *The Gentleman's Daughter: Women's Lives in Georgian England*. Yale University Press, 1999, p. 52.

[184] Pepys, Samuel. "Sunday 28 May 1665." *The Diary of Samuel Pepys*, www.pepysdiary.com/diary/1665/05/28/.

[185] Archives, The National. "Currency Converter." *The National Archives*, The National Archives, Kew, Surrey TW9 4DU, 1 Mar. 2006, www.nationalarchives.gov.uk/currency/default0.asp. Of course, take that with a huge grain of salt as there is quite a lot of issues converting old money into modern.

[186] Johnson, p. 106.

[187] Ibid, p. 112.

[188] Ibid, p. 106.

[189] Rochester, p. 81-85.

[190] Ibid.

[191] Ibid.

[192] Ibid.

[193] Ibid.

[194] Ibid.

[195] Ibid.

[196] Ibid.

[197] Ibid.

[198] Rochester, p. 145-151.

[199] Ibid.

[200] Ibid.

[201] Rochester, p. 86-87, though this copied version comes from https://andromeda.rutgers.edu/~jlynch/Texts/charles2.html.

[202] Qtd. In Johnson, p. 255.

[203] Timbs, John. *Doctors and patients, or, Anecdotes of the Medical World and Curiosities of Medicine.* London: Richard Bentley and Son (1876), p. 151.

[204] Greene, p. 110.

[205] Ibid, p. 145.

[206] Ibid, p. 188.

[207] Rochester, John Wilmot. "The Farce of Sodom, or The Quintessence of Debauchery." *Wikisource, the Free Online Library,* 1689, en.wikisource.org/wiki/The_Farce_of_Sodom,_or_The_Quintessence_of_Debauchery.

[208] Ibid.

[209] Ibid.

[210] Ibid.

[211] Ibid.

[212] Ibid.

[213] Ibid.

[214] Ibid.

[215] Ibid.

[216] Qtd in Dabhoiwala, p. 102.

[217] Qtd in ibid, p. 105.

[218] Ibid. p. 105.

[219] Ibid, p. 118.

[220] Clark, Peter. *British Clubs and Societies 1580-1800: The Origins of an Associational World.* Clarendon Press, 2000, p. 2.

[221] Ibid, p. 5.

[222] Palliser, D. M., et al. *The Cambridge Urban History of Britain.* Cambridge

Brian M. Watson

University Press, 2000, Volume 2 in general, but especially chapters 2 and 10.

[223] Clark, *Clubs*, p. 157.

[224] Andrew Gordon Craig, "The Movement for the Reformation of Manners, 1688–1715," unpubl. Ph.D. diss., University of Edinburgh, 1980, p. 1.

[225] Reformation Society. *An Account of the Societies for Reformation of Manners in England and Ireland: with a Persuasive to Persons of All Ranks to Be Zealous and Diligent in Promoting the Execution of the Laws against Prophaneness and Debauchery for the Effecting a National Reformation.* 3rd ed., Printed for B. Aylmer and A. Bell, 1700.

[226] Craig, p. 35.

[227] Ibid.

[228] Ibid, p. 32.

[229] Reformation Society, *An Account.*

[230] Ibid.

[231] Dabhoiwala, p. 59-60.

[232] Craig, p. 119.

[233] Defoe, Daniel. *Reformation of Manners: a Satyr.* Publisher Not Identified, 1702.

[234] Qtd in Dabhoiwala, p. 66.

[235] Ibid, p. 72.

[236] Stone, p. 93.

[237] Pepys, Samuel. *A Pepysian Garland.* Edited by Hyder E Rollins, Harvard University Press, 1971, p. 72–77.

[238] Shoemaker, R. B. "The Decline Of Public Insult In London 1660-1800." *Past & Present*, vol. 169, no. 1, Jan. 2000, pp. 97–131., doi:10.1093/past/169.1.97.

[239] Langford, Paul. "Chapter, 8 Personal Nobility." Public Life and the Propertied Englishman: 1689-1798, Clarendon Press, 1998, pp. 540–575.

[240] Tosh, John. Manliness and Masculinities in Nineteenth-Century Britain. Pearson Longman, 2005, p. 61-82. Also, Doror Wahrman, *The Making of the Modern Self.* Yale University Press, 2004

[241]

[242] *Political State*, xxviii (August 1724), 207. Available at https://books.google.com/books?id=NXZYAAAAcAAJ&lpg=PA207&ots=R25ayFDQdW&dq=Why%20is%20poor%20Curll%20hunted%20down%20by%20the%20Society%20for%20Reformation%20of%20Manners%20for%20his%20unprofitable%20starving%20Bawdry%3F&pg=PP7#v=onepage&q=Why%20is%20poor%20Curll%20hunted%20down%20by%20the%20Society%20for%20Reformation%20of

%20Manners%20for%20his%20unprofitable%20starving%20Bawdry?&f=false

[243] Baines, Paul, and Pat Rogers. *Edmund Curll, Bookseller*. Clarendon Press, 2007, p. 156.

[244] Gibson, Edmund. *A Sermon Preached to the Societies for Reformation of Manners At St. Mary-Le-Bow, on Monday January the 6th, 1723*. John Wyat at the Rose in St. Paul's Church-Yard, 1723.

[245] Baines and Rogers, p. 13.

[246] Straus, Ralph. *The Unspeakable Curll*. Chapman & Hall, 1927, p. 4.

[247] Ibid.

[248] Johns, Adrian. *Piracy: the Intellectual Property Wars from Gutenberg to Gates*. The University of Chicago Press, 2011, chapters 2 and 3. 'Charles II, 1662: An Act for preventing the frequent Abuses in printing seditious treasonable and unlicensed Bookes and Pamphlets and for regulating of Printing and Printing Presses.', Statutes of the Realm: volume 5: 1628-80 (1819), pp. 428-35. URL: http://www.british-history.ac.uk/report.asp?compid=47336.

[249] Qtd. in Straus, p. 101.

[250] Ibid, p. 105.

[251] Mudge, *Flesh*, p. 145.

[252] Ibid, p. 201.

[253] Ibid, p. 147

[254] .Ibid.

[255] Ibid, p. 149.

[256] Ibid.

[257] Ibid, p. 149-150

[258] Ibid, p. 152-54

[259] Ibid, p. 152-55

[260] Ibid, p. 156.

[261] Ibid, p. 15.

[262] Ibid, p. 171.

[263] Ibid, p. 166.

[264] Ibid, p. 173.

[265] Ibid.

[266] Ibid, p. 176.

[267] Wagner, Peter. *Eros Revived: Erotica of the Enlightenment in England and America*. Paladin, 1990, p. 213.

[268] Stauss, p. 100.

[269] Baines and Rogers, *Curll*, p. 179. *Heydegger's Letter* was a defense of the popular masquerade parties that had taken London, especially upper-class

London, by storm, and were seen as particularly offensive and dangerous by the Society for the Reformation of Manners.

[270] Rogers, Pat, and Paul Baines. "The Prosecutions of Edmund Curll, 1725-28." *The Library*, vol. 5, no. 2, Jan. 2004, pp. 176–194., doi:10.1093/library/5.2.176.

[271] Baines and Rogers, *Curll*, p. 159. And Strauss, p. 104.

[272] Strange, John. *Reports of Adjudged Cases in the Courts of Chancery, King's Bench, Common Pleas, and Exchequer: from Trinity Term in the Second Year of King George I. to Trinity Term in the Twenty-First Year of King George II*. II, Printed by A. Strahan and W. Woodfall, Law-Printers to the King for G.G. and J. Robinson, W. Otridge, 1795, p. 791.

[273] See INGRAM, MARTIN. *CHURCH COURTS, SEX AND MARRIAGE IN ENGLAND, 1570-1640*. CAMBRIDGE UNIVERSITY PRESS, 1994 AND Addy, John. *Sin & Society: in the Seventeenth Century*. Routledge, 2014.

[274] Dabhoiwala, p. 43.

[275] Ibid, p. 44.

[276]

[277] Baines and Rogers, *Curll*, p. 160-61.

[278] Commonwealth Legal Information Institute. "English Reports: DOMINUS REX v. CURL." English Reports 1795. www.commonlii.org/uk/cases/EngR/1795/1184.pdf (accessed May 1, 2013).

[279] Ibid.

[280] Ibid.

[281] Ibid.

[282] Strauss, p. 121.

[283] Meibom, Johann Heinrich. *A Treatise of the Use of Flogging in Venereal Affairs Also of the Office of the Loins and Reins. ... By John Henry Meibomius, M.D. Made English from the Latin Original by a Physician. To Which Is Added, a Treatise of Hermaphrodites*. Printed for E. Curll, 1718, Preface.

[284] Ibid.

[285] See Wagner, *Eros*, chapter 1.

[286] Baines and Rogers, *Curll*, p. 291.

[287] Qtd in Mudge, *Flesh*, p. 260.

[288] Ibid, p. 268.

[289] Ibid, p. 266.

[290] Ibid, p. 262.

[291] Ibid, p. 279.

[292] Youssef, H. "The History of the Condom." *Journal of the Royal Society of Medicine*, vol. 86, Apr. 1993, pp. 226–228., www.ncbi.nlm.nih.gov/pmc/articles/PMC1293956/pdf/jrsocmed00099-0056.pdf.

[293] Qtd in *Mudge*, p. 266.

[294] Ibid, p. 278-79.

[295] Ibid, p. 262.

[296] Ibid, p. 281.

[297] Stone, *The Family*, p. 6.

[298] Ingram, Martin. "Courtship and Marriage, C. 1500–1750." *The Routledge History of Sex and the Body: 1500 to the Present*, edited by Sarah Toulalan and Kate Fisher, Routledge, 2016, pp. 313–327.

[299] The couple still had a good deal of negotiation power, however, and could sway their parents, as much research has shown. See, for example Outhwaite, R. B. *Marriage and Society: Studies in the Social History of Marriage.* London: Europa Publications, 1981. Stones model here is offered as a generalized outline.

[300] Stone, *Family*, p. 31.

[301] Qtd. In Mudge, *Flesh*, p. 281.

[302] Ibid.

[303] Stone touches on this, but see also Fass, Paula S. *The Routledge History of Childhood in the Western World*. Routledge, 2015, chapters 3-5, and LASCARIDES, V. CELIA., AND BLYTHE SIMONE FARB. HINITZ. *HISTORY OF EARLY CHILDHOOD EDUCATION*. TAYLOR AND FRANCIS, 2013.

[304] Stone, *Family*, p. 174

[305] Ibid.

[306] Contributors, Multiple. *Onania: or, the Heinous Sin of Self-Pollution, and All Its Frightful Consequences*. H. Cooke, 1756.

[307] Qtd in Stone, p. 515.

[308] McKeon, Michael. *The Secret History of Domesticity: Public, Private, and the Division of Knowledge*. Johns Hopkins University Press, 2007 discusses this at great length in chapter 5.

[309] Bailey, Beth. "The Vexed History of Children And Sex." *The Routledge History of Childhood in the Western World*, edited by Paula S. Fass, Routledge, 2015, pp. 191–210.

[310] Stone, *Family*, p. 656.

[311] Ibid, p. 257.

[312] Richardson, Samuel, et al. *The Novels of Samuel Richardson: Complete and Unabridged;* Heinemann, 1902, *History of Pamela*.

[313] "LETTER WRITING AND THE RISE OF THE NOVEL: THE EPISTOLARY LITERACY OF JANE JOHNSON AND SAMUEL RICHARDSON." *THE PEN AND THE PEOPLE: ENGLISH LETTER WRITERS 1660-1800*, BY SUSAN E. WHYMAN, OXFORD UNIVERSITY PRESS, 2011, CHAPTER 5.

[314] Ibid.

[315] Richardson, Samuel. *Pamela*. London: J.M. Dent, 1914, title page.

[316] Ibid, preface.

[317] Mudge, Bradford Keyes. *The Whore's Story: Women, Pornography, and the British Novel, 1684-1830*. Oxford University Press, 2000., p. 187.

[318] Ibid. and Mackie, Erin Skye. *Rakes, Highwaymen, and Pirates: the Making of the Modern Gentleman in the Eighteenth Century*. Johns Hopkins University Press, 2014.

[319] Mudge, *The Whore's Story*, p. 70.

[320] Richardson, *Pamela*, preface.

[321] Ibid, p. 257.

[322] "NOVEL PLEASURE." *THE CAMBRIDGE COMPANION TO EROTIC LITERATURE*, BY BRADFORD KEYES. MUDGE, CAMBRIDGE UNIVERSITY PRESS, 2017, P. 130.

[323] Ibid, p. 213.

[324] Dabhoiwala, p. 173.

[325] Fysh, Stephanie. *The Work(s) of Samuel Richardson*. Newark: University of Delaware Press, 1997, p. 57-58

[326] Footnote from: GOODING, RICHARD. "PAMELA, SHAMELA, AND THE POLITICS OF THE PAMELA VOGUE." *EIGHTEENTH-CENTURY FICTION*, VOL. 7, NO. 2, 1995, PP. 109–130., DOI:10.1353/ECF.1995.0021: "Dr Peter Shaw, The Reflector (1750), quoted in A.D. McKillop. Samuel Richardson: Printer and Novelist (1936: Chapel Hill: University of North Carolina Press, 1960). pp. 101-2. McKillop, in fact, identifies Shaw's remarks as plagiarism of a passage from the Danish dramatist Ludvig Holberg's Moral Thoughts (1744)."

[327] For positive reactions and the cultural phenomenona see Fysh, Stephanie. *The Work(s) of Samuel Richardson*. Newark: University of Delaware Press, 1997, p. 57-58. For negative reactions see Mudge, *The Whore's Story*, p. 186.

[328] This section of indebted to my article for *The Edinburgh History of Reading* 'Hellfire and Cannibals: 18th and 19th Century Erotic Reading Groups and Their Manuscripts' (forthcoming). Anon. *Supplement To The Historical Portion Of The 'Records Of The Most Ancient And Puissant Order Of The Beggar's Benison And Merryland, Anstruther', Being An Account Of The Proceedings At The Meeting Of The Society, Together With Excerpts, Stories, Bon-Mots, Speeches, And Songs Delivered Thereat*. 'Anstruther,' Printed for Private Distribution, 1892, p. 15. In Peakman, Julie. *Mighty Lewd Books: The Development of Pornography in Eighteenth-Century England*. Palgrave Macmillan, 2014, Peakman argues "However, the Beggar's Benison *Supplement* was probably a money-making scam by the nineteenth-century pornographer, Leonard Smithers, the minutes a fabrication of Smithers himself. According to Kearney, the book was printed by Smithers on the disbanding of 'Beggar's Benison', in London in 1892. To take any book published by Smithers as a serious factual account would be stretching credibility. Not only did he operate as a bookseller, selling a variety of salacious material, but he was

a notorious publisher of pornography, commissioning both translations and new writings." Stevenson agrees that the records should be treated very skeptically, but argues extensively in favor of the mastubatory rituals; I find his argument convincing.

[329] Cleland, John. *Memoirs Of A Woman Of Pleasure*. Printed for G. Fenton, 1749, p. 5.

[330] Ibid, p. 7.

[331] Ibid, p. 18.

[332] Ibid, p. 20-23.0

[333] Ibid, p. 44.

[334] Ibid. p. 49.

[335] Ibid.

[336] Ibid, p. 67.

[337] Wagner, *Eros*, p. 239.

[338] Cleland, *Memoirs*, p. 86.

[339] Ibid, p. 111.

[340] Ibid, p. 115.

[341] ANON. *A CONGRATULATORY EPISTLE FROM A REFORMED RAKE, TO JOHN F------G, ESQ ; UPON THE NEW SCHEME OF RECLAIMING PROSTITUTES*. PRINTED FOR G. BURNET, 1758.

[342] Ibid, p. 299.

[343] Ibid, p. 300.

[344] Ibid, p. 323.

[345] Wagner, *Eros*, p. 240-42.

[346] Sherlock, Thomas. "A Letter on the Earthquakes in MDCCL." In *Discourses Preached at the Temple Church*. Oxford: Clarendon Press, 1812. 325-338, pgs. 325-27.

[347] Mudge, *The Whore's Story*, p. 214.

[348] Ernst, Morris L. *To The Pure: A Study of Obscenity and the Censor*. New York: The Viking Press, 1929, p. 109.

[349] Phillips, John. *Sade: the Libertine Novels*. Pluto Press, 2001, p. 4.

[350] Ibid, p. 7.

[351] Ibid, p. 8.

[352] Ibid, p. 9.

[353] Ibid, p. 8.

[354] Ibid, p. 13.

[355] Ibid, p. 97.

[356] Qtd in Phillips, p. 100.

[357] This quotation seems to come up wherever Justine is mentioned, but without proper sourcing.

[358] Ibid, p. 94.

[359] De Sade, Marquis. *Justine, Philosophy in the Bedroom and Other Writings*. Translated by Richard Seaver and Austryn Wainhouse, Grove Press, 1965, p. 574.

[360] Ibid, p. 578.

[361] Ibid, p. 579.

[362] Ibid, p. 580.

[363] Ibid.

[364] Ibid.

[365] Ibid, p. 581.

[366] Ibid, p. 582.

[367] Ibid, 606.

[368] Ibid, 612.

[369] Ibid, p. 619.

[370] Ibid, p. 622.

[371] Ibid, p. 633.

[372] Ibid, p. 646.

[373] Ibid, p. 841.

[374] Ibid, p. 696.

[375] Ibid, p. 760-61.

[376] Ibid, p. 929.

[377] Ibid, p. 935

[378] Wyngaard, Amy S. "Sade, Réage and Transcending the Obscene." *The Cambridge Companion to Erotic Literature*, edited by Bradford Keyes. Mudge, Cambridge University Press, 2017, p. 2120

[379] Ibid.

[380] Dabhoiwala, *Origins*, p. 108.

[381] George III, King . "By the King: A Proclamation for the Encouragement of Piety and Virtue, and for preventing and punishing of Vice, Profaneness and Immorality." In *Part the First: Address to the Public from the Society for the Suppression of Vice, Setting Forth, With a List of the Members, the Utility and Necessity of such an Institution and its Claim to Public Support* . London: Printed for the Society, 1803, pg 24.

[382] Ibid.

[383] British Broadcasting Corporation. "William Wilberforce." BBC - Religions. http://www.bbc.co.uk/religion/religions/christianity/people/william-wilberforce_1.shtml (accessed September 14, 2013).

[384] Scott, John. *An Account of Societies for the Reformation of Manners, and*

the *Suppression of Vice with Answers to Objections Against Them Second Edition, Enlarged.* W Rawson, 1807, p. 4.

[385] Robert Issac Wilberforce, *The Life of William Wilberforce* (London 1838), I, pg. 132.

[386] Society, for the Suppression of Vice *Part the First: Address to the Public from the Society for the Suppression of Vice, Setting Forth, With a List of the Members, the Utility and Necessity of such an Institution and its Claim to Public Support* . London: Printed for the Society, 1803, pgs 34-35.

[387] Qtd in Ashbee, Henry Spencer. *Index Librorum Prohibitorum; Bio-Biblio-Icono-Graphical and Critical Notes on Curious, Uncommon and Erotic Books.* London, Privately Printed, 1877, p 117-126.

[388] Ibid.

[389] Thomas, Donald. *A Long Time Burning; The History of Literary Censorship in England.* New York: Praeger, 1969, p. 114-5.

[390] Society, For the Suppression of Vice. *Society for the Suppression of Vice, Consisting of Members of the Established Church. WIth a Brief Abstract of Proceedings in 1802.* Bridge-Street, Blackfriars, London: Printed for the Society, 1803, p. 5.

[391] Ibid, pgs 5-6.

[392] Ibid, pgs 6-7

[393] Ibid, pg. 24.

[394] For the advice to their members, see SSV, *Part the First*, pgs. 62-64. For their police handbooks, see Society, For the Suppression of Vice, *The Constable's Assistant: Being a Compendium of The Duties and Powers of Constables and other Peace Officers, chiefly as they relate to the Apprehending of Offenders, and the laying of Information before Magistrates.* Villiers Street, London: Printed for the Society, 1808.

[395] Society, for the Suppression of Vice *Part the Second: Address to the Public from the Society for the Suppression of Vice, Containing an Account of the Proceedings of the Society from its Original Institution.* London: Printed for the Society, 1804, pg. 26.

[396] Quinlan, Maurice J. *Victorian Prelude, a History of English Manners.* Hamden, Conn.: Archon Books, 1965, p 204.

[397] Paul, Charles K. *William Godwin: His Friends and Contemporaries.* Roberts Brothers, 1877, p. 80.

[398] SSV, *Part the Second,* pgs. 16-17.

[399] Ibid, pg. 25.

[400] Thomas, Donald. *A Long Time Burning; The History of Literary Censorship in England.* New York: Praeger, 1969, p. 213.

[401] SSV, *Part the First,* p. 37.

[402] SSV, *Part the Second,* pgs. 16-17.

Brian M. Watson

[403] Mason, Diane. *The Secret Vice Masturbation in Victorian Fiction and Medical Culture.* Manchester University Press, 2014, Chapter 1.

[404] Ibid.

[405] This according to Roberts, M. J. D.. *Making English Morals: Voluntary Association and Moral Reform in Nineteenth-Century England.* Cambridge, UK: Cambridge University Press, 2004, p. 75. Roberts was able to examine the bank records of the SSV, held at Hoare's Bank in London.

[406] Qtd. In *Victorian Prelude*, p. 221.

[407] Anonymous. *The Lustful Turk.* New York: Masquerade Book, 1990, p. 10.

[408] Ibid, p. 23.

[409] Ibid, p. 14-15

[410] Ibid, p. 23.

[411] Ibid, p. 51.

[412] Ibid, p. 54-56.

[413] Ibid. p. 57.

[414] Ibid.

[415] SIGEL, LISA Z. *GOVERNING PLEASURES: PORNOGRAPHY AND SOCIAL CHANGE IN ENGLAND, 1815-1914.* RUTGERS UNIVERSITY PRESS, 2002, P. 9 AND 43.

[416] Anonymous. *The Lustful Turk,* p. 58-60.

[417] Ibid, p. 87.

[418] Ibid, p. 88-9.

[419] Ibid, p. 104-5.

[420] Ibid, p. 106.

[421] Ibid, p. 115.

[422] Ibid, p. 139.

[423] Ibid, p. 148.

[424] See MARCUS, STEVEN. *THE OTHER VICTORIANS: A STUDY OF SEXUALITY AND PORNOGRAPHY IN MID-NINETEENTH-CENTURY ENGLAND.* BASIC BOOKS, 1964 FOR DISCUSSION ON PORNOTOPIA.

[425] Anonymous *The Lustful Turk,* p. 149.

[426] Ibid.

[427] SIGEL. *GOVERNING PLEASURES,* P. 19.

[428] Ibid, p. 20-21. For the estimation of the numbers of pornographic shops, see Sigel's citation of "Letter from Mr Pritchard to Lrd Campbell," Jauary 1858, Social Evil Extracts Album, part 1, NVA Papers, Fawcett Library.

[429] Qtd in MENDES, PETER. *CLANDESTINE EROTIC FICTION IN ENGLISH, 1800-1930: A BIBLIOGRAPHICAL STUDY.* SCHOLAR PRESS, 2000.

[430] Qtd in Thomas, p. 423-424

[431] Ibid, p. 429.

[432] "An Act for the Punishment of idle and disorderly Persons, and Rogues and Vagabonds, in that Part of Great Britain called England.." legislation.gov.uk. www.legislation.gov.uk/ukpga/1824/83/pdfs/ukpga_18240083_en.pdf (accessed October 3, 2013), p. 669 no. IV. [PDF]

[433] Manchester, Colin. "Lord Campbell's Act: England's First Obscenity Statue." *The Journal of Legal History* 9, no. 2 (1988): 223-241, p. 226.

[434] Hansard's Parliamentary Debates, HL Deb 11 May 1857 vol 145 cc102-4. http://hansard.millbanksystems.com/lords/1857/may/11/sale-of-poisons-and-poisonous (Accessed October 3rd, 2013).

[435] Ibid.

[436] Hansard's Parliamentary Debates, HL Deb 25 June 1857 vol 146 cc327-38 http://hansard.millbanksystems.com/lords/1857/jun/25/second-reading (Accessed October 5th, 2013)

[437] Hansard's Parliamentary Debates, HL Deb 03 July 1857 vol 146 cc864-7, http://hansard.millbanksystems.com/lords/1857/jul/03/committee. (Accessed October 5th, 2013). Discussion of SSV lobbying in M. Hardcastle (ed.), *Life of John, Lord Campbell*, London, 1881, vol II, p. 353.

[438] Roberts, MJD. "Making Victorian Morals? The Society for the Suppression of Vice and its Critics 1802-1888." *Historical Studies* 21, no. 83 (1981): 157-73, pg 170.

[439] HL Deb 25 June 1857 vol 146 cc327-38.

[440] Ernst, p. 128.

[441] Fuller, Wayne Edison. *Morality and the Mail in Nineteenth-Century America.* Urbana, Ill.: University of Illinois Press, 2003, p. 103.

[442] Ibid.

[443] Ibid, p. 104.

[444] Trumbull proposes that he killed himself, but other sources are more divided. Trumbull, C.G. *Anthony Comstock, Fighter.* New York: Fleming H. Revell Company, 1913, p.62.

[445] Horowitz, Helen Lefkowitz. Rereading Sex. New York: Knopf, 2002, p. 372 seems to suspect however, that Comstock may have always had his eye on the YMCA as a "religious clerk with his career in a dry-goods company at a standstill."

[446] Ibid, p. 372.

[447] Ibid, 374.

[448] Qtd. From the New York State Police Record, in Horowitz, p. 375.

[449] Ibid, 370.

[450] Hansard's Parliamentary Debates, HL Deb 07 December 1857 vol 148 cc226-7. http://hansard.millbanksystems.com/lords/1857/dec/07/return-moved-for (Accessed October 5th, 2013).

[451] Qtd. In Thomas, p. 263.

Brian M. Watson

[452] Some of this comes from WATSON, BRIAN. "THE VICTORIAN WITH A SECRET." *NOTCHES*, 12 DEC. 2017, NOTCHESBLOG.COM/2017/12/12/ THE-ARCHETYPICAL-VICTORIAN-WITH-A-SECRET-HENRY-SPENCER-ASH-BEE/. ANOTHER LARGE BIT OF IT IS INDEBTED TO indebted to my article for *The Edinburgh History of Reading* 'Hellfire and Cannibals: 18th and 19th Century Erotic Reading Groups and Their Manuscripts' (forthcoming).

[453] Gibson, Ian. *The Erotomaniac: the Secret Life of Henry Spencer Ashbee.* Faber, 2001.

[454] Swinburne, Algernon Charles. *The Swineburne Letters. Vol. 2 : 1869-1872.* Edited by Cecil Y Lang, vol. 2, Yale Univ. Press , 1974, p. 20 fn.

[455] in Ashbee, Henry Spencer. *Index Librorum Prohibitorum; Bio-Biblio-Icono-Graphical and Critical Notes on Curious, Uncommon and Erotic Books.* London, Privately Printed, 1877, p xvi.

[456] Ibid, p. lxviii.

[457] Ibid, p. lxx.

[458] Gibson, *Erotomaniac*, p. 153.

[459] Qtd in Gibson, ibid.

[460] The second half of Gibsons biography is dedicated to this idea. See also LEGMAN, GERSHON, AND HENRY SPENCER ASHBEE. "'PISANUS FRAXI' AND HIS BOOKS." *BIBLIOGRAPHY OF PROHIBITED BOOKS*, JACK BROS-SEL, NEW YORK, 1962, PP. 5–51, MENDES, PETER. *CLANDESTINE EROTIC FICTION IN ENGLISH, 1800-1930: A BIBLIOGRAPHICAL STUDY.* SCOLAR PRESS, 1993, AND OF COURSE MARCUS, STEVEN. *THE OTHER VICTORIANS: A STUDY OF SEXUALITY AND PORNOGRAPHY IN MID-NINETEENTH-CEN-TURY ENGLAND.* BASIC BOOKS, 1964.

[461] Ashbee, *Catena LibrorumTacendorum*, pg. 185. Published as Volume III of Ashbee, Henry Spencer. *The Encyclopedia of Erotic Literature, Being Notes Bio-Biblio-Icono-Graphical and Critical, on Curious and Uncommon Books.* New York: Documentary Books, Inc., 1962.

[462] Anonymous. *The Romance of Lust.* New York: Grove Press, 1968, p. 3. Some Grove Press editions of this work falsely attribute it to Edward Sellon, who write several erotic books for William Dugdale, including *The New Epicurean* noted above.

[463] Ibid, p. 5.

[464] Ibid, p. 13-14.

[465] Ibid, p. 15.

[466] Ibid, p, 25-26

[467] Ibid, p. 27.

[468] Ibid, p. 30 and then 68-69.

[469] Ibid, p. 262.

[470] Ibid, p. 298.

[471] *La Petite Morte* (French): 'The sensation of orgasm as likened to death, literally, the little death.'

Futuumeshi (Japanese): 'The moment after orgasm in which a man can think clearly.'

[472] Some of this section is indebted to WATSON, BRIAN. "'A POISON MORE DEADLY': DEFINING OBSCENITY IN THE WEST." *NOTCHES BLOG*, 25 AUG. 2016, NOTCHESBLOG.COM/2016/05/10/A-POISON-MORE-DEADLY-DEFINING-OBSCENITY-IN-THE-WEST/.

[473] Ernst, Morris L. *To The Pure: A Study of Obscenity and the Censor.* New York: The Viking Press, 1929, p. 128.

[474] ARNSTEIN, WALTER L. "THE MURPHY RIOTS: A VICTORIAN DILEMMA." *VICTORIAN STUDIES*, 1 SEPT. 1975, WWW.JSTOR.ORG/STABLE/3826732? SEQ=1#PAGE_SCAN_TAB_CONTENTS.

[475] WOHL, ANTHONY S. "THE MURPHY RIOTS." *THE VICTORIAN WEB*, 4 APR. 2002, WWW.VICTORIANWEB.ORG/RELIGION/MURPHY_RIOTS.HTML.

[476] "Regina v. Hicklin."Wikisource. https://en.wikisource.org/wiki/Regina_v._Hicklin (accessed November 12, 2013).

[477] The National Archives (UK)."Records of the National Vigilance Association."The National Archives. https://www.nationalarchives.gov.uk/a2a/records.aspx?cat=106-4nva&cid=0#0 (accessed November 15, 2013).

[478] Knowlton, Charles. "Fruits of Philosophy: A Treatise on the Population Question." Gutenberg.org. http://www.gutenberg.org/files/38185/38185-h/38185-h.htm (accessed November 20, 2013).

[479] Ibid.

[480] From the Preface to the First Edition, a copy which is available online: Ellis, Havelock. "Studies in the Psychology of Sex, Volume 2."Project Gutenberg. http://www.gutenberg.org/files/13611/13611-h/13611-h.htm (accessed November 20, 2013).

[481] See Ellis, Preface to the First Edition of the Second Volume of *Studies in the Psychology of Sex*

[482] Travis, Alan. *Bound and Gagged: A Secret History of Obscenity in Britain.* London: Profile Books, 2000, p. 9.

[483] DuPont, Ellen. "Henry Havelock Ellis." The Embryo Project Encyclopedia. http://embryo.asu.edu/pages/henry-havelock-ellis (accessed November 27, 2013).

[484] Forster, E. M. *Maurice; A Novel.* New York: Norton, 1971, p. 159.

[485] Ibid, p. 250.

[486] Ibid, dedication.

[487] Lawrence, D. H. *The Rainbow.* New York, NY: Signet Classic, 2009, p. 152, 182.

[488] Ibid, p. 164.

Brian M. Watson

[489]Ibid, pgs. 240-1.

[490]Ibid, p. 330. Furthermore, it would be possible to make an argument that, as Anton is Polish, Ursula's maternal side, the fact that she is able to resist marks the triumph of the maternal over the paternal lines.

[491]Ibid, p. 332.

[492]Ibid, pgs. 469-70.

[493]Ibid, p. 352.

[494]Ibid, pgs.353 (my emphases) and 176.

[495] Travis, p. 130.

[496]Qtd.In Travis, p. 132.

[497]Qtd.In Travis, pgs. 132-3.

[498] Ibid.

[499]Qtd in Travis, p. 134.

[500]Lawrence, D. H. Sex Literature and Censorship: Essays. New York: Twayne Publishers, 1953, p. 88.

[501]Ibid, p. 69.

[502] Ibid.

[503]Ibid, p. 70.

[504]Ibid, pgs. 74-5.

[505] Ibid, p.   72-73.

[506]Ibid, p. 92.

[507]Ibid, p. 83.

[508]Hall, Radclyffe. The Well of Loneliness. New York: Anchor Books, 1990, p. 146.

[509]Ibid, p. 13.

[510]Ibid, p. 13.

[511]Ibid. p. 16.

[512]Ibid, p. 18 and 26.

[513]Ibid, p. 54.

[514] Ibid, p. 105-6.

[515]Ibid, p. 98.

[516]Ibid, pgs. 155-56.

[517]Ibid, p. 200.

[518]Ibid, pgs. 202-05.

[519]Ibid, pgs. 433-34.

[520]Ibid, pgs 436-37.

[521] Travis, p. 55

[522]Souhami, Diana. The Trials of Radclyffe Hall. New York: Doubleday, 1999, p. 11.

[523] Travis, p. 57.

[524] Souhami, p. 197 and Travis p. 64.

[525] Woolf, Virginia. *The Letters of Virginia Woolf, Vol. 3: 1923-1928*. Ed. Nigel Nicolson and Joanne Trautmann. New York: Harcourt, 1978, p. 555.

[526] Ibid, p. 520.

[527] Travis, p. 64.

[528] Ibid, p. 53.

[529] The Times."Alleged Obscene Novel. Proceedings at Bow-Street." The Times (London), November 10, 1928, p. 9.

[530] Woolf, Virginia. *The Diary of Virginia Woolf, Vol. 3 1925-1930.*Ed. Anne Oliver Bell with Andrew McNeillie. New York: Harcourt, 1980, p. 207.

[531] Travis, p. 66.

[532] The Times. "Novel Condemned as Obscene." The Times (London), November 17, 1928, p. 5.

[533] Ellis, Havelock, Lord Charles Darling, Stephen Foote, E.M. Forster, Virginia Woolf, and Carrol Romer." The 'Censorship' of Books." The Nineteenth Century and After DCXXVI (1929): 433-450, p. 437.

[534] Ibid, p. 444.

[535] Ibid, p. 447.

[536] Taylor, Leslie. ""I Made up My Mind to Get It": The American Trial of "The Well of Loneliness" New York City, 1928-1929." *Journal of the History of Sexuality* 10, no. 2 (2001): 250-286. http://www.jstor.org/stable/3704816 (accessed December 10, 2013), p. 256.

[537] To clarify, these are my suggestions, not Taylor's.

[538] Qtd. in Taylor, p. 283.

[539] Koetzle, Michael. *1000 Nudes: Uwe Scheid Collection*. Taschen, 2001, p. 11.

[540] Dupouy, Alexandre. *Erotic Art Photography*. Parkstone Press, 2004, p. 82.

[541] Koetzle, *1000 Nudes*, p. 9.

[542] Dupouy, *Erotic*, p. 38.

[543] Koetzle, p. 11.

[544] THOMPSON, DAVE. *BLACK AND WHITE AND BLUE: ADULT CINEMA FROM THE VICTORIAN AGE TO THE VCR*. ECW PRESS, 2007, P. 19-20.

[545] Qtd in ibid, p. 21.

[546] Ibid, p. 13-14.

[547] *"Mousquetaire au restaurant" [Mistitled]*. Ogg Thedora -- Original Unknown., 1920. https://en.wikipedia.org/wiki/File:Mousquetaire_au_restaurant_part_1.ogv.

[548] STEWART, POTTER. "JACOBELLIS V. OHIO." *FINDLAW*, 22 JUNE 1964,

Brian M. Watson

CASELAW.FINDLAW.COM/US-SUPREME-COURT/378/184.HTML.

[549] Ashbee, Henry Spencer. *Catena Librorum Tacendorum: Being Notes Bio-Icono- Graphical and Critical, on Curious and Uncommon Books*. London, Privately Printed, 1885, p. xlii.

[550] Ibid, p. xl.

[551] Ibid, p. lvi.

[552] SIGEL, LISA Z. *INTERNATIONAL EXPOSURE: PERSPECTIVES ON MODERN EUROPEAN PORNOGRAPHY, 1800-2000*. RUTGERS UNIVERSITY PRESS, 2005, P. 8.

[553] Kennedy, Maev. "Lawrence 'Obscenities' Finally Get a Showing." *The Guardian*, Guardian News and Media, 22 Nov. 2003, www.theguardian.com/uk/2003/nov/22/books.arts.

www.ingramcontent.com/pod-product-compliance
Lightning Source LLC
Chambersburg PA
CBHW021613270326
41931CB00008B/684